Leave the Lights on When You Go

Leave the Lights on When You Go

A Memoir

Janis Ahlenberg

Sky Street Press

Copyright © 2019 by Janis Ahlenberg

All rights reserved. No part of this publication may be reproduced, distributed, or transmitted in any form or by any means, including photocopying, recording, digital scanning, or other electronic or mechanical methods, without the prior written permission of the publisher, except in the case of brief quotations embodied in critical reviews and certain other noncommercial uses permitted by copyright law. For permission requests, please email ahlbjan74@gmail.com.

Cover and interior design by Tabitha Lahr

Published 2019
Printed in the United States of America
ISBN: 978-1-7328462-0-3
E-ISBN: 978-1-7328462-1-0
Library of Congress Control Number: 2019900498

For information, email: ahlbjan74@gmail.com

To everyone I love.
You're in these pages.

Contents

Just Us 15
My Mother's Other Children 32
Love Is the Answer 48
Mother's Little Helper 58
My Brother and Me 76
Love Alone 94
Max 111
Where Does Love Live? 117
Margo 129
Bad Times with Mum and Dad 135
Marisol 143
Family Trust 151
Christmas Presence 158
The Ramp 166
Life Be Loved 176
Fifty-Cent Time 184
Be With Me When I 194
Tragedy 204
Poor Once More 205

Empathy	215
Reckonings	224
Way After Sunset	228
When Music is Your Only Way	236
The Reluctant Supplicant	243
It Has to Be Love	252
Time	264
Page One. Page One. Page One	269
End of the End	272
No Song to Write About It	287
After All	294
Good Day Darkness	309
Taking Power	310
New Day	319
Not So Sure About Thee	324
Love Is Not Enough	330
Don't You Turn Your Back On...	335
Book of Love	341
Flowers In the Teapot	348

Acknowledgments

Special thanks to Dr. Bruce Carruth and Chris Welles Feder, who read this manuscript in its relatively final form and encouraged me in detail. Without you, my story might not have seen the light of day. Mindy Lewis and Walter Bode are deeply appreciated for their caring help in shaping and editing. My son and daughter-in-law read certain stages of chapters and had useful opinions, as did my friends Kim Sarasohn, Penny Rosen and JoAn Relich. Thanks to my first writing group in that university town so long ago and early on. I'm grateful to Karen and Mike Braziller for their reading and support. Bill Thomashower, thanks for your valuable advice.

Olga Cheselka has steadily aided in my continued personal development throughout this autobiographical journey.

Deep friendships have sustained me: Carolyn Edelman, Jeanette Hooban, Carolyn Yoder, Diane Adler, Natalie Finkel, Susan Freeman, Dorothy Langer, Jeffrey Israel, and all in my Sunday Book Group: Eva Werbell, Connie Kagel, Carol Harracksingh and Linda Feigelson. You all have my permanent gratitude.

Thanks to Brooke Warner and her team, copyeditor Krissa Lagos, and proofreader Chris Dumas, for guidance.

Author's Note

There's a reality substrate here, of course, but this is my story. I'm writing from my own experiences and perceptions. I've portrayed events and dialogue from careful diaries, but I've had no corroboration of these recollections. Memories are subjective. And I've lived a long time with these memories.

All names and places are changed, including my own, to protect relationships I care about.

"It is a joy to be hidden and a disaster not to be found."
—D. W. Winnicott

Just Us

My seven-years-younger brother and I perch high up on the rock ledge, above this heaven-sized New England lake, looking out over the family vacation cottage—a modest brown dwelling on the water's edge—that my parents built as their second home just after I left at eighteen.

Steve and I haven't known each other as adults. It's not that we never commiserated on occasion, but all the family confusion back in 1962 separated us and we lost touch. Just being here now—I'm here to escape the ongoing storm of my miserable divorce, following a thirty-year marriage—is an act of reorientation and surrender.

I can't stop falling, Alice-like, through deepest time into the old, luxurious feeling of our family past, the glory of which might be something of my own creation. It happened so long ago. The first-born child gets the youngest and—if lucky—most wondrous-feeling parents. They're your introduction to basic everything: colors, sounds, tastes, smells. Sun, sky, house, summer, road, pond, spoon, dog, bird—first astonishments to hold forever. They are first life, first love.

"This feels like sitting in a ship," I had exclaimed to my folks and Steve earlier when we were all out on the deck and I was swimming in the fairy-tale feeling I once had had, when we had only one small home and my parents were beautiful and strong. I was imagining "just us," forty years ago—the reflection of our four ghosts lavished out upon the water by reach of this extended deck. Dad, in probably his finest engineering feat—after my era in the family—somehow managed to cantilever this platform off the living room.

Dad has remained long and lean. Mum has grown comfortably frumpy-dumpy. She still has her pretty face and her hair has turned a glowing white; it sweeps like an angel's wing. They're getting old. Steve, middle-aged, as I am, has remained young and good-looking like my father—tall, with sandy hair and sky-blue eyes. We are again that once good-natured lot—just us four, laughing the way we did long ago. It feels as if I'm stealing something I thought I'd outgrown, but didn't get enough of before it ended too soon. I reflect how it was this, the best of our parents, that nourished our beginnings—no matter what happened beyond that.

My folks always cherished child imaginations. They took seriously my wish when I was three to follow what I'd called a "shunder flower" and find the pot of gold at the end of the rainbow. One Sunday afternoon, my young parents set out in the car, with tiny me in the backseat, to find that impossible rainbow's end.

At an outdoor carnival, around that same time, they were both so really there with me when I lost my first balloon. We shared one broken heart—all three of us cheek-to-cheek, watching, as that balloon lifted out of reach for a slow, defiant length of time and eventually became a speck. We spoke not a word, recognizing this primary lesson in loss—that you can never get back something you just had in your hand a minute ago. What was happening to me was happening to them.

An even earlier memory hangs on: when I was a toddler and my two parents stood waist-deep in Lake Crockett and threw me back and forth between them, making me scream with delight. They were young then and caught me well, each turning me in mid-flight to face the other with arms outstretched, their exuberant faces—mirroring my own—full of anticipation, to dip, but never drop, me. That experience taught me trust.

Steve joined this bubble of enchantment when I was seven, and glad for the end of being an only child in a lonely place.

We had simple travels and adventures then. My folks took my brother and me to "Indian places" in the wild, maintaining that this country and all of nature—anywhere we went, everything we could see (the soil, the land, every rock, tree, and leaf)—belonged to the actual natives, the real Americans, the Wampanoags. Somewhere within I'm forever sliding down flat, water-smoothed rocks in a long, winding waterway through Willard Brook Park, an old-soul forest that my parents found. I felt their pleasure in sharing the love of a place, watching our joyous expressions, joining in our happiness, all of us together in the glory of that moment. Steve was delirious. "What a puppy day," he said.

For five years, "just us" was that family of four. Battles over money were not the blind rages that came later over the looming monthly mortgage or "owing our lifeblood" to Sears for the washer and dryer.

Steve and I were magical children, and our parents sometimes, on weekends, let us turn them into magical children, too. Here, today, we can recall the richness when we lived back on Eden Avenue and our paternal grandparents and sometimes-caretakers lived upstairs. On Saturday mornings, we got Mum and Dad to put on Indian headdresses and war paint and we all carried homemade tomahawks and explored our immediate part of the planet: the small wooded quarter-acre across the road. We practiced walking on dry leaves and twigs without making a sound, and anyone who did was "It." We sat on a giant boulder passing our make-believe peace pipe back and forth, making up stories and wondering about life in a silly language with expressions like "How now" and "Thunderthud" and other phrases we invented. We didn't have books, and TV was new.

Anything wrong then was roundly ignored. Our "make-believes" were freedom and fun.

On our way out to our powwow in the woods one day, Mum forgot her feathered headdress as we headed out the door. When I reminded her, she quickly reached for the nearby lampshade and placed it on her head. It was a joke, of course, and Steve laughed so hard he peed his pants. Swarmed by these memories now, I want to feel we are back to that old way of being, having a return to glorious times. Just us: two young adults and two children—I'm nine and Steve is two—on one of those treasured weekends after my folks' long workweeks at the Watch Factory that "wore out their nerves."

Here I came knocking, amazed that they'd found their way to owning this second home.

"You just missed the cat," my mother said as she greeted me with a warm embrace. "She died."

"I've missed you too, Mummy," I hugged her back.

My father stepped forward and embraced me. "She doesn't know our cat, Lorraine. Is that the first thing you say?"

"I know that, Horace," my mother said, "I mention it because it just happened Tuesday."

I was surprised to see Steve—here from the West Coast—sitting out on the deck against the blue. I've hardly known my brother for decades. I was puzzled to learn that he comes here often.

Steve retired at forty-seven from his real estate law practice in Los Angeles, and he's had at least a semi-resolution with Joanne, his partner of some fifteen years. Though he praises her wit and intelligence with some frequency, she never joins him in coming to the lake house. He and I speak on the phone sometimes and he tells me about the family. He recently gave me good financial advice. Occasionally, he emails photos of something he's just prepared for his dinner: a ceviche in a cut-glass goblet set out beside a glass of Riesling, or a deep dish brimming with feijoada. He prides himself on his cooking. Like me—but seven years later—he became an educated citizen of the world, a savvy gourmet with refined tastes. Since his early retirement, it seems, he's spent every September and May here on the lake. My parents come for long weekends then. The cottage is rented out in summer, when the region becomes tourist-filled and noisy, and it sits empty in winter, when the rugged dirt road is iced and forbidding.

Stepping into this house is like entering the lake itself. One long glass wall faces out on vast water. That afternoon, it framed the deck, my brother, and the sky.

Following the sweet commotion of embraces, Steve waved us out to join him. We all sat down and toasted one another with glasses of homemade lemonade. My parents seemed to have once again become the decent people they once were. I found myself basking in the long-ago warmth. *It's okay*, I thought, *I've been a wife and mother myself, I'm a well-analyzed therapist, I can afford an irrational dip into the past. Who is ever free from longing?*

I wasn't expecting to return to the Cowabunga tribe now. There was much to catch up on. My divorce after thirty years. But my folks went on mourning their cat. Her empty bowls were stacked beside us. I had entered their world, their continuous present. So I joined in.

The cat, they said, had traveled the country many winters with them in their Wally-Byam-Trailer-Club days, after my father retired.

"She took us all the way from middle age to this," my mother said, glancing with surprise at my aging father, as if she hadn't noticed him for a while. She tossed her chin toward the potbellied boulder that anchored the shore. "She's there now, still with us. We're always looking at her. The rock was already there. Now Snowy is there too."

A respectful silence naturally followed.

Even mourning the cat, I could see that my parents suffer comfortably and matter-of-factly. Their friends are dying. They said: "Oh, poor Shirley, finally got to do all that traveling, then drowned right in her own bathtub. It was her heart. So sad to see Shirl go."

"Yes, we miss Jilda too. Oh my, yes. She was a good egg. Such a good egg."

"Yeah, we're droppin' like flies."

"It's the way it is," said Mum.

"Nuttin' you can do," added Dad.

That put those feelings, all neatly folded, in place. Then they went about setting the table and reading aloud from the local want ads.

"Someone's selling a rotary saw for $10," Dad said. "It's a Dewalt. Hand me the phone, Lorraine. I gutta call this guy."

We could have been sitting again with our picnic basket on the spit of beach at Bussa's Pond, on Dad's US Navy blanket, made of the real wool that moths prize. One sun-kissed day, two-year-old Steve motored around the blanket with the pure energy of a budding boy. Dad took off his watch and headed into the water, smiling. I—wearing war paint and a feather in my crown—followed in to see him make one of his fabulous dives, leaving a still spot where he'd knifed in and disappeared. There he was—a tall man on the raft—and then he was not there, leaving not a ruffle on the water.

My father had set the underwater record in the Navy when "trying out" for World War II. He held his breath for a minute and twenty-six seconds—the reason he subsequently found himself in a submarine under attack off the Philippine Coast, and sorry to be there.

I waited for that "creature from the black lagoon."

Sure enough, a subaqueous creature was at my toes; fingers shoveled under and flipped me backward in a splash of glee. We dripped our way back up to the blanket, where my mother handed out bologna sandwiches, deviled eggs, and Twinkies.

As soon as my father sat down, Steve flew and landed on his back, making noises of a stinging bee. Dad's watch lay facedown next to the picnic basket. Not much was required of us, a plain family—just us—that didn't think to want anything we didn't have, sitting quietly in a bowl of contentment, taking in the pond. The reeds on the far rim of the pond appeared etched on the sky; comfortable clouds drifted past.

With little knowledge of a world beyond us, and no sense of anything to come, everything was all right. Not much bothered us in my hometown, where my father's parents had located themselves. We never saw anyone better or richer. Not much happened in the way of accomplishment, except in sports. No one valued or thought about being smart. My father did talk about a place where people were "very smart." They were all geniuses in a place called MIT, a world sufficiently far away that we were safe. Here in the familiar, we were cozy. No demands. Just us; just here.

For the longest time, I clung to my glorified vision of us three, then us four. Just us. How we were. I chose to remember the tranquil times. Our family had its "royal period" then, when my mother—despite her migraines and spells—set spots of visual pleasure all around. A smoky rose carpet printed with ballroom swirls of 1940s dancerly plant shapes spanned the living room. Her prize gardenia, in its mossy Italianate stone pot, reigned over all on a tiny round table, so operatic and splendid it was a pleasure to have to walk around it. I thought of its thick, sensual fragrance as essence of "Mummy." We had an upright piano then, and Mum played by ear the beginnings of Chopin's most famous polonaise and Strauss's "Blue Danube Waltz." These were her ways of being with us.

This elegant era took place in a stage Mummy set while she was still slim and pretty herself. The living room was a kept place, a testimony to belief in order and respect. There were doilies on side tables. The most unforgettable objects were a pair of chrome ashtrays on the coffee table that reflected in the glowing mahogany veneer. Each had a round, gleaming chrome-plate base, and from the center of each one sprouted two crossed, mirror-image, graceful chrome extensions vaguely resembling herons' beaks, or parted elegant fingers, headed in opposite directions, as if taking coordinated flight from one another. These artful shapes conjured plants, birds, shapely driftwood. They could be larks rising "at the break of day." Their parted "beaks" captured the essence of receptivity; their lengthiness was sheer movement—like throats reaching; their purpose to bear forward, like a torch, the pausing cigarette, probably with a chevron of lipstick at its tip. Mum was the beautiful smoker then. But she cast it all aside (the smoking, too) when life became pressing.

My mother was shut off in many ways. I assumed she had her reasons—an innocent person afflicted with life. She refused to feel difficult emotions and gained further traction in that with Dad, who would follow her anywhere. She gave of herself in the ways she could. The lace curtains over the living room windows were always in motion, as if at her behest; something about the way they breezed into the room, fluttering with outdoor freshness in that burnished light, was pure Mummy. Every December an elaborate Christmas tree, with Italian bubble lights that could thrill a child forever, reached to the ceiling. Then she spent money maniacally, with Dad groaning and begging in her wake but the two of them relishing the pleasure of giving Steve and me everything we wanted, including bikes and puppies. Christmas was how she made up for being mean, we said, how she made up for the rest of the year.

Christmas over, we needed extra magic. Mum was spent from holiday effort and heavy debt, and when she exploded and disappeared behind her slammed bedroom door, Steve and I produced our spring-loaded Pez dispensers to save the day. Dad would pronounce that Mummy was "all nerved up again." The gardenia, robust and undisturbed, maintained its royal station in the middle of everything, and Steve and I surrounded the plant to mock-shoot each other with Pez candies and then die rambunctiously, twitching on the floor. This allowed Mum a grace period until we all returned to our tranquil state.

My father's heart visibly lifted when Mum emerged from their room to cook dinner. And soon we were all seated at the kitchen table, with Dad making wisecracks and pouring salt on our food.

All was made well for two weeks every summer, when Dad got his vacation. We went to North Truro with Aunt Sunday and Uncle Pye (Pierre), where Cousin Claude and I chased each other over the Cape Cod sand dunes. We traveled the Mohawk Trail in western Massachusetts, where I climbed up and embraced the bronze statue of the handsome young Mohawk brave in sun salute and could not come down and end that moment, no matter how my father pleaded (I felt a need to stay riveted there, as if I'd connected with a past life). We once camped on Lake George in the Adirondacks and explored Fort Ticonderoga and Fort William Henry. Those happy experiences comprise a permanent investment in the coffers of my well-being.

Then, somewhere in time, Mum began a living room renovation that involved ripping the wallpaper and plaster off the walls and exposing the studs and lath, leaving dust and peeling paint everywhere. She became a tornado, tearing the house down with the promise to begin anew. It gave her moods an outlet. She planned plumb walls and handsome wallpaper, an elegant new carpet and a new couch. But her plans went astray and all was interrupted when the glory fell out of our existence and we entered the land of nitty-gritty.

"You're having a three-headed baby?" I asked on a summer day in 1957, when my mother stopped me in the kitchen in our first and only home in our modest Rhode Island mill town. She was so hugely pregnant, she'd had to stop driving and couldn't go anywhere.

She'd just told me that "the doctor's X-rays showed three heads." At my quizzical response, she became stern: "There'll be no complaints from you. Don't even try to be funny." She said there would soon be triplets born to this family—sent by God. "We can't take care of you anymore."

I thought I had to be dreaming.

She said I'd have to get a job.

"But I'm only twelve."

"You can still sleep in your bed," she continued. "You can still eat at our table. But you'll have to pay for your clothes and movies with your friends." One of her pin curls had escaped the field of tight hair circles bobby-pinned in rows all over her head, and that errant blond tendril shook—strangely, comically, as if to mark her words. My eyes flew to the cobalt blue Fiestaware teapot on the windowsill that Mummy and I both loved. We sometimes sang the "Little Teapot" song and do-si-doed around. That day, her bursting belly leaned forward and eclipsed the teapot, causing me a siege of panic until she swayed again and that happy touchstone came back into view.

Teapot, a voice said inside my head, anchoring me, as Mum explained in the voice of a stranger the work she had lined up while her motion made the teapot appear and disappear. She wore one of my father's tent-sized T-shirts, which hung like scaffolding over the pregnancy. I silently criticized this "around-the-house" outfit she'd adopted, as if to announce defiantly that we were entering into a ragamuffin life. She'd replaced decent slacks and makeup with baggy, paint-stained pedal-pushers, discolored white ankle socks, and ugly wedge shoes; her pale mouth clamped a lit cigarette in one crisp corner.

Table, my inner voice continued, while my heart clanked away and my voice uttered sounds of protest out loud.

My fingers traveled along the table when our conversation was done. *Doorknob.* I continued my way into the front hall as if my hands were all that was left of me. I knew, with certainty, that my life, my family, and all that was familiar was about to change, and like someone blind I felt my way toward the front door, touching the walls and descending the front steps. *One step. Two step. Three step. Six. Grass. Cement. Step. Road.*

Standing in the road—that trail of hot, sun-softened tar where few cars ever came—my noonday shadow reduced me to a point far away beneath my feet. Our house looked like a white fort—its windows and doors sealed with tight black trim—and it seemed to have risen away up an imaginary hill. I tried to pull my nerves from that box with its once-friendly upper-story dormers like two sleepy eyelids, to withdraw all my faith and my trust. But I was forever nailed to that moment. My mother's words made me think I was a grown-up now. *Look at me,* I thought with unbearable shame. *I'm twelve years old, and I still need my mother.*

I was suddenly charging around town with my best friend, Darlene, every afternoon, pushing Mrs. Sorilla's six-month-old Baby Ed in a carriage in front of us, harmonizing "Let It Be Me," and looking for out-of-town boys driving by. They'd stop and talk, but we couldn't go with them with a baby in a carriage, so we'd all make promises to meet again. *All we have to do is dream,* we sang about those thrilling stranger-boys.

By seventeen, I'd cared for the children of numerous families who worked in the mill. I'd worked in the Town Diner, the Five-and-Ten, and several departments of the ribbon company, too. I felt my work was due to disastrous necessity, and I didn't protest. But I felt dislocated, outside everything—my school, my family, my town.

Mum didn't go on with her remodeling. The living room remained in that "unfinished" condition for the rest of my time at home. She said we should get used to the mess, there was no point in improving things now. A new odor prevailed: dirty diapers and the souring baby food that was trapped in the slots of the triple-seated baby butler my father built. I spent Saturday mornings—stuck home babysitting anyway—scraping gunk from those hard-to-reach places. I became the self-appointed mess-keeper. Everything seemed hopelessly out of control. The chrome ashtrays disappeared, the piano went to the cellar, and the gardenia evaporated.

My eighteen-year-old self escaped from my family and my town—leaving Darlene and my classmates behind—and I've been post-eighteen ever since. I found my way to Boston and got jobs and a degree in English literature from Northeastern University. I barely got accepted, given my sparse college prep and poor SATs, but they liked my personal essay. A ten-year rift with my parents followed my departure, as they refused both financial and emotional support for my aspirations. Then something of a reunion followed, after I married. My marriage still has a wild-animal hold on me—even while I'm back here in my past, reclaiming my youngest parents and my life.

Before my folks and Steve and I could begin catching up, another car came clattering and tumbling down the driveway and this little hour got taken over by the very phenomenon that ended our family as it was. The "second family" kept emerging from the car like a troop of circus clowns and soon came squealing out on the deck in full force. The three arrived in the same manner of chaos by which—at birth—they assumed central place in the family forever.

Not that they weren't thrilling new surprise babies. In 1957, I couldn't resist holding and kissing each sweet little miracle. But I soon complained. Bassinets and bathinettes took over our four small rooms, and every inch of space became occupied by baby clutter. A full chorus of infant wailing carried on, and my parents were up—running around in the middle of the night, bumping into each other like Moe and Curly, making formula and changing diapers—while Steve and I, in our bedroom off the kitchen, beat our fists and cried into our pillows.

In my childhood home, where I had always complained that "nothing happens"— "nobody, nowhere, nothing, nohow" was my refrain—something had certainly happened. At twelve, I could only feel bewildered. It was impossible not to feel the god in new life. The three dewy babies had miraculous tiny lips and fingers, huge eyes, and tender dispositions. I couldn't resist their baby breath and smells, their murmurs and mouth shapes. They were innocence and newness. Margo and Marisol were mirror images, with shocking Jean Harlow hair. The whole town lined up to see them. Max was a redhead—a serious, sober baby—but not "identical," and therefore less noticed. This caused that little boy to withdraw and retreat from the gaudy publicity.

"They've put this town on the map," Lois Wishinsky, the bakery owner, pronounced. It was a moment of glory for the down-and-out denizens living all around the dozen-acre, brick bastion that was once the prosperous wool mill. The wool industry had moved south, leaving a ghost complex inhabited primarily by weeds and briars and now and then by short-lived small businesses. Triplets were rare then, a celebrity event. News photographers from Providence clustered on the scabbed road outside. Our German shepherd—our female Rina-Tina-Tina—could no longer nap on that sun-warmed stretch of tar in the morning.

Max—a middle-aged, slightly balding man now—stood, silent, staring and unaffected, on the deck, like Kaw-Liga (rhymes with Elijah), the wooden cigar-store Indian of the Hank Williams song. But the two adult sisters had arms full of bowls and baking dishes and bags with handles and were wailing again. I tried to be generous, noticing how these two identical platinum blonds were still as gorgeous as when they were children. But they were coming at us from every angle, forcing a banquet and demanding our attention. Food and praises to God were being pushed at us unmercifully. "Do you want some pandoody? Apples from heaven." "Pineapple yogurt flume." "There's lamb hanks with punilla. Eat. God loves you." "Squash with prunes and tomatoes, the love of Jesus, and alabaster pie." "This is salad nisseewissee. Have some now. But first we owe thanks to the Lord."

"No. Chill the salad first," shrieked Margo.

"Chill the Lord," asserted Steve.

"You start the moment of silence," screamed Marisol. "I'll put the salad in the refrigerator. Everyone join hands."

The two invoked God in prayer and squabbled about whether He was here in this house or out over the lake, looking down, while we original four sat open-mouthed, as if we were being conquered. Max remained stationary while the two sisters argued without stop. Steve and I refused to join hands and pray to anything.

"Stop the music!" my mother's voice soared.

The moment hung. Then a plastic bowl of pudding plopped facedown on the kitchen floor and the squawking resumed.

"You kids stop this fighting!" Mom demanded. "Right now! I'm putting my foot down. Everyone be quiet. Cut it out and shut up!"

But the noise had risen, and soon I noticed my father—looking paler than the Arctic sun—blubbering in his metal rocker at the far corner of the deck.

"Stop that, Dad," I barked reflexively. "What's the matter with you?"

"I just want everyone to get along and love each other," he said.

"Be a grown-up, Dad," I snapped, putting my longings aside.

Just after my mother announced the "three heads," my father flew off the road on a crazy midnight drive and stopped just short of the river, his car crumpled in the arms of a grand sycamore. He spent weeks in the VA hospital, uncertain whether he'd lose his leg. Instead he lost his mind.

Home on crutches, Dad was a washed-out figment, paler and whiter than his worst imaginings. (Dad thought us all too pale-skinned and seemed to fear we could vanish into "thin air.")

His hair stood on end and his eyes bulged; he didn't smile and he seemed to look right through you. Later in my life, when my husband heard the story, he speculated that my father might have had passive intentions of ending it all, that he'd "had a nervous breakdown, but kept right on going."

Dad went back to work for a while, but he became alarmed about money when the deluge of infants arrived. He began taking home piecework from the machine shop where he worked by day and stayed up past midnight in our cellar, grinding and polishing metal parts for oil rigs on his lathe, drill press, and milling machine.

It's a mystery to me why he might have panicked and lost his grip, as he'd had enormous good fortune finding work in the machine shop. He must have thought we wouldn't have enough. Just before my brother was born in 1952—when I was almost seven—my parents were laid off after years working in the Waltham Watch Factory and then at Raytheon. Until then I'd been left in the care of my grandparents by day. My mother didn't look for work after Steve was born. But my father's search, during a serious stretch without money, yielded a serendipitous experience.

He was interviewed by two young MIT graduates, just starting their own business outside Providence. JW was a vibrant young Irish American and Viki a reserved and taciturn Japanese American. (We didn't know about the internment of Japanese in World War II, but that could have explained Viki, who didn't socialize and never came to office parties.) The pair recognized my father's mathematical and mechanical talent, despite his lack of higher education, and offered him a job in their new machine shop if he'd attend a two-year college program on weeknights—at company expense—attain an associate's degree in mechanical engineering, and remain with the firm for ten years.

"Daddy's a genius!" my mother exclaimed when my father came through the back door that day looking like he'd just stumbled out of the forest, lost no more. He stood there with dignity and a disbelieving smile, occasionally searching overhead as if dollars might start raining down.

But his leg wasn't healing. He'd developed osteomyelitis (an infection of the bone marrow) and had to have a steel rod inserted with a drain hole for pus. Soon, he had to stop working in the shop by day. His gray work outfit developed rents and grew threadbare, and he looked ghostly as he stumped along on crutches—a sound that lobs around in my head to this day.

Even in this state—home all day—he managed to "hand-build" that triple baby butler, since no such thing could be found on Earth, and a glow of contentment burst through when he fed the three babies all in a row in the morning with a single bowl and spoon. "Here comes the happy-pappy zpoom," he chanted in a singsong voice. "It's the zoom-boom-goody-guppy-puppy-zpoom." All three mouths flew open like baby birds'; they were angelic and trusting, and it was impossible not to sigh. Dad's own mouth opened wide with each extended spoonful. A nurturing man in a perfect state of empathy.

These three babies—the towheaded identical girls and the little redheaded boy—had newspaper staffs pleading for help in naming. Slews of letters arrived, as did enough cloth diapers for a small country (Pampers didn't exist then); potties and playpens added to the clutter of our home until there was no room to walk. Photographers still clustered on that scrap of road.

"Are you the sister?" a pad of paper and ready pencil was shoved under my nose as I waded through.

"No," I answered. "I'm a stranger."

"Have ya gut names for 'em yet?" asked another.

"Yeah. They're Be, Bop, and Lula," I threw at them and ran up the back steps.

There was a universal assumption that all three names had to begin with the same first letter, and no other thought about it. We had hundreds of responses to choose from: Pamela, Patricia, Patrick; Sarah, Sandra, and Samuel. My parents didn't know Marisol was a Spanish name, or perhaps it simply didn't matter—they liked it. The package suggestion was Marisol, Maritza, and Manuel.

It took three months to name the triplets, during which time Margo, Marisol, and Maxwell were called A, B and C, in the order of their birth.

My mother told me that we lacked health insurance because it was unaffordable, and now, given the accident, the births, and three incubators for premature three-pound babies, we were about to become poor. I was thoroughly alarmed. But when someone from the shop came to our door one day with a baseball cap brimming with two hundred one-dollar bills, I was one mortified twelve-year-old. Mum, at her most stern, informed me that the shop had "just saved us losing our home."

Now, here, Steve was scolding Max about the boat. Max stared into space as if nothing was happening and seemed not to speak—but Max makes his presence felt in other ways.

Max has let the family rowboat sink by the dock—outboard motor and all—three Septembers in a row, and each time Steve has rescued it from the bottom of the lake. Last September, he warned Max that he wouldn't rescue it again. And Max left the boat out anyway. Rain filled it, the boat went under, winter came, and the lake froze over.

"You're fucking forty-two years old," Steve said, as if that should be convincing.

The lake itself grew agitated. That's when I slipped out the door and climbed the rock face behind the house, to sit high up and face the mystery of the ancient water.

My Mother's Other Children

But some part of my parents enjoyed this spotlight. From birth, "the babies" became their sole focus and source of angst and pride.

"Yeah, they got their fifteen minutes of fame," says Steve after he too escapes the melee and heads up the steep path behind the cottage. We've left the squabbling and pleading to mount this rock face above the lake, where we can see them all out on the deck. Except for Max. Max has retreated inside to stare at the ceiling.

We agree our parents should have won the "stupid prize" in family planning. Three babies were just too many to comprehend, when I was twelve and Steve was five, in a family of four that was barely doing okay. We—the two oldest—were far apart enough to have had few of the advantages of siblings, and when our mother, at thirty-six, delivered this unexpected litter, our two lives changed so much that we lost touch. Our parents mishandled that whole whopping change.

"They were the worst," I reflect. "But look. They couldn't possibly have planned it. Most families weren't planned then anyway. I was the unplanned pregnancy that forced their marriage in the first place. 'Choice' wasn't a concept. What saved them was their decision to pronounce the three a blessing. Mum got religion and Dad went along." We are settled on our precipice, facing out on the sweep of water, above the resounding cottage.

"Listen to them. That's just Margo and Marisol down there," says Steve. "It sounds like a massacre. Those echoes travel miles out over the lake."

"Even up here it's deafening. Everyone knows they're here."

"We'd get a perfect shot," he quips, making me reflect on our bow-and-arrow period, that brief window in which our childhoods overlapped, when we prowled that wooded quarter-acre across the road with Mum and Dad. Dad had made bows and arrows with cut branches and strings for him and Mum and they used Tupperware for tom-toms. Steve's and mine were store-bought and seemed like the real thing. The only redemption if you were "It" was to discover a lady slipper. Then you could be Chief Butterscotch or Tincture of Merthiolate or Spark Plug or anything you wanted for the day.

"Oh, give it up and sign the peace treaty, Massasoit," I say. "The palefaces usurped the land long ago."

The cottage sits small below.

"Do they all come up here every weekend?" I ask.

"No. They came to see you."

"But I came to see Mum and Dad. I was pleased to find you here too. But who invited everyone?"

A pine breeze kisses past. We sit here, sun-warmed, perched above it all, and Steve tells me things I didn't know.

"Sometimes Margo and Marisol come up here together," he says. "You should see. I'll be out on the deck just loving the silence. Then they get here and it turns into a barnyard. Those two thrive on crisis and hysteria. They whip each other into a constant frenzy. I can't hear myself think for the whole weekend, 'til they're gone."

I'm watching Margo wade into the lake in a blue bathing suit below. First she stands serene against the blue. Blue against the blue. I think of that blue of Mum's everlasting teapot and make up an instant jingle—*The hour struck three and broke the teapot. It was just a matter of time*—as Margo launches herself into an athletic crawl toward the horizon.

"You should see what goes on." Steve tells me that in the off-season, one of the three will drive up to spend a few days alone on the lake and slop ruin everywhere. Rotting food and dirty dishes are left; spills flood the counters and dribble down the cabinets, off the living room side tables, the coffee table, and the couch to the floor. The refrigerator ends up full of garbage; the bathroom is filthy, drains are clogged with hair, the toilet overflows, used towels are flung around. Steve spends September and May cleaning and cursing.

I become thoughtful. "I remember when they were all three hospitalized and diagnosed back when they were still teenagers. I heard about it then. But it doesn't explain . . . I mean, I've never experienced the likes of Margo and Marisol's screaming. And those messes. Maybe we have to understand that they can't help it."

"That doesn't mean it's okay."

"I'm just saying it's probably not about them intending harm."

"Oh, no? There's harm to me. I get here and have to clean for days before I can settle in. Every time."

"It's easy for me to say they can't help it. I wasn't here, I was out of the fray. I never lived with this. They're so childlike, so infantile."

"And spoiled. Spoiled since they were born. Margo and Marisol never lifted a finger. Never washed a dish. Never. When we got a dishwasher, those two were supposed to load and empty it. Well, they wouldn't. They never did. Never. Not once. You should have heard the screaming and fighting. I felt like shooting them all with my BB gun. Ma finally did the dishes. Every single night."

"No one insisted . . . ?"

"They did nothing. Ma and Dad both picked up after them and kissed their asses. Every time they screamed they got their way."

"Why?"

"I dunno. You tell me. Because they're triplets? And that was so special?"

"I'm thinking it was guilt, that they actually wanted to drown them in the bathtub."

It seems that the trouble began when Max and Margo both dropped out of state college in their first year. They couldn't go out into the world, couldn't leave home. Somehow my parents had managed to send them off to college and to pay for it. They'd even given them cars. I don't know when their economic situation improved so, or when their values about education changed. But Margo fled the university, threatened by menacing pictures on the walls in her dorm that communicated disturbing things to her, and she talked of suicide. When my mother tried to force her return, Margo started punching her while Mum was driving on the highway, sending the car off the road and down into a roadside marsh. The police intervened and took Margo to a mental hospital.

Then Max was caught hiding in the closet of a woman's apartment and was arrested, taken to jail and subsequently had a stay in the same hospital as Margo. He was medicated, and later released and mandated to live in my parents' home. He moved into the little room off the kitchen, which had been mine and Steve's shared bedroom. Marisol had chosen not to go to college and—right out of high school—married a drunk who beat her; but she had the good sense to leave, though she had a breakdown first.

Thus began the nightmare I was not part of, since by then I was long gone and out on my own. When I left at eighteen, I didn't look back. Dad signed for my LBJ National Defense education loan, told me he was proud of me, and said bye. Mum and I never spoke during those years. I found friends: a group of fellow "orphans."

No one knows why all three became derailed in their late teens. An obstetrician friend of mine told me the incidence of brain disorders in multiples increases enormously once there are more than two. Factoring in two-month prematurity, low birth weights, three incubators, and my mother's age (thirty-six was considered dangerously old to give birth at the time), it's all the explanation anyone has.

Steve claims that there's no history of multiples on either side of the family. The triplets were subjects of medical research. Margo and Marisol are from a single zygote that split into two embryos: that made them identical mirror images, right down to their mirrored-handedness (one left, one right) and opposite unequal foot sizes. Identical twins have virtually identical DNA. Max is their fraternal triplet—a separate zygote from the start—just a sibling who inhabited the womb with his two sisters, and the last born. I can see that he has what are called the negative symptoms of schizophrenia—that withdrawn, staring-into-space, blunted manner. No one ever knows what Max is thinking.

"Max was the caboose," says Steve.

I called them the M&Ms.

Mental illness runs in families, probably most families. We have our share on Mum's side. Mum's mother, Mimay, produced six children, then took to bed and locked into a permanent lovegaze with her Infant of Prague statue on the bureau at her feet while her children went out to beg for food. Not to mention some sadder family members. Dad's are all in Finland and Sweden, where we've imagined them quiet and repressed.

Now in middle age, Margo and Max—both on disability—live with Mum and Dad. Those four are an enmeshed lot, all of them living at Eden Avenue.

"I'm glad I got out when I did," I tell Steve. "It had to be awful . . ."

"Oh, they like mental illness here. I'm telling you, it's their specialty. Ma would be right in there praying with them if you weren't here. She went through some kind of conversion, too, and watches some lunatic evangelist on television every Sunday morning. Dad just goes along with anything Ma says. They're like Holy Rollers. Sometimes I think they're all wackos and I wonder what the hell I'm doing here. You don't get loved in this family if you're not mentally ill."

"Yet you come here a lot. Having moved clear across the country."

"It's the place. I had my best growing-up years here."

"Oh?"

"You were gone. You wouldn't know. The family had its best life in this house, on this lake. Ma and Dad had friends; they all went dancing. All the kids grew up together. Those were boating summers."

A breeze slaps something dry against my cheek. "Ouch!" Startled, I grab a dried-up luna moth, still exquisite, but dead. Another breeze whisks it out of my hand and dances it down the rock face.

How amazing to comprehend that beyond my existence here, Dad earned a better position when the machine shop became a company. Steve was part of both families: just us, the factory workers, and just them, the family with the second home. Mum tells me what they hand-built up here was their dream home.

Steve says that with age, the three have mellowed. Max and Margo may still live with our parents, but Marisol became an LPN, got a job, and moved out at some point. Steve was in college when they all had "nervous breakdowns." But he knew that our sisters lived in states of pure delusion, accusing every man they saw of assaulting them.

"They reported men all over town," he says. "The police were their babysitters when they were in their twenties. For years."

"Did that end?"

"No. But it's toned down."

"The least to blame, really," I say, looking at our feet bracing us against the rock, shuffling in the sand and mica, "are the three." I gained this perspective in twenty years of psychoanalysis. The point was to get my anger into the right place. It belonged to my parents. I'd left home angry at three babies. Not until I had a baby of my own did I fully understand that it's not a baby's intent to trap and tie you down. And with your own, you've signed on for the responsibility.

I recall my father's childhood friend, Olga, just following the triple-header birth, saying, "Horace, you better hang it out to dry."

Steve, at five, wouldn't have taken that in.

Someone else, pointing to Dad's crutches, said, "He heard he was having triplets and he jumped out the window."

Dad didn't laugh. Dad had stopped laughing.

But again, in spite of his low point, Dad managed to hand-build a triplet stroller. He welded pipes and metal tubes onto a twin stroller to make a third seat for Max in front of the original two. When Darlene and I, at thirteen—at our most cool in tight black peg pants, mascaraed lashes, and Tangeed lips—tried to push the stroller into town, there proved to be a weighting problem. We had to stop—interrupting our perfect Everly Brothers harmony of "When Will I Be Loved"—to coax and reposition the wheels, but they stuck and turned in every cleft and crack in the road.

When we finally made it to town, people flocked around us and carried on.

"These are the triplets," the chorus went. "The Ahlenberg triplets." Their awe increased while I died of embarrassment, moving along these bouncing, squirming products of conspicuous fecundity and the pulsing primal scene. This was altogether too much spectacle and limelight for a teenager. I refused to push the stroller again.

Darl and I were both heady with our dreamed-of womanhood swiftly taking flower, rushing us into our own sexuality (Elvis had appeared and changed our lives)—but I was full of caution as well. Two of my older friends, who were fifteen—Janine and Martha—were already knocked-up young mothers-to-be, about to have baby daughters and name them after me. Though sex was a powerful constant on my mind, I was also excruciatingly aware of the consequences. On top of it all, this picture of me trying to command the impossible stroller cast me as the pathetic servant.

Darlene understood exactly how I felt. In eighth grade, she was the new girl in town. She appeared out of nowhere one day and we felt like long-lost loves. She had blue-black hair and eyes so black that even when she faced the sun and I studied closely, the pupil and the iris were indistinguishable. When I asked where she got her eyes, she said she was Scottish. My eyes, on the other hand, were as light as glass. Darlene said they had rays of yellow behind the blue, and that on different days they looked gray, blue, or green.

Darlene had a funny accent—she'd say she had to "warsh" her hair—which she attributed to having once lived in Baltimore. She had moved to Rhode Island to live with her much older, married sister, her sister's husband, and her five-year-old niece, Rose. She cleaned house and babysat for Rose on evenings and weekends in exchange for room and board. Darlene's sister was tall, slender, and blond, with a narrow face—a completely different type. Much later in life, I'd wonder what their connection really was.

Darlene and I were both outsiders in our school. Because we worked, we couldn't participate in extracurricular activities. Those activities included only sports and Glee Club in our very basic small town. Our class of ninety-two had about fifteen "popular" kids—the cheerleaders and the football, basketball, and field hockey stars. We were below envy. We saw those people as having a superiority we could never understand. It felt awful to think about them, so we didn't. Other kids forced to work outside school seemed marginal and pathetic, however, and Darl and I shunned them. The rest of the kids we never saw somehow. They came to school and left.

Darlene was the only friend I brought home. One day, when we were upstairs sitting on boxes that held my mother's S&H Green Stamps booklets, in my grandparents' unused spare room, Darlene watched through the window as my father walked up the backyard walkway from the car. "He don't look so happy," she commented. I was saddened by his troubled look.

When I was twelve and Dad had his car accident and went out of his mind, he walked around in his underwear. His doctors told him to. The point was to keep the wound in his leg dry. He wore BVD underwear that looked like they'd peep open with the slightest move. Every time he entered the kitchen or living room, stumping along on those crutches, I got up and left the room—furious, without knowing why. Dad, in that disturbed state of mind, took my abrupt exits to mean that I hated him and eventually told me, "When you hate, you get hate right back."

We were at a stalemate. I was relieved when he had to spend time in the hospital again. With a house full of babies and nowhere to put them, of course, we were all at our most displaced.

Somewhere in there, Mum began working nights as a hat-check girl, and I suppose it fell to me to take care of the babies. When Dad was home from the hospital, it was him, in his underwear, and me on duty all evening.

The underweight babies spent their first two months in incubators, and that left me alone in the house when Mum was visiting them and Dad was also in the hospital. I don't recall where Steve was. Alone in the house and full of "prurient interests," as the nuns put it, I prowled through my parents' bedroom drawers. In among the whites in Dad's BVD drawer, I found *Playboy Magazine* (the first issue I'd seen) and a paperback copy of *Lolita*—a book banned in this country, I knew. Dad otherwise didn't read anything but *Popular Mechanics*, so I knew this book must be hot. I sought out the steamy passages.

That experience changed me. I found myself turned on by

what I read, yet horrified by Humbert Humbert, a man my father's age with a girl my age. I became at once sexually obsessed with and repelled by boys (my junior high school classmates) and men. Alone, I learned to know my own body and feel it in my control. I became my own "mistress." I owned myself. Janine and Martha—married with their two little Janices—were my cautionary tales.

I also fastened on Nabokov's description of the "nymphette," whose physique was superior. She was bird-boned and delicate, unlike me. I was almost sorry to be a girl for a while. Then every boss I had and every man who drove me home from babysitting jobs at night had boundaries that felt porous, their attentions more focused than they should be. One gave me gifts to be kept secret from his wife and one turned the light on in his car so we could linger outside and he could show me photographs of his inventions. I didn't know if I was imagining things, but I was both thrilled and cautious.

Dad and I turned away from each other for a long time—but later, he proved to be my more invested parent. Overall, no one was bad, just bewildered.

Margo's motion on the horizon is so fluid and seamless, she could be stitching the water to the sky.

"What a good swimmer," I comment. "Totally in her element."

"I don't want to look at her," Steve grunts.

But Margo's swimming has started a little eggbeater in my heart. Here, she is royalty to my parents and maybe she was that once to our simple town as well, but to the world—hardly. The public misled the triplets. Even with her superb, purposeful swim strokes, and with my full admiration, Margo is just a speck down there, as alone and vulnerable as anyone over her head in an incomprehensible vastness. I can't stop myself from feeling the full weight of her complicated life. None of it is their fault. They didn't ask to be born. They didn't ask to be three. My balance wobbles as I add up the pain of everyone.

"I feel the aggravation, too," I agree with Steve. "But think how hard it was. They held the stage as the triplet show. What concepts have they had of 'I' and 'me'? And now think how hard it is for all three, trying to have lives."

"It's easy for me," he responds. "I have no problem. They're useless and it sucks that we got stuck with them. No problem at all. More trouble than they're worth."

My sisters' beauty is ravaged by their plight. Margo is tall and well proportioned, yet her glorious, thick hair is unkempt, her creamy complexion dulled like that of a smoker, and her mouth a slash of fury. This is due to her illness and the medication she could never dare to be without. How can we understand?

If my anger should have gone to my parents for sacrificing me, I've never managed to get it there. Moreover, I fear that letting go of my resentment of the triplets could have me drowning in sorrow.

The setting sun's rays hit the silver on the ledge, making sparks jump and dance before us as we shuffle our feet. They also cause Margo, wading back to shore, to twinkle like some luminescent water-creature surfacing from the deep.

My empathy juices dry up quickly.

That evening in the lake house is a noisy nightmare. It isn't just the crowding and chaos of lunacy. My sisters—born-agains—turn everything into a sermon on a Hallmark God. They express horror that we don't pray to this god who then won't love us. They plant themselves in the middle of the room and scream, as they've done since they were born. All contact, even with myself, is cut off.

Steve wonders how much of this noise is them "being spoiled as all hell," and how much is mental illness. "Doesn't mean I have any more tolerance either way," he's quick to add.

"Maybe they're making the world look and sound the way they feel," I suggest. "A loud, chaotic mess. Turning themselves inside out. And Max? Just makes quiet messes?"

"He's mixed." Steve shrugs. "He does a lot of repairs on the property. He's built all these bluebird boxes and the bird feeders. He knows his birds."

"So he contributes."

"He makes messes too. I find the lawn mower sunk in the mud and rusted. Blowtorch in the basement next to an open can of gasoline. Guy runs on about a tenth of a hoof of horsepower. But then we go fishing together. Then I like him."

Finally, Steve and I both separately tell the M&Ms to shorten their visit and let us have Mum and Dad to ourselves.

"Oh, okay," is my sisters' response, as if we've suggested something delightful. Childlike, they gather up their bowls and casserole dishes and sweep out the door, blowing kisses and sweet "I love you's." Max, meanwhile, disappears without notice. Then, in this clean brown-and-blue setting, we become again that quiet, unassuming family we once were.

I know full well I'm trying to recover impossible losses. I've always liked my parents, even when I've hated them. I resolve to come back here two weekends a year and repeat these good times, with all of us laughing and enjoying one another.

My father asks about my long drive. What route I took. Not the most important thing about my recent history, but I answer.

"Did you take 287 to 87?"

"Yes."

"Then 89 all the way."

"Yes. Yes. Dad, you have a mind full of maps."

We all agree about Dad's map-mind and chortle away. My parents seem mildly amused all the time. Dad used to say that one life in this universe wasn't "more than a fart," and the two of them would break up laughing.

They roll.

It was my destiny to wake up young from this easy contentment, curious to know what there was to know, and the extent of knowledge. We were not an inquiring lot. We didn't aspire. My father did well over time, finding his way to owning our first and only home. His parents did well too, finding their way to America from remote regions of Finland and Sweden. But I had more abstract yearnings. When the beginnings of rock and roll reached in, Elvis's "Heartbreak Hotel" stormed my heart, Little Richard brought burning energy, and Ian and Sylvia purred pure love in "Love Is Strange." They, along with Chuck Berry (oh, stop here) and The Coasters, indicated life beyond this place. Voices on the radio populated my world with soul mates.

Not so alone in my vague ambition, I finally set off at eighteen, an age when it seemed you should done with your parents anyway. But my departure was not wholly my own choice. I thought I was leaving a poor family in ruins. In fact, my burdened parents had pushed me from the roost.

Northeastern University had a co-op program that alternated school and work terms, and provided a new terrain of opportunity. I was deeply interested in understanding human motivation and personality. I began my co-op job, working double shifts (sixteen-hour days) at McLean Hospital, a private mental institution, as a psychiatric aide. During the school term, I worked many part-time jobs, but McLean was my co-op job. I was an English major with a sociology minor, and I was eager to work with the mentally ill. My triplet siblings would have been six then. No hint of what was to come.

I sought out that job not only out of interest in the human psyche but because I'd heard that the patients there were wealthy. I wanted to meet rich people, to know how they lived. I'd never known or seen anyone who was rich. I wanted to know their relationship to the wider world. I wanted to borrow from that larger view.

I wore a white uniform. On my first day, I met Mike, a Yale student. Both new to this environment and scared, we stood together on the ward we were assigned while a patient—a wild-looking Brazilian woman named Astrid—circled us, looking us up and down, smoking angrily, and muttering curses with dry, spitting gestures. A stereo in the background played "Donna Donna" by Joan Baez, then appearing in nearby Cambridge coffee houses. I dreamed of seeing her, of hearing that magnificent voice in person. But inside this hospital, all else felt far away.

Mike and I clung to each other. By the end of the week, we had both impersonated that amazing ward character many times over, each of us capturing the high drama of her crazy, wild disgust. We did this, of course, off the premises and out of sight. We found we were good imitators. We soon became an act. There were other patients worthy of parroting. "Real characters." We got good at free association, at LOAs and FOIs (loosenings of associations and flights of ideas), and made up brilliant soliloquies. We loved our patients, but we were comic and young and cruel. It was our eighteen-year-old way of handling the alarming extremes we saw.

When Mike invited me to Yale, his suite-mates gathered to greet me. Following introductions and showing me the campus, Mike's friends begged us to do our act. Mike invited me to go first, doing exotic Selena. I spread my hair over my face, then cast my eyes far out to some vision only I could behold, held a make-believe cigarette, and free-associated in breathless "schizophrenese":

"Eric loves me and he leaves me and he leaves me and he loves me and he goes away and takes my heart off and my head off and my heart off my head and my head off my heart and even then not enough. He takes my eyelashes and fingernails and my tears turn to teeth and rake my knees. And he says he's never coming back, and I will have to drown myself. That's okay with Eric if my body lies face-up or -down in a bloody bog. He's got his motorcycle and I should understand he only works here. He's not locked in. But don't worry about me, I tell him. I'll just cry 'til I'm gone."

I told them about beautiful Selena, who sat stringy-haired, rocking and lamenting, when her medication wore off. She was only semi-real. By now, we were adding our own soup of primary-process thinking. I told them she had Eric, an aide who worked there, mixed up with her motorcycle-riding boyfriend, who was barred from visiting. When on medication, she got dragged off to occupational therapy, where she created plaster statues of herself—wrecked, gaunt, and twisted with torment.

Mike and I had perfected my imitation of her in the cafeteria over many suppers. I shudder to recall our antics, but I have compassion for those two eighteen-year-olds. We were puzzling out life in all its mysteries, some so haywire we couldn't even get to the question.

One day, Mike and I were sent with a male nurse in a car to pick up a woman living on Beacon Hill. She came from a prominent Boston family that was having her committed.

She was alone and terrified when we arrived at her apartment off Mt. Auburn, with its floor-to-ceiling windows and tapestry drapes. I could hear my small voice addressing a woman in her forties, "Mrs. F, you must come with us. Your family wants you to have the treatment you need."

She resisted all my pleas, as well as our leader's commands. She said her family wanted to annihilate her.

"Why would they want to do that?" I asked in all sincerity, but fearing it could be so.

Then the police came, and this patrician woman was forced by two burly women into the police car. It was awful. Was it permanent, I wondered? Her confinement? Her state of mind?

Mike and I wandered the grounds on break, a designed landscape, a thought-out property with splendid old trees. Our imitation of our patients was also about walking in their shoes, imagining being them. They walked in privileged surroundings. But privilege didn't guarantee mental health. It was a crushing revelation.

A classmate worked at Metropolitan State Hospital, just across Trapello Road. Every now and then she and I met and walked the grounds of one or the other institutions.

"We should never go crazy," I said to Judy one day, facing the foreboding state hospital. The shaggy tips of untrimmed firs chafed our cheeks. "We'd end up here in this snakepit, not at McLean."

"I don't think people choose to be insane," she said.

"Well, I'll never allow myself to go nuts. At thirty-eight dollars a day, my family couldn't afford a single day at McLean. I'm condemned to stay sane."

Shortly after the triplets turned eighteen, two of them became patients at McLean. By then, however, my family had health insurance that covered the costs.

Working sixteen-hour days and sometimes six days a week eventually had me feeling that McLean was my world. Sometimes I'd get outside the buildings and onto those magnificent grounds to walk with a patient who needed supervision, wasn't free to go alone. *Who is the rich one?* I asked myself.

When the school term began, I had other part-time jobs: temp-typing, selling lingerie, hostessing in one hotel restaurant, cashiering in another. These jobs felt like sidetracks. I didn't feel I was partaking of the world. I knew of the Peace Corps and wished for that opportunity, but I couldn't even afford not to work.

Graduation meant secretarial jobs for most female humanities majors, even those from the best schools. And where would we go from there? Most people then had never imagined a female physician, lawyer, pilot. I thought women could not do the things men could do.

Love Is the Answer

In February of 1967, at twenty-two, I met David, twenty-five, an urbane and ambitious young neurology resident at Boston City Hospital whose energy and intelligence were magnetic, as was the conviction and promise in his eyes. He raved with passion about the lifetime plasticity of neurons (nerve cells) in the human brain, which had long been thought to grow fixed and immutable with age. "Neuroplasticity" became our mantra. It expressed all our idealism, optimism, and hope.

I was honored to be chosen by this worthy fellow who had, I told a college roommate, a life "a thousand times more interesting than mine." And that was fine with me. Women's lives were supposed to be the lesser. We were taught to just comfortably exist and enjoy our own beauty. He liked me in the ways I liked myself. And I did the same for him. I loved it that he looked to a future in a bigger world, and I felt I'd gladly share that bigger world. I'd already developed sophisticated ways, but I was missing something and didn't know what it was.

The life I began with David had nothing to do with my first one. I hadn't envisaged finding a life partner. I was not future-oriented. Hardly did I hold marriage and family as ideals. I didn't picture the thing before the person. Then this buoyant optimist came along and easily filled the place I hadn't known existed. That was David. I'd never met anyone like him.

He was reading three books when I met him: *Endurance*, about the polar explorer Ernest Shackleton's attempt to cross Antarctica on foot; *The Rise and Fall of the Third Reich: A History of Nazi Germany*, by William L. Shirer and Ron Rosenbaum; and *King Solomon's Ring*, by Konrad Lorenz, which described the phenomenon of ducks and geese imprinting on humans.

I'd set out seeking strangers—people different from myself—with the hope of leaping into something unimagined. This motive may have begun early, with a conversation I had with Dad when I was four, back when we lived with my grandparents in a tiny house just behind the one we later moved to on Eden Avenue. It's a conversation that may or may not have happened.

I asked my father one day if I had "to listen to him."

"About what?" he asked.

"Like about going with strangers?"

"Yeah. You shouldn't do that."

"But I never see any strangers."

"Yeah, well then, don't worry about it."

"But what if I do see some strangers?"

"Well, don't go with them. That's all. Even if they try to give you candy. Don't go with strangers. Don't get in their cars. That's what you have to know."

"Is it okay to just look at them?"

"Well, if you stand far away and don't talk and don't take candy." Dad explained further that he and my mother couldn't tell me much about life. "There's a lot we don't understand," he said. "We get along the best we can. I can fix things and Mummy's a good cook and she can sew. But there's a lot you'll have to find out for yourself."

Strangers became an intrigue. A song on the radio, "Some Enchanted Evening," promised me that I would someday meet a stranger, and stirred my hopes for adventure.

On one of our first dates, David and I were walking in the city when a middle-aged man in a suit collapsed to the sidewalk ahead of us. David ran to him and seemed to make a quick assessment: checked his pulse and breathing, made sure there was no trauma or injury from the fall, said it was probably a vasovagal reaction, and instructed me at the same time to search the man's briefcase for medications he might be taking. People gathered around, offering instructions. "I'm a doctor," David informed the crowd. Everyone fell quiet and stepped back. "Someone call an ambulance," he said. The man was sitting up, answering David's questions by the time the ambulance took him.

    I was stunned by David's confidence and authority. I'd never seen such competence. David was the perfect stranger, who soon became the most familiar person—ever—in my life. We glided into marriage.

    That phase of life with my husband was a new way of being—among excellence—that erased those past poor roads and starved houses... erased them as they had erased me. I blossomed vibrantly among welcoming new friends in better climes. Much as I wanted this happiness to be complete, however, I was nagged by insecurity as it became clear that my relatively poor education had left me underdeveloped compared to these new people. I refrained from expressing myself, not knowing what deficiencies would show.

    I didn't feel lacking with David. I felt his interest and his respect. But in the wider arena, I fought feeling like my husband's appendage, a non-entity who could hardly speak. No matter how much reading I took on, I lacked a beginning. I'd indeed made a leap.

One day, David received notice that he was one of fifty young MDs who'd been selected to serve their military duty by working in research labs at the National Institutes of Health in lieu of going to Vietnam. David was made an ensign in the Navy. He didn't have to wear a uniform, or do anything military. We moved to DC. Once or twice we dined at the Officers' Club, just because that was our privilege. We never saw the contradiction when we marched regularly on the Capitol to protest the war.

David's further good fortune was to be working in the laboratory of someone about to win the Nobel Prize for catecholamine research, which opened up the whole understanding of neurotransmitter reuptake in the brain. David did stellar work on the pineal gland and its related circadian rhythms that year. That whole two-year stint led him into neuroscience.

His ascent surprised him all the way. One night he arrived home with a letter in hand and announced in a disbelieving voice that he'd won a traveling fellowship. He could work for a year in a laboratory of his choice anywhere in the world.

A laboratory in Cambridge, England welcomed him. Neither of us had ever been overseas. I recall that flight: hours traversing the ocean we'd only known on a globe or a map, sitting in the clouds, level with the sunrise, looking down on castles on the greenswards below. It was a wondrous year.

On our return, we settled in New York City, where David set up his own Division of Developmental Neurology in a major city hospital.

Before Cambridge, we'd had a deep experience of the sixties together—all its music, its "doors of perception," high times, close friends on the same trip with us—it's magic even to recall those days. We did things we'd never imagined: technical rock climbing, canoeing, hiking in the mountain wilds. I began writing for a women's liberation magazine called *Off Our Backs* in 1969, when we lived in DC.

Then came England. Then in New York I did some ghostwriting and—without recognizing the contradiction—became a dependent wife, waiting all day for my husband to come home.

Having our son opened a stretch of new happiness. I put off being nagged by my personal shapelessness.

After I married David, something of a reunion with my parents followed our ten-year rift. My parents—now in their retirement trailering days—visited us and our son, Jason, in New

York City or in our cabin in the Catskills. We cooked dinner, drank wine, and talked about their trailer travels and even world affairs. David educated them about the frontiers of medicine. My parents were more aware by then. Dad told us he watched *60 Minutes* and loved Jane Pauley, co-host of the *Today Show*. Jason—my parents' only grandchild—was the star delight, chasing the live Maine lobsters they'd brought across the kitchen floor. We were all secure. I no longer needed my parents. They were off the hook with me. We completely enjoyed one another. And I treasure those times.

In 1969, when I joined the group at *Off Our Backs*, the foremost of the first "women's liberation" newspapers of the sixties, David actually helped me develop some of my ideas for an article. We had a good time making fun of the gender mores of the day. Yet he wouldn't make the bed—never did—or do the laundry. I finally bought a comforter and took away the top sheet so the bed could be made in one swoop. I promised to hold it against him forever that he'd never cooked a meal or cleaned a toilet. But that was all good-natured play then.

Though I continued to earn a living (since age twelve, I've never not worked), suddenly financial reality was not pressing. David encouraged me to spend time writing. The arrival of our son gave me further reason to be at home, but when Jason was six I became concerned about my pattern of hardly going out and saw a therapist. She helped me take on a return to school for a master's degree in clinical social work, so I could help others in the way I was being helped. Then I followed with institute training. I was in my early forties when I became a psychotherapist with a focus on children and parental guidance. Certainly my interest had been fostered at McLean, which had opened the profound domain of human psychology to me.

For so long, my marriage and family contained the most deeply shared sense of life. But our son was moving on, my husband was making his mark in his career, I felt I was just emerging into the world as an adult, and we had now moved from the city to a university town.

I know I'm running from a piece of life that doesn't so easily break off. I go on writing about the confusing family I left behind before there was David, thinking it's possible to find answers in the remotest beginnings. The question remains: Why did the divorce have to be? What drove those tempests?

I'm returning to my first family now, a practicing psychotherapist. Just divorced after thirty years, and I've lost all our friends. My son has grown up and moved on. The smoke cleared, I looked around, and no one was there. I think my world will surely replenish itself in time. But for now, I've realized that I still have parents. That's how I came to be sitting on that craggy scarp above that glacial lake with my brother, watching down from above it all, fixed on Margo, swimming far out in the lake. She was the firstborn triplet, when I was twelve and Steve was five. One family became two families. And I lost my parents then.

Margo, with her constant phone calls, is the one who led to my being there on that granite shelf with my back pressed against its mossy rise. She's always called me, since the time I left home. Most times I've ignored these as intrusions. But her calls gained more presence when I no longer had David and began living in a house that was mine alone.

Her childlike voice filled my living room one day on the speakerphone:

"Hi Janis. It's Margo. Do you have ridges in your fingernails? I do. Marisol does. And Dad does. Ma doesn't. Max and Steve won't tell. Please check your nails and call me right away. I love you. Bye."

Her call came just as the tea-stained light of late afternoon sifted down through the trees and mauled me with a beastly mood. Why? I'm half a person on my own. David and I were that kind of couple. Two of us made one. And I've become too serious. My sense of humor is shot, and I'm dark.

I pulled on my sweatpants like someone moving through glue. I was trying to create a life I could live. But lately, my mind goes bad every day about three. My motor conks out.

This day I talked to myself like I do to some of my depressed patients. *Move physically to a different space: go outdoors, to a museum, a pond, anywhere other—preferably larger—than where you are. Not to escape the reality of a mind-state that might need to be embraced, might be pressing for cruel lucidity, but to air that persistent mood, to experience it in another setting, against another play of scenery and light. Feel what it is, say, on the path along the local waterway, or on a cut through deep forest. Run or walk vigorously. Flex and feel the colors, flavors, strains, and nuances of a stuck disposition. Know these mood-troughs won't last. Misery comes in waves. It will lift. It's not all of you. Knowing this when you're most down is key. Put notes around. Know that no one escapes the pain.*

And remember there is music. There is always music.

I felt around in the front closet for those rigid walking shoes that wouldn't soften with use and time, wouldn't mold to my feet and become mine. Even their stiff laces wouldn't go through the holes. It was as if they'd hardened against me, required my feet to conform to them—they'd stayed wrong. I asked myself how I'm a psychotherapist who helps anyone.

That cobalt-blue Fiestaware teapot—now mine—sits high up on the baker's rack in my kitchen. The lid is chipped from a recent washing, leaving a glaring white dot, like a cold sore on a lip. The sight of it marred after all this time seemed a vision of mortality itself and dragged me under.

Where was resilience? Acceptance? Letting go? Ability to laugh? I was having a bad time. The door groaned as I let myself out.

"*Abierto, cerrado,*" I recalled our dear friend Romelia, who had helped when I was an uncertain new mother, saying. A good thing, when you're bleak, to remember good fortune, even to say out loud what makes you grateful.

At the end of the walkway, I stuck those walking shoes toes up in the trash barrel.

Soon I was at a table in Main Street Café, sitting over a steaming latte with a heart centered in the milkfoam. *No one needs to know I don't always follow my own advice.* Coffee-caffeine—drug of assurance, consolation, unconditional love—is not the cure I recommend to others. The whole raw-nerve of me was soothed all along its processes, traveling from my center, out through fight-or-flight, to knowing that yes, we have to die. Each day draws us closer. Knowing and mourning that would mean living more fully.

I strolled back to my home-office studio with a buzzed and lighted mind, renewed and ready to sit in my office wearing dress heels, a neat suit, and gold earrings, looking collected and ready to bear the weight of other lives by talking, shooting baskets, or animating stuffed animals, soldiers, pirates, and dolls. I'm a child analyst, who uses play therapy. I treat the child in everyone: varieties of Humpty Dumpties—the hopeless, the alone, the never-loved, the over-loved, the conflicted, some who languish, some with poor lives. There's need for me, and I'm committed to my work.

"Hi Janis," said the speakerphone. "They're vertical ridges from the nail beds to the tips of your fingers, and mostly in the center of the nail. Look especially at your thumbs. Call me when you get this. You must not be home. Love you."

Later—alone with my two cats under the moon—I felt how the infinite dark of night replaces little life with enormity of mystery and magic. I wandered around, touching the things I've planted: tall, moon-glowing fountain grass; bursting peonies; mosses under my bare feet. *It's just loneliness*, I thought, excusing the mood that had plundered the afternoon. *Makes you funny in the head.* I wondered how David—now my ex-husband—would see me here. He too must have marveled that I'd finally been able to leave, to extricate my small self from his large self. But I was missing him, too. And where was I now? With him I'd had a place. And maybe I'd been a fool to leave. Women of my generation had left their husbands in droves in earlier years—searching for never-formed identities—only to regret it later, when they'd become whole enough to have perspective. Would that be my fate, too? After all? We'd lasted for thirty years.

I ran through that tight thought-circle like a gerbil on a wheel and wondered what was to become of me.

Holding on to yourself can be a challenge. Creative optimism helps. But the war-torn heart deserves its laments. Coming to terms—getting well—is not done by magic. Healing is accomplished in small measures: steps, words, knocks, stitches, heartbeats, hums, and especially concentrated breaths, all while you seek higher ground in that realm of choice larger than yourself.

But all the strategies against loneliness I've attempted have proven low-yield. Volunteer work, groups, clubs, tours, the chamber music concerts that I love—none have opened up a social world. I know life will begin again. I need animal-level patience and acceptance.

My animal-models are the two meowing felines who plant themselves in my opened suitcase as I pack for my return to Mum and Dad. I hit Qwerty and Elemeno with bras and nightgowns, causing them to stand up, turn around and sit, ready for more. They seem to know so well that time-present is all we have. I know this in the deepest way as a therapist. Though I specialize in dwelling on "spilt milk," it's for the purpose of cleaning it up as best you can, so you don't slip in it and break your neck.

"Hi Janis: If you have ridges in your fingernails, you can file them down. Don't pick your hangnails and don't trim your cuticles. You'll be sorry. Drink plenty of water. Call me when you get this. I don't know where you are. But you must be somewhere. Love you."

Since time-present was ringing empty, I decided to visit my parents. Not to return to the past, I thought, but to continue the reunion that began after I was married—to discover who we were now, Mum and Dad and I. But the past is a force of profound insistence. Don't I know this well.

With no more husband, and newly on my own, I was returning to where my folks and I had left off in our first life together. In their vacation home, the one that had never contained me. They were too old now to come to me. Time for me to go to them.

Mother's Little Helper

The next May—after seven hours on the road—I find Dad at the bottom of the steep driveway, slogging in the mud, trying to jack up an unfamiliar car that looks like it's dripping pea soup. He is surrounded by a flock of nuns in white habits. They were out exploring, ignored the large *DEAD END. PRIVATE. DO NOT ENTER* sign, and slid down the runny mudway to where the land tables out just short of the lake.

Dad has lain out chains, but it takes hours to turn the car around and get them off up the hill.

"Daddy had to hold his curses," says my mother as we take our seats on the deck.

"Jesus," says Dad. "I was so pissed off at them and that back wheel just kept spinning deeper. And every time I went to say 'shit' or 'goddammit' or 'what kinda stupid assholes drive down a dirt-road hill in mud season that says Keep the Hell Out or You'll Be Shot?' . . . I had to bite my tongue; they looked like angels praying fa' Chrissake."

"You know Daddy never fixed anything without cursing to high heaven," adds my mother. "It's how he gets anything done."

I remember very well that steaming plume of curses when Dad was fixing something under or behind the washer, the dryer, the car, his "Goddamn shit-pissing SOBs," and

"Christallbastards" and "everything-to-hells." "Fuck" was never used in those days, by anyone—which gave that expression unimaginable power, to be gasped by lovers in reaches of passion beyond all words or possibly by someone out-of-their-mind frustrated. The unspeakable. Like Yahweh.

Dad among the nuns is the funniest, given how he disdains religion, as did his parents (they tolerated Mum's tepid Catholicism). He won't call himself an atheist, however, because he says it sounds like another religion. Dad sees the possibilities in all religions or none, but has always declared himself Nothing. Not a Pagan? Not a Heathen?

"I'm Nothing," he declares with satisfaction, enjoying his modest little place on Earth. We all look out to the lake, the far island, the sky.

Somewhere—after the babies became children—Mum and Dad must have recovered their focused, hard-working selves. They couldn't have known what complications were to come. Mum told me they "hand-built" this place. They cleared the property that was a swamp and a woods. The six of them camped out on the shore while they waited to be able to afford the cement blocks and lumber.

On this—what we don't know is to be our last "just us" weekend—we get to the sad subject of my divorce and the family's loss of David while Steve ransacks the attic, looking for his .22. We speak about all of us aging. And at the end of that cooling afternoon, Steve and I bring up the question of whether they've made their last set of plans. We rehearsed it earlier, sitting up above the house and the lake.

"What'a you saying?" my father asks.

"They're wondering what to do with us," my mother says, taking it on.

"Do with us?"

"They're wondering where to plant us."

"Huh?!" my father suddenly grins and his Adam's Apple does a little jig. "Well? Right over there." He nods toward Snowy's monolith on the shore.

JANIS AHLENBERG 59

We all crack up.

All the while, it feels as if I'm stealing something I should have outgrown but didn't get enough of before it ended too soon. "Just us" feels like a warm ganache, lumped with the dread of losing my parents. After all the hardship and alienation, we seem restored: "Mummy and Daddy" are their original selves, not those strangers; Steve and I are children again. Our visits have a sense of joy and urgency; it's Mum and Dad, Steve and me, as it once was. But time doesn't stop, even on this heavenly water.

It's 1997. A few days after Steve and I leave them at the lake, Dad has a stroke, leaving his left side paralyzed. Yesterday he was making repairs on the cottage roof, and he woke up this morning with his mouth drooping on one side. The Emergency Medical Team managed the long, winding dirt road and the dried-up mudslide in minutes. My parents tell me that David—the neurologist—got on the phone and guided the local lakeside hospital team through decisions in handling the initial crisis. David's medical assessment proved true. He calls to tell me that the stroke was to the right side of the brain and that Dad's mind and speech—largely properties of the left brain—will remain relatively intact. "If you have to have a stroke," he says, "this is the better one."

I'm moved by David's actions, even with my locked-up heart. I can't thank him enough. But our conversation is short and to the point—and quickly over. We've erased each other for now.

David had a health scare himself when he was diagnosed with carcinoma of the thyroid when Jason was six. Some surgeries followed, some uncertainty, and then it seemed to be a low-grade, chronic, "indolent" condition. But I've never completely relaxed about what might happen to him in the future. He apparently has someone new in his life, and though that upsets me and I'll try to take the high road, it suggests that he is well.

This visit is different. Mum and Dad are on Eden Avenue for good. Now they can't get to the lake. Dad won't dare the deck stairs, or the three-hour trip. And Steve won't come to Eden.

This is my first time back to this basic house where I grew up in forty years. I drive past the same two-story dwellings, slumped together like old drinking buddies along the river stopped still by duckweed, then up the long road to the place where we became one of those houses with kids bursting out the windows.

I heave a sigh as I park where the road peters out in front of the house. Weeds have claimed everything. The house has been through time, through generations, through care and long neglect. The windows look opaque, as if blinded. It's hard to believe anyone is inside. In what shape will I find them now, pounded by time?

The wet grass is knee-high up to the front steps. When I was six, my father and grandfather built those steps together. Janine Jarvi, my childhood friend, and I set our footprints in the wet cement of the bottom step. How many melting Fudgesicles and Dreamsicles dripped down into our toe prints when we sat on those stairs?

Those were competent steps, strong and plumb-lined, with skilled stonework in the risers. The footprints are gone now. The steps have heaved; mosses and stubble grow out of the cracks. Margo has planted things in the flower boxes Max installed under the windows: weeds and geraniums embrace in a messy tangle. I know about the flower boxes because of many phone messages, my consistent backdrop to almost every day. Margo's phone calls have followed me since I left for good at eighteen. She let me know when our beloved German shepherd died. She let me know when John Lennon died. Just before I left this time came these:

"Hi Janis. I ran over a squirrel on my way to my therapist today. I could see it twitching in the road. I was really upset. Anyway, I never know where you are. I love you. Bye."

"Hi Janis. I'm in the cemetery. I've been here all afternoon looking for Nana and Grandpa and I can't find them. Do you know where else they'd be? Love you."

"Hi Janis. My back is better, but I have to keep lying down most of the time. I'm still dog-sitting for my girlfriend, so if you call me here, let it ring once, then call back." (This, so men stalking her won't get her to answer.)

"Janis. There's a rapist who has moved into this area. I'm glad I'm not sitting for my girlfriend's dog anymore. Love you. Bye."

Last night's message from Margo was: "Call back right away! Dad's suicidal!"

I called Steve, who's up on the lake for the month. "Hot dogs!" he informed me. "It's about hot dogs. Dad's been served hot dogs now that Margo's run away, refusing to cook anymore. And he's frantic. He hates hot dogs."

Margo has announced that she's sick of feeding everyone, because they complain about her cooking. She's pronounced a boycott and run away to the monastery that takes people in for a night or two (and recently lifted its restraining order against her).

No one answers the bell. The doorknob falls off in my hand. I push the door hard and there inside, in a dizzying reach back in time, is the sun porch with its ever-shifting installation of castaway things. There's the usual stack of cardboard boxes of old clothes, shopping bags spilling empty bottles, fallen heaps of newspapers, an assortment of broken ironing boards, odd ice skates, croquet mallets, hula hoops, and a bookcase stocked with trinkets and oddities in mayonnaise jars and coffee cans. The top shelf holds what must be Max's current supply of underwear—a place away from the cellar, the dusty and cobwebbed old coal-bin below where, Steve has told me, Max now lives.

One lumpy couch sits against the wall, buried under an array of needlepoint pillows across from two old televisions, one stacked on top of the other. On the wall above the couch—to my unbelieving eyes—are my Virgin Mary and Mummy's Jesus, Jesus still bearing his flaming, blood-dripping heart. Our "holy paintings"—paint-by-number oils on canvas—were accomplished over many yawning gray afternoons when it was "just us" and the world was so small it felt like we lived inside a locket. Mum did her painting on the coffee table, while I lay on my stomach on the floor. We had the junk room in the sun porch then, but not the accumulations of the subsequent population.

Under my footsteps, the floor groans in the same old places. I'm walking into a sore memory. I left a miserable teenage self here—went away, and stopped being the girl who'd had this life.

I do know that the "just us" era—before the babies—was not always the star-bright way I've polished the memory. Mum became strangely troubled at times and could blow her top—often on cleaning day—when she brought out the fire-breathing Electrolux. Her quickening footsteps provided the only warning; her voice rose to fill the house; an explosion followed; and her treasured copper-bottom pots and pans (paid for with years of collecting—she and I pasting them into booklets—those S&H Green Stamps) lifted like a flock across the kitchen, crashing against the walls to fall dented and disfigured on the floor. Anyone in the way got hurt. If I managed to dodge the missiles, I worried about my baby brother.

None of us understood. No one asked. Quiet followed, as if there had only been some weather conniption.

If I was hurt, I ended in a ditch of sadness. I sniveled the morning away in a state of sorry confusion behind the stuffed dusty-rose armchair in the living room. That chair was a stout matron with a generous lap and demure mahogany cabriole feet. I crawled behind her, my crying so enormous that it sought a small space. I extended my legs on the floor under the chair, my back against the wall, and sobbed seeming hours away with my face pressed hard against the raised waffle-weave of crisp fabric that felt like toast. When I finally sobbed my way back to comfort—got cleared of Mummy's last eruption—I emerged, my wet cheeks branded with waffles. It hurt most that Mum refused to ever talk about it.

Those painful disconnects happened over and over again. Too many times to count, my mother lit out like thunder and "got out the stick"—but in time I turned sly and nimble and learned to get away. When I grew a little older and spunkier, the sight of the vacuum cleaner was my cue to head out the back door, through the field across the yellow dirt road, and into another woods, where I would find Lola and Mary Ann Marquese jumping joyously from rock to rock in the brook. All up and down the road by day, it seemed, mothers raged. Thelma Marquese was the loudest; her voice flooded the neighborhood.

As a favor to Mum, who is fundamentally a "good egg," I keep memories of her "tear-asses" (my father's term) in a separate mind-compartment, one that might look like our old cookie jar: a large ceramic mouse with a smirk. I maintain this generosity toward Mum because I believe understanding could free her from being judged. She couldn't help this behavior that seemed so common for women in the 1950s, and under those layers, at the core, is the "Mummy" I love. That's the Mummy who loved "how I looked," according to my aunts and the neighbors to whom she evidently bragged, though she never told me.

We did know that her tirades were caused by medication. Otherwise, what could explain her sudden need to hurt and leave me breathless on the floor? There she was in the evening, after all, making popcorn for the two of us to eat while we watched *I Love Lucy, Milton Berle, Lone Ranger,* or *Boston Blackie* together. According to Mum, her "diet pills" were what caused these bouts of violence that ended her up behind her slammed bedroom door while we three tiptoed around the "headache" that had spread through the house like the tide.

She calmed down altogether when she pronounced the triplets' birth a "calling" and declared there was no point in cleaning anymore. She simply let the housework go.

The mess was awful. Feeling frantic, I tried to maintain a sense of order, and my cleaning efforts increased. But Mum had let go of all that; my helper efforts mattered only to me. Mum and Dad moved on to become film producers, recording the babies day and night, with Steve dancing through every frame, making faces. My father hobbled around with one crutch and a movie camera. My mother coached him on the sets and angles, and little 1, 2, and 3 wore matching outfits that Mum handmade, with ruffles and bow ties. My parents thought they'd hit the jackpot. "The babies" became their sole focus, their panic, and their glory.

My sadness hardened and gathered moss with time and seeped darkly into my bones—a quiet storm that just held steady in my soul, which I've gone on weathering every day. What else? The whole story gathered up and went into hiding when I moved to a different orbit, but it snuck up behind me and laid hold all these years later. I suppose I'm talking about the divorce.

My divorce is a cataclysmic change. I'm trying to escape it, when I should dwell in it for a while. But a divorce has no center; how do you live in the heart of your divorce? It's a heart closed up. All you knew and trusted has vanished.

My act of courage in moving beyond my marriage was a call to enlarge life. I mean to be moving ahead into new frontiers. What am I doing here in my first past? I seem to need to unfold this old story before I can come up for air again.

I find the living room in yet a new stage of squalor. There is the lumpy couch strewn with forgotten shirts and dish towels, layers of dust everywhere, and a carpet thick with debris. I've known none of the interim incarnations.

My parents and I enjoy warm hugs. They're glad to see me. I'm moved by their endearing sweetness and gentle voices and decide they're living in a different chaos from the one I last knew here: a late-life undoneness, a permanent letting go. I can see by the disarray that no thought of order exists. But they are happy and fun, the way they were when David and Jason and I enjoyed them and welcomed them when they came through twice a year, leaving their Airstream—presumably with one Snowy inside—hooked up to a waste-line in a trailer park and driving to us in their car.

I take my mother grocery shopping. The refrigerator holds an abundance of rotting foodstuffs and those hot dogs my father hates.

"Birds of a feather," she comments as we cross the yard, pointing to some sparrows, "over there, having a convention in Max's strawberry patch."

Set in the middle of what looks like a hayfield—a merriment of encroaching meadow—this patch is an act of strawberry intention embraced by the contrasting wild. The mountain laurel Max has planted out front is also eclipsed by overgrowth.

"Look at them," my mother goes on. "Thick as thieves."

As we slowly cross the yard, we upset the policing blue jay, which calls out its warning. A local cat is crouched in the overgrowth. The blue jay lands like a dart among the strawberries, scattering the other birds. The cat hunkers down, ready to spring.

"Fools rush in . . ." my mother warns. But the cat slinks away. "A word to the wise," she finishes as she climbs into my passenger seat, her bracing hand an old bird itself.

"Wish there was someone here who mowed," I reflect, distressed by what I see as I look around.

"That's the truth," my mother says with conviction. "No one like that around these parts anymore. Not for love nor money." She fastens her seat belt. "No point fighting uphill battles."

"So, you just don't expect anything from anyone," I say as we move down the road.

"There's no point," she says. "Let sleeping dogs die. There was a time when I didn't know that. Live and learn, I always say."

We haven't been alone together in a car since my mother was the one driving and we harmonized "You Are My Sunshine" in robust voices over the winding back roads cut with rivers, lined with apple orchards and haunting, abandoned New England mills to visit my aunt Sunday and my cousin Claude. Once Mum told me, when I was young enough to have two front teeth missing and we were riding in our car, that when she's hurt she likes to crawl away like a lone animal, to be by herself to lick her wounds.

On those drives together, we followed the route of her peripatetic childhood some fourteen miles away in a French-Canadian town. She and her five younger siblings would take up their few belongings and move with their mother to some abandoned house, where "Mimay," my grandmother, would promptly take to bed. Then my mother and Aunt Sunday would scour the neighborhood for bread that they soaked in water to fill all their stomachs. Still, they all got rickets. They'd stay until someone found them "squatting" on property they didn't own and threw them out. It seemed to take a year or two each time before they were discovered and had to move again.

"There was the house where we couldn't afford a Christmas tree," my mother would say, nodding toward a now-empty lot. "I'll never forget that one." And: "There's the one that had a wood-burning stove. We had some warmth that winter."

This was her life until she began work in the shoe factory. Mimay pulled all her daughters from high school at age sixteen and made them work. Then they paid room and board to live at home. The sons got to finish high school, but Romain, a top student, was not allowed to accept a full scholarship to Notre Dame. "The shoe factory was good enough for me," Mimay said, "and it's good enough for my kids."

My mother claimed not to hold this against her mother. "Mimay was just an ignorant woman, Janis. She didn't know better." This harsh, New England French-Canadian, working-class mentality went on for generations and kept them down. Mum said it was FDR who saved them with the Works Progress Administration. FDR was the source of their bread.

Back then—on our way back from Aunt Sunday's—we always stopped at the A&P and bought cake mixes and food coloring and made layers of green, pink, or blue, decorated according to whatever was on our mind that day.

Mum chose good- or ill-fortune stories from the local newspaper. We spent a whole day sad together once, when Mum found the story of a boy who'd gone out on the ice to pick up a piece of Christmas tinsel and drowned. Mum thought he was just so excited by the glitter that he couldn't resist trusting the ice.

"He got punished just for loving something and wanting it," she said.

Our cake was deep-chocolate sad that day, with a blue-frosting pond, one squiggle of silver sprinkles for the tinsel in the middle, and green trees bowed with grief around the edges.

Our happy cakes had frosting scenes depicting people bowling, playing baseball, and having picnics.

After the babies, our baking and our day trips just ended.

In the supermarket, I lose my aging mother twice, and both times find her stooped low and talking to a soulful Bassett hound, leashed to a column in front of the store. For a moment, I hope she isn't telling him about her unpaid bills. But that was decades ago, when she talked to any stranger who would listen. She appears to be saying tender things to the dog. I take her by the hand. Mum never got over her heartbreak when our Rina-Tina died; she couldn't consider having another dog.

We bring home dinners for the week and together make chicken breasts in Parmesan with sherry—a recipe from Mum's good-cooking days.

We eat in the living room, Dad in his Barcalounger, Mum and me on the lumpy couch. We can't eat at the kitchen table; it's too cluttered with tools and pill bottles, a large potato with sprouting eyes, loose mail, and some partially folded laundry. A healthy Christmas cactus thrives over all. My mother's green thumb persists. Lush African violets and gloxinias preside atop shaky piles of debris.

Max's dirty dinner dishes appear on the table later, spilling over onto an old family photo album. Margo's footsteps sound on the stairs as she ascends to her quarters on the floor above. She continues her boycott and stays upstairs.

My parents and I recall our powwows in the woods. Steve once reigned as Chief ItchyBum for a week, because he'd started shitting in the woods before Mum could snatch him out of the poison ivy.

Today, Day 2, I begin a thorough cleaning of the refrigerator, which takes hours and gallons and chisels and scrubbers. I wear holes in the two pairs of yellow rubber gloves I brought.

"There's no point," says Mum.

"The Board of Health will condemn you," I warn.

Mum was always a fan of "elbow grease." And my need to order the chaos here is an old ball and chain. My cleaning feels like a continuation. From age seven, I had "the dishes." No dishwasher then. Mum's attunement to the child imagination also had its cruel side. She designed a Cinderella nightmare for me. The sink was in the pantry and I hold a body-memory of standing on the stool for what felt like the live-long day, my hands in red sauce–acned water, daydreaming through the window into our neighbor's pair of apple trees. The trees shed their blossoms, like dissolving ball gowns, and our neighbor began and finished mowing his lawn (there were only manual mowers then). Every dish and pot used by the four of us was to be washed by me.

Sometimes my grandparents came down from upstairs and joined us for Sunday dinner at noon. There was no appealing Mum's dictate, no way ever to say "Mum, this is too hard." Over the course of hours, my clothes became soaked, my hands red lobsters that played at nipping each other. The water turned cold and gelid. Tomato sauce perfectly red-rimmed the soap bubbles.

Morning turned to afternoon. Dishes kept coming. There was no accomplishment. The job was never done.

The arrival of three babies forced a new level of demand. My father continued looking disoriented, like someone wanting to take flight. Mum set about hanging plaques on the walls with appeals to merciful heaven. One began, "Lord of all pots and pans and things . . ." and begged for housewifely domesticity and the patience needed for that.

Dad, out of work by then, couldn't stand just being "laid up" with a bum leg. He got out his electric saws and drills and in one titanic project—driven by his curses, with babies squiggling through—he moved the sink from the pantry to the kitchen, put in counters and cabinets, and built a large picture window above the sink. I don't know how this was paid for.

Dad always adored my mother, who hated being adored. Being loved made her mad. The kitchen renewal was a gift to her, and for that she berated Dad for being Finnish and having no religion—the subject they'd always agreed was off-limits. Dad was still in his "not-himself" phase (as I thought of it), and I woke up one Sunday morning to hear bloody screaming. I flew from my room off the kitchen to find my father beating my mother with a shoe. I forced myself between them. Mum then went off in the car for hours and my father retreated to the cellar. I suppose I took care of the babies.

Later, when both were back, a low-level bickering began over what would be for dinner. With babies underfoot, my cleaning became maniacal, as if to control the shouting and a burgeoning rage of my own. They seemed not to know what else to do but take out their confusion on each other, while my scrubbing and washing speeded up and soon covered everything in sight.

"Go fry your ass!!!" my father finally shouted, ending this new petty argument.

My sponge stopped still—as did both diatribes. A hush followed. Mum was headed for her bedroom, and from the back I saw her shoulders shaking. Dad went to her and suddenly the two fell together—not crying, but laughing. Shouting one minute, laughing the next. That's how it was. I wiped my hands on my nightgown and retreated to my room to imagine the rest of my life.

My mother broke the stuck-argument phase with my father by getting that job working nights as a hat-check girl at her brother-in-law's working-class country club back in her own hometown, a small, predominantly Catholic city. She was in her element again. Dad was back at the shop by that time, and arrived home in time for Mum to take the car to work. Occasionally, he had the job of cooking dinner, if Mum hadn't managed a meatloaf or a stew before leaving.

I worked at the diner after school, home by six. I walked in one night to find Dad at the stove with a tall open can of B&M Boston-baked beans standing upright in a pot of boiling water. I thought this a low point.

"Dad, this isn't a nice supper," I protested, objecting to his presentation. He'd been a short-order cook in the Navy and made fantastic breakfasts every day—eggs sunny-side up (sometimes on top of hash), bacon, creamed chipped beef on toast (called shit on a shingle), the babies' cereal. "Cook a supper that makes us want to eat?"

But Dad motioned to slabs of Spam crisping in the broiler below and made a joke of his efficiency. My father was back to being himself. I called him Spam-happy. That made me Spam-happy too.

I wonder how my folks recall our past.

Over forty years later, the old truth tumbles out when Mum and Dad and I sup here together again. Mum and I are on the couch, in the clearing among boxes holding newspapers and cracked and dusty plaster statues of birds, fish, and children. Framed photos of "the babies," at every stage, surround us; many are newspaper clippings captioned "Ahlenberg Triplets Turn Four"; "Three Turn Seven"; and "Sweet, Sweet, Neat Sixteen."

We are not entirely alone—Max and Margo drift in and out like hallucinations—but for now, there is a clearing in the traffic. My mother has poured us wine in chipped, unmatched glasses.

After a few sips, I hear myself speak.

I find myself talking to my folks about our long-ago rupture and that decade that we hardly saw each other. I've long believed we'll all just die with it undigested, like boulders in our stomachs. I tried once on the lake, over ten years ago. But when my mother understood what I was saying, she put on country-western music and got my father up to line dance, leaving me and David sitting at the dinner table. On they went, swanning to the music, back and forth across the floor. I was stunned. I decided then that we would simply never talk about that long rift or how I'd survived when I was young, broke, alone, and new to cities.

"Mum and Dad, did you make me go to work when I was twelve, cut me off without a cent, and then make me go away for good at eighteen and not see me for almost ten years?" I press my back hard against the lumps in the couch.

"Oh, no," says Mum. "We wouldn't do a thing like that."

"After being warriors together?" I continue. "Kimosabes?"

"No. That doesn't sound like us, does it Horace?"

I stumble on. My voice feels like it's coming from someone else. "We were about to have triplets, Mummy." I falter but forge on. "You took me aside one day and said the doctor's X-rays showed three heads? I was twelve!"

My mother shakes her head no.

"I remember exactly what I said that day," I insist. "I said you were having a three-headed baby. You became very stern and said that there would soon be triplets born to this family because of God, and that you couldn't take care of me anymore. Do you remember that?"

"Oh, no," she says, surprised but flat. "I don't."

"You told me I'd have to take care of myself now, that I'd have to get a job."

"What?" my father shouts.

"You said I could still sleep in my bed and eat at your table, but I would have to earn money to pay for my own clothes and pizza and movies with my friends. That was what you said. Did you mean to get rid of me? Because that's what you finally did."

"I would never say something like that. I must have been kidding."

"Well, you weren't," I soldier on. "Because you already had jobs lined up, first taking care of Baby Ed Sorilla weekday afternoons, all that summer and then every day after school. Do you remember?" The light feels dull and pulsing. I feel unreal. I think this isn't happening. "I moved on to other jobs." No one knows this happened but me. I've long lost touch with the old friends still here.

"Oh," she says again, "I don't think so. You're remembering wrong."

My father's voice rises again. "What are you saying? This is the first I've ever heard of this." His good right arm is flying around and pounding the air. "What are you telling me? How come I never knew about this? Where was I that I didn't know?"

"That's what I'm asking you." I'm surprised how alive this is for me. "I went on to have jobs forever after. In my freshman year of high school, I babysat for the Boylan family every day after school. There was never any more money from you. Do you remember?"

"No!" He is yelling.

My voice is calm, my heart frantic. The light is throbbing. A voice is telling me, "They're almost eighty," and another voice is saying, "But this was your life." I hear myself remind them how the taxi came every afternoon of that year to take me two towns away to a swarm of seven kids, when all I wanted was to be on the phone with Darlene, watching TV and talking about the kids dancing on "American Bandstand." There were times I locked all seven little Boylans outside.

"You know," Dad says, "I hate hearing these things now, when I'm old."

"I know, Dad. Believe me, that was a consideration. I'm not sure I've done a wise thing." I hear a stitch in my voice. There are stories I don't tell of fending for myself, how stranded I was in Boston at eighteen, the protection I sought from strangers.

"Just help with my confusion, Dad. I never understood what happened. Or knew what you were thinking. Did you wonder what was happening to me once I was gone?"

By now, Mum and I are drunk. My father is ranting. "This is unbearable, to think of you in those situations. How come I didn't know?"

I'm sick at heart myself. "Well, probably you denied it, Dad. You didn't want to know. You had to be overwhelmed. Bewildered. Confused. Three babies. Your accident." I remind him that he was in the hospital that day Mum stopped me in the kitchen to tell me I was on my own. "Mum was at her wit's end too. She was colossally pregnant and couldn't drive, couldn't fit behind the steering wheel or reach her foot to the gas pedal. The car was totaled anyway. Neighbors drove her to visit you. As for me, you both didn't know. Couldn't know. How could you really know? With such changes, it was probably impossible to think of me and . . . know . . ."

"Well. What I wanna know," he booms, "is, what was I doing out in Subic Bay in a submarine getting bombed when I had a baby at home? And that was you. I saw you when you were born. I saw you at ten months. Then I didn't get to see you 'til you were two."

I've launched my father off into the far past. After waiting all this time, it was never a matter of timing. Suddenly, my mother jumps up, announces that she "does not have to listen to any of this," plucks a handful of tissues to dab her eyes, turns her back, and heads out the door.

"Wait, Mummy," I plead. "Please stay and talk about this. Only you and I were there." But Mum has vacated the scene. My heart has landed in a swamp.

Early the next morning I have to leave, as planned, to drive north to see Steve at the cottage. These two visits were fit into the five-day slot I had in my work schedule. I didn't intend to open this up with my parents and then have to go. But that's what happened.

After coffee, I head for Mum and Dad's bedroom to hug them good-bye and tell them I love them. I'm trying to understand this love, a helpless love, a child-love, an old and early love. I'm not going to get the answers I came for. Then the giddy wish comes over me that we could join in a chorus of "Ten Little Indians," as we used to do to end our powwows in the woods. Only this minute do I fully realize that the song eliminated the Indians, one by one, down to none. We never thought about that.

Dumbfounded out of sleep, my parents sit up in bed—mute—like two headstones.

My Brother and Me

I drive down the long driveway. The lake house with its deck looks like a snoozing brown dog with paws extended toward the water.

"What'd you, come through Siberia?" Steve asks when I arrive.

"No, I stopped for breakfast." I set my small travel bag down on the deck and pour my tension into the lake. "Hello to you, too. It was a long drive."

"Well, I've already gone walking."

"Without me? Come on, it's only ten. I asked you to wait for me."

It's an old family game: a kind of peek-a-boo. "You thought you were going to get something of me, but—surprise—you're not! I won't be where you expect, but I may turn up someplace else." So, we both keep people waiting and wondering. We run away, disappear. I thought I had it under control. I should have called him.

"So, who won?!" I jest.

My brother looks tan and handsome. He's like our father, with that sandy hair that doesn't gray. The TV is on Fox News; the sliding glass doors are open onto the deck so the news can be heard. Steve apparently thrives on world affairs. Since retiring at forty-seven, he's done successful investing and gutted and renewed his three-story Los Angeles walkup, taking the top floor for himself and renting out the three apartments below. When he's there, he spends his early-retirement days calling into and speaking on radio talk shows. He's had conversations on the air with California Senator Tom Hayden, among others. I'm surprised that he likes Senator Dianne Feinstein, a California Democrat.

Steve launches right into these views before, or in place of, anything personal like "How are you?"

We are leading up to the 2004 election.

"I think this John Kerry is downright dangerous." My brother yells when he speaks. "Why did he boycott Allawi's talk before Congress? He's making the claim that he will continue the war in Iraq to the point of establishing the country. Allawi is the person he'd have to work with. So, why would he snub him? What's wrong with this guy?"

My brother—this once-rock-music journalist for the *Providence Journal* in his college days in the late-sixties (Dad read some of his articles and said, "When I see the words he uses, I can't believe it's him")—has become conservative, or maybe libertarian. My parents warned me.

"Well, I think a lot of people would say Allawi is George Bush's puppet." I don't mean to take the bait. I don't want to talk about politics.

"George Bush's puppet?! The man has survived eleven attempts on his life. This is a brave man. He's the one Kerry has to know to be able to establish the country before getting out. What do these people want? Do they think George Bush should put someone in there who doesn't agree with him? Doesn't like him? Give me a break!"

"Look," I say, "I don't have your knowledge or interest in world affairs. I'm not retired. I don't trust W. Too much Evangelical Right and dead-set on reversing Roe vs. Wade, which I wrote, marched, and fought to uphold in my early twenties in DC. And I don't like this war in Iraq. Anyway, let's talk about something else."

On he goes with his satisfied smile. He enjoys being frightening. "They should just evacuate all of Fallujah. Make people go through checkout points and then bomb the hell out of the rest of the place."

"You believe in might as the way to handle the world's problems."

"Yeah, and you want to give everyone yoga and understanding."

So, with things larger than ourselves in mind, we settle into the Adirondack chairs on the deck. Side by side, we stare speechless across toward Sunden, the pristine island that makes the near horizon feel touchable. I tell Steve that I've spoken with Mum and Dad about something no one in the family ever knew. My words feel absorbed by the spread of deep water between us and the island, which is conservation-protected—a piece of God and trust, hope and beauty, in a crazy world. This is the place of loon calls. The pure, aqua, see-through lake laps the sandy shore, which has a naturally bonsai-ed pine rooted in the sand. Mountains loom. The place feels eternal.

"What happened when I was twelve was this . . ." I repeat the whole saga of Mum stopping me in my tracks in the kitchen that day. "I never talked about this to anyone in the family. Not to them. Not to you. Not to the triplets, of course. But I've talked to friends, and certainly, over many years, to David about it. So finally, we talked about it: Mum and Dad and me. I had to finally say it, or forever give it up."

Steve is listening. I didn't think I'd get this from him. So, I go on.

"Mum said she was surprised and didn't remember saying this at all, which is what I thought she'd say." Encouraged by his listening, I continue about the X-rays and the three heads, but then I stop, expecting a wall. My brother's not a listener. "I was twelve," I add.

"Yep, that's Ma," Steve says.

"So, you understand. I didn't know if you would. Then Dad started saying he didn't remember any of this and why didn't he know. He got quite riled and started ranting."

"Yep, that's Dad. He's still riled and ranting."

"This morning? What did he say?"

"Well." Steve talks slowly, in his laid-back mode. "He talked about how upset he is: something about how you had to walk six miles home from your job at midnight or rely on strange men to get you home."

I didn't think I told Dad this. It must have been the wine. "What about Mummy?"

"Nuttin'."

Steve got himself a college education, like me. But he never changed how he speaks, a kind of loyalty to himself and his past. I sound like someone in film or television. I felt phony for a while, but when I moved to Boston at eighteen, it seemed necessary to drop my broad New England accent.

We talk all afternoon about our family experiences. Steve tells me how he stood up to Dad as a young adolescent—just shouted in his face while walking backward up the driveway—and Dad walked toward him, throwing stones. Our father could become deranged. Ditto Mum; she once threw Steve into the car and locked the door. He, about four and too young to know he had the power to unlock, tried to kick out the windshield. She did the same to me twice, at age three and four, and I remember the paralysis of my rage and despair.

Our conversation feels like a ride through the afternoon and all the unspoken territory of our childhood—a slightly different experience, a slightly different take. That's how parents could be then, we agree. Kids weren't precious, they were a fact of life. Kids were facts!

Soon we reach an oasis of silence and validation. A woodpecker hammers the tree before us, whose branches appear to hold the lake in its outstretched fingers. The light has changed.

The sky is pistachio drenched with pink. The sacred island before our eyes maintains the still presence of a witness.

"I need to ask you a question," I say.

"Yeah?"

"Why do you have your gun out?"

"I'm shooting the red squirrels and the chipmunks."

"Oh, God. Why? You did this when you were—how old? Nine? I couldn't wait for you to get over that stage. I thought you did."

"Yeah—these guys are tunneling under the house. They're perforating the land under there. They've got to go. They're destructive."

"Perforating the land! Is there no other way? Why do things have to be so disturbing?"

No answer. Just a comfortable, self-satisfied air.

We laze as the pink saturates the pistachio.

The lake house sits on sacred ground, I'm sure of it. The pulse and strength of Native American spirit lives here. Across the gargantuan body of water from this modest human dwelling on the water's wooded edge, that protected island rises up from fathoms below, a gentle mountain of wilderness that gets haloed by the moon with a pathway drawn up to it in liquid light. The night shrieks with loons.

The phone rings. We remain listless, as is our conditioned response. Predictably, Margo's voice blurts out on the speaker. The message records and resounds out over the deck.

"Let her talk to the fish," I comment.

"Janis, I want you to know Dad is very upset. He's been crying. And I think telling all this stuff is just a stupid thing to do. And . . . . . I know" (her voice blurs, but remains loud) ". . . didn't want me to be born. And Ma told me . . . once in a family therapy session . . . that they didn't want me to be born . . ." (They went to family therapy? But of course. In conjunction with all those mental hospitals.) "And you said that once too in a fit of anger . . . and no one should be saying these things. I don't know where you are and why you're not answering. I love you. Good-bye."

"So, now I'm supposed to feel terrible for her," I say.

Long silence from Steve.

"I can't get to be alone with my parents."

"Nope, it's not gonna happen."

"There's just no way anymore to have my own private visit with Mum and Dad."

"You'll never be alone with them again." Steve is terse, with an attitude of having been through it all and being above it now.

"Pity and fury. Pity and fury," I continue. "That's how I always end up feeling about them, the M&Ms. The babies." No nuances. I didn't want to be thinking about them.

"They're always front and center. It's beyond control."

We set out in the motor boat (Steve's own sleek model that he stores shrink-wrapped in a commercial boathouse, not the one he has to rescue from the bottom of the lake) to dine miles across the water at a new, upscale restaurant. Steve drives the boat. We sit drinking martinis on the upper deck, looking out on the lake and watching a wedding take place on the lawn below. Steve starts making comments about buxom women at the wedding.

"Stop being immature," I retort.

He looks pleased at the comment.

"Do you see that couple down there?" I continue. "They look like David and me in our thirties. That's just how we were. What happened?"

"You know, she's not a bad-looking woman," Steve says. "Not a bad-looking woman at all."

"Can't get beyond your one note," I lament.

"You're still talking about a marriage that's over and gone. Maybe I don't want to go there with you."

"You think I won't sometimes be reminded of a thirty-year period of my life? That I wouldn't still be trying to make sense of the breakup? My marriage will always be part of me."

"You're divorced. That's it."

"So, this is one of your 'Get-over-its.'"
"Yup."
"Well, I don't get over things. But at least I'm not a one-note."
"I don't know about that."
"I'll claim two notes. More, if I had anyone to listen."

We move on to enjoy ourselves, talking, as always, about the family as it now exists—our parents and "the babies"—as well as the wedding below. Steve empathizes with the little boy ring bearer, struggling with his confining suit. And we both can't get over bridesmaids dressed in black, once the curse-color to wear to a wedding.

Steve engages our waiter in a conversation that goes on for way too long about the town, the structure and history of the building we're in, local people and news. Now they move on to state affairs. Not much I can contribute. I recognize Steve's way of distancing the person he's with: he's fencing me out, putting me on the sidelines. I wonder if he does this with Joanne. But maybe she manages him better than I, since she stays with him.

I begin feeling the painful dislocation of being a stranger in this place that holds such meaning for my brother and the rest of the family. Stories of his adolescent summers, full of water-skiing and boat parties and dances and friends and families together, make me wish I'd had the carefree summers of youth that my siblings did, that I personally cared about this mountain town and felt part of it. But this place belongs to that second family. It was a surprise for me one day to put together these well-off years of theirs with my concurrent poverty in Boston. How do my parents feel about this now? I thought it would relieve us all to talk about it. I have these puzzle pieces on different planes. David was the one who finally paid off my college loans and all the impossible debts of my youth that my low-pay drudge jobs couldn't touch.

David and Jason and I were here in 1995 for my parents' fiftieth wedding anniversary. Steve and David and I had paid for a family surprise party—planned by my sisters, with the assumption that we would foot the bill—aboard a cruise ship that travels the lake, winding through mountains over some six hours, with dining and champagne. The lake house was a surprise. I had thought they'd remained poor. But the family sat and treasured their memories here together—while I sat in silence, nursing my abandoned soul, and got a 'Get-over-it' from David, who handled his own disappointments that way.

"You were a teenager, out living your own life," Steve exclaimed when I expressed my unfulfilled longing. "You were partying and having fun. What eighteen-year-old wants to be with her family in their summer vacation home?"

This one! I thought to myself. I'd never finished being twelve.

Towering mountain shadows fall into the valley and through the windows of the restaurant. It makes for a mood that is deep and serene. There's a feeling in this New England state—a timeless feeling. People sitting at tables are silhouetted against the trees and mountains, old couples with decades-long histories, facing one another, dining in the twilight, looking calm and true—as if moments in these mountains on this lake are indelible.

Back down on the town dock, we stop for a brief conversation with a professional fisherman, a handsome, friendly man. Then there is a burly, bare-chested guy on the other side of the dock, standing in his oversize boat, a small bouquet of white posies on his dashboard.

"Nice flowers," Steve says.

The man gives a coy smile. "I'm cultivating my feminine side."

We all laugh.

I'm pleased with our easy conversation with strangers, reminding me that Steve and I are of the world. Our deteriorating parents and the M&Ms are strictly of their own world. There was a time when my parents would have talked to the fisherman. Not now. Mr. Feminine is another story.

Steve points out that Mr. Feminine is driving an ocean-going motor vessel, and these are now taking over the lake and one's entire experience here. "Those boats are so noisy when they go by, you can't have a phone conversation in your house even with the glass doors drawn closed," he says. "And you can't be in your own standard-size boat on the weekend. The wake of those monsters can turn you over. They're dangerous. Their waves can break your dock."

Our parents don't know this day and age, I reflect. They knew the respectful, understated aristocrats of the past, but they don't know the rude, grotesque wave of new-rich folks who've moved in and built castles on the shore and seem bent on demolishing Nature and life on the lake as the family knew it. We two look from a point of years behind us upon a new world of black-and-white weddings and boat drivers who rip up the lake by fiat of boat-salesmen lobbies. Now, too, we know fine restaurants, in addition to the old clam shacks and submarine sandwich shanties. We like the restaurants. Our parents are not part of any of this; they're scoped down to their last little spot of time.

Back at the house, we climb out of the boat and sit on the dock under a large gibbous moon. The dock is so low, it's like sitting on a tongue rolled out to taste the water.

The milky way is brilliant this night, the loons are sharp and clear. We talk about the years I don't know about. When the M&Ms were young adults, there was always a crisis: police taking one or more of them out of the house—sometimes in restraints—at all hours of night. Max did strange things, like remove all his possessions to the trash barrels at the end of the driveway, that worried my folks. Margo and Marisol believed that men were sexually assaulting them, exposing themselves, breaking into the house to get to them. It seems this has never stopped. Margo, especially, continues this delusion. My sisters seem to live in a state of pure infantile narcissism. Neither their beauty nor their intelligence saves them. They received so much attention from strangers growing up that it may have ironically left them feeling unprotected, open to anyone. It also gave them an inflated sense of importance and entitlement. After all, they put a town on the map, and brought that parade of news photographers from all over. Both learned to telephone the police when anything upset them, at any time of day or night. To this day, the police are called regularly, like ancillary staff. The two Valkyries even got access to the office of a high-ranking senator more than once. Marisol was dating one of his aides. That person's influence was used to get Margo sprung from an institution, to the regret of all—even Marisol.

Finally, when my father retired and bought their trailer, my parents joined the Wally Byam Travel Club and started spending October through April of every year traveling the country with five thousand other white-haired people. All five thousand went to Mexico together once, and David commented that this was "like invading a country." But we gave them credit. They really just up and ran away from home, leaving the local police to manage the mess.

My parents returned to their nightmare every June. "It's our cross to bear," my mother said stoically, drawing on her fluffy visions of God's will and the need for acceptance—tacked up on those plaques and picture-messages all over the kitchen walls—and wishing they were back in Arizona in their trailer.

"Well, when you think how sad the whole thing is," I say to Steve. "Those had to be nightmare years for Mum and Dad. And the triplets, they hardly have lives. I now understand the meaning of Margo and Marisol working for the Right to Life Movement. I wish I'd never clobbered them with my beliefs. I don't need to tell them I think abortion should be a choice."

"I think it should be mandatory," says Steve.

What would he and I talk about if we didn't talk about them?

My reveries sail off to contemplating the stars. How often do we do this anymore? Sitting side by side before this gigantic screen reminds me of going to drive-in movies with Mum. The last movie we saw together—before drive-ins became the place to go with boys—was called *Imitation of Life*. We'd gone there mad at each other, arguing and fuming, then stewing in malignant silence. The movie ended with the pale-skinned actress running down the street after her black mother's coffin, crying about her betrayal and rejection of her mother and her mother's race. Mum and I faced forward in parallel, sobbing so hard we fogged the windshield, crying—we thought—for those poor people on the screen. We made one more last cake—chocolate and white marble layers with a two-faced frosting profile, the Rubin vase in blue, the chocolate face on one side, the white on the other—for old time's sake.

Sunday, midday, my brother says, "Think I'll call Dad."
    Call Dad! I forgot my promise to call him. I never call Dad.
    "What'cha doin'?" Steve sounds tender and playful. "Didja eat your banana?"
    I think he and Dad speak many times a day. It's a running phone conversation that never stops. They're friends. Dad's daily thought stream runs right into Steve's ever-present ear. Steve does the same with him. He keeps up with the family's daily life.
    "Well, then how are you?" Steve's voice turns serious. My ears perk up. Then silence. He's listening to a long story. I start gesturing for him to reveal what's being said, to give me indicators. He doesn't. He keeps listening with a straight face. Finally, he says, "Did she leave? What happened?" There follows another silent listening. I hold my breath. Suddenly, Steve bursts out laughing.
    I finally say, "Can I please speak to Dad?"
    He easily gives me the phone. Not what I expected. No teasing. There used to be teasing between us. Long ago.
    "Dad, how are you?"
    "Not so good. Things have been very bad here."
    "I'm sorry to hear that. What's on your mind?" I brace myself, ready to bear the consequence of my actions. I've caused an old man to regret his life.

"Well," he says, "Margo came to us last night and said that once in a family therapy session, Mummy said she didn't want her. And Margo was so upset. I don't understand how she could think we would ever have said that. I'm so upset, I can't even eat."

"Dad? Can I say something here?"

"Doesn't Margo know we love her and care about her? That we'd never say such a thing? She went upstairs and wouldn't come down. She was crying and I was crying. I couldn't stand that my own daughter . . . she's my daughter, and—"

"Dad. Dad," I break in. "I think Margo just needed your attention because the focus was on me this weekend."

"We're not perfect, we know, but we'd never hurt Margo. She should know . . ."

"Dad. Listen! I told you some difficult things the other night that we've never talked about. I got a little spot with you for the first time in forty years. Margo has had all your attention since she was born, and she can't stand attention on someone else. That's what's going on."

"Well, Margo's a good person. She has her problems and we have our fights, but we would never say we didn't want her. That just never happened. She should never . . ."

"Well, I'm sorry there's been such a ruckus. I guess you're upset."

"Janis, I can't believe all those bad things happened. I didn't know. I can't think about you walking six miles in the night and taking rides with strangers. I can't think of you working all the time when you were young. I think I'm too old for you to tell me now. I didn't tell my parents about the things they did."

"I've never known whether to talk about it or not. That's why I waited so long."

"Well . . .? All I have to say is"—he's back to his everyday tone of voice—"it doesn't affect me. That's all. It doesn't affect me."

"What the hell does that mean?"

"It doesn't affect me!" His tone is slightly petulant.

"You mean you don't want to feel these feelings?"

"Yes. That's right. And I can't stand Margo being so hurt and upset."

"I think I waited too long to bring up what was on my mind. We've had many good times since those things happened. I just wanted to reconnect with you for real—from that broken place. We're all old now."

"I can't hear these things, I don't want to know about the bad things now."

"Well, I'm going home tomorrow, but I want to keep in touch with you. And I'll visit again, probably next fall. We'll have more good times."

"I just can't stand to hear about the bad things." His voice sounds tearful.

"Do you want to hear about the good things?"

"No!"

"What do you want?"

"I want to watch the baseball game."

I return to Steve.

"That's how it is," he says. "You're not going to get in. It's the four of them under one roof, like peas in a pod, and that's all there is. No one else gets in. Marisol isn't in either. Anyone who moves away is out."

"I didn't realize the extent of it. It's like a walled fort."

"Dad's not someone to handle things in words. He needs action or something beside the point to get to any truth. He can't handle direct confrontation."

"Maybe they were the last people I should have told. I was talking to their blind spot. Like telling a stone that you're cold. I'm sorry Margo had to be there, to step in and steal the show."

"She is such a pain in the ass."

"Well—finally—I'm on the other side. I've always wondered what it would look like after telling them. And the other side of the mountain looks just the same."

We watch TV and talk. Our focus keeps moving to our other siblings. We relish our obsession with their bizarre relationships—to each other and to life. "They" includes my parents, now that they're less rational too. We enjoy resenting Margo and feeling superior.

"If you came back to get what you didn't get, fuhget it," Steve offers. "You ain' nevvuh gonna get it now."

We return to the TV, watching political events, with Steve's running commentary.

A couple hours later the phone rings.

"Hi Janis, thiz Dad. I was just sitting here thinking about you."

"Hi Dad. What's up?"

"Well, Mummy is making a nice meatloaf here, and I just want to say thank you for going and getting those groceries." His voice is tender and intimate. "I know that was hard after your long trip and I'm so happy and thankful to have this food. Mummy's just getting the meatloaf out of the oven and she's smiling and it was just a wonderful, thoughtful thing you did. I appreciate it. You are a very kind person and I know that."

"Thanks, Dad. I was happy to do that for you. And it gave me a chance to be with Mum. Enjoy your meatloaf."

"Yup, I'm going to enjoy it. I love you, Janis."

"I love you too, Dad."

Steve and I are back sitting on the deck, facing forward, so we talk to the lake.

I think Steve might have wondered how I earned money at twelve. I start to explain my babysitting for people outside our family. I bring up Baby Ed and recount his mother working in the factory and my bringing Baby Ed to Darlene's house, where no one else was ever home by day. I assume he remembers Darlene, how she and I liked to harmonize like the Everly Brothers. I tell the story of our spending afternoons making crank phone calls to boys from out of town. "Most often we gave cute Baby Ed a lot of hugs and attention. But once we left him in Murphy's drug store and set off looking for boys in cars. When we remembered, we ran all the way back and Mr. Murphy was holding him and about to call the police. Poor Baby Ed. I wonder what happened to him in life. Another abandoned child."

"Janis, can you just stop talking about this!?" Steve explodes.

"What?"

"I don't want to hear any more about your past. You're obsessed. All you're talking about is you and the family. You can't let go. It's enough. It's time to get on with your life. Get over it!"

"Isn't it understandable, when I've held it in for forty years?"

"It's enough! I can't stand hearing about it anymore."

"You must have always wondered why I disappeared. I'm sure I didn't even say good-bye. And I could never tell you what happened. I didn't want to be the girl that happened to."

"Oh, give me a break. You've told me this story a zillion times."

"What? I never told you. How much have I even talked to you over the years? I sought professional advice, and I was advised that there were good reasons to keep it to myself. I gave it the most careful consideration many times over. No. I never told you."

"You told me."

"I can't imagine why you're saying this."

Steve, though loud, has his unassailable calm and slight amusement: "You told me so many times I could repeat it word for word."

"OH, SHUT UP!" I pick up his running shoes and throw them over the railing.

He smiles with glee.

The loons grow louder when night begins.

"Hold on." My brother grabs his .22, propped by his side. "I've gotta get Osama bin Laden over here." He shoots, then stands in silence.

"Is this what comes from growing up shooting rats in the dump? I can't stand you killing those chipmunks."

"Yeah. I know."

"Your anger is the reverse side of mine. Either that or you took mine. My anger is suffocated under some wet blanket. Nothing sets it free. And you're an animal murderer."

"I'm not an animal murderer. You have to shoot these guys or they destroy your foundation. Jack next door gets out there with his .22. Sometimes we're both out here shooting at the same time."

"Hope you don't shoot each other."

He fires another shot. "I got him. There's the other one." He moves to the other side of the deck. Another shot. He sits down, triumphant.

The sky darkens. Loon wails fill the night.

The phone rings. It's Dad again. "Is Janis there?" He sounds tender and desperate.

"Hi Dad."

"Are you sure you're not coming back this way?"

"Oh, Dad. I miss you too. But I have work Tuesday night."

"He wants groceries," Steve pitches from the sidelines.

"Well, Janis, I realize you only get to see us sometimes, and it's short because you work. Everybody else is here all the time. Steve can come for a whole month because he retired. You have to say what you have to say and then you have to go. And I think that's really hard on you."

"Well, thanks for thinking of me. It means a lot. I'll see you again soon."

"I want you to know that I love you. You're my first child and I'll always love you."

The phone rings again. It's Margo. We both listen.

"Hi Janis, I don't know where you two are. I bought eighty bulbs at Costco. Maybe you want some. Ma wants some. They were having a sale. So call me back as soon as you get this message.

Oh—and Dad is feeling much better tonight. Ma said that awful thing to me just after she had breast cancer"—she giggles—"anyway. And Ma and Dad and I talked last night for a long time and we all felt better. She didn't just say that to *me*, anyway—she said it to all three of us. So, it wasn't just me. Well, I don't know where you are. I love you."

"She doesn't say what kind of bulbs," I comment. "Tulips, I assume, not light bulbs."

Steve wanders over to the sliding glass doors to look out over the deck. "I actually feel bad shooting these chipmunks and squirrels," he says.

"I am *so* consoled to hear that. Please don't shoot the squirrel that runs back and forth across the beach with a nut in its mouth. I've grown attached to it."

"I wouldn't shoot them. There are two of them."

"Why? I'm glad, but why?"

"They're a pair. I don't want one to have to watch the other one die."

Steve whistles "Blue Moon of Kentucky"—Creedence Clearwater Revival–style—while he makes stir-fried chicken and vegetables. We sit at the table with the moon rising in our faces.

Dad comes on the speaker again: "Janis, did you just try to call me? The phone rang. I thought it might be you."

"Well, Dad, I'm thinking of you too," I answer.

"Are you still going home tomorrow?"

"I do have to leave early in the morning."

"Well, I hate to see you go. I'm gonna keep your phone number and call you. I get free minutes because I'm a senior citizen. I don't call you because you're busy and the work you do is important. I call Steve all the time, because he's not busy."

"Okay. I'll look forward to hearing from you. I love you both. Bye."

After watching a movie and talking about Jason and his music career, I tell Steve, "I'm going to crawl over there and sleep in my clothes on that couch, where I can hear the loons. I'll be leaving before dawn and I won't wake you when I slip out early in the dark. So, I'll say bye now."

A little later, on his way to the bedroom in back, Steve says, "Janis?"

"Yeah?"

"Are you awake?"

"Yeah."

"I just wanna say . . ."

"Uh-huh."

"In the morning. When you go . . ."

"M-m-m-m-h-m-m-m."

"When you go . . ."

"M-m-m-m-m!"

"Leave the lights on when you go."

Love Alone

On the long drive home, my thoughts are directed to the steering wheel and the road.

My love for my parents is involuntary and should be a contradiction, if they don't merit forgiveness for their negligence and their denial... which they don't. Love is the mystery. And what is love? I ask this question often now. Maybe with my folks, it's about having humble expectations; then the smallest positive morsel is relished. But I'm not willing to just spin my wheels, other than to guide this moving car. I turn on Country Joe and the Fish (Porpoise Mouth 1967)—among the most stoned music of the late sixties, to my mind. I sing the lines as I've always mistaken them—I have a white dove (not ducks) flying on past the sun, their wings flashing silver at the moon—lending suppleness to my mood. Country Joe became David to me over the hundreds of times we listened. With the American flag painted on his front tooth. It's true. David is also John Lennon, Jimi Hendrix, Jim Morrison, and Paul McCartney (he loved his humanity). I could be Janis. These thoughts always tickle me—another configuration of love. Love that stays silly and doesn't get old and doesn't go away.

From their perches in the trees, red-tailed hawks stare down like guides along the highway. I need to shut down these memories as I'm driving to my present home. I'm going through so much change, I don't know where to turn. It would be so good to have close friends. Life has required leaving so many people behind. I'm about reconnecting now, starting with my parents—the first rupture.

Thinking about David is disquieting. Thinking about any of the past is disquieting. It's hard to reflect on that befuddling story of babies who can't be blamed. Certainly there were new pressures—and three babies at once would overwhelm most any family—but Mum was enraged long before they arrived. What I want to know, above all, is how all these pasts are the sum of me now—divorced, in a new place I don't yet know. How do I add up? I want to believe there is more and better of myself, a larger, improved me to come.

Home at last, I park alongside my gleaming white-picket fence and pull my suitcase on wheels up the bluestone walkway over the mosses filling in the cracks, encouraged by my own patient efforts. Mosses do well when encouraged. My gardens have my focus and ambition.

Then I see that David has replaced the train station parking permit—a hang-tag that we share—under the wooden turtle at my door. I'm touched. The feeling turns sad. I unlock and open the door, and am immediately flown at by two Tonkinese cats, excited by my return. The phone on the kitchen wall is ringing. I pick up the phone.

"Hi Janis," Dad says. "I thought you'd be home by now."

"Hi Dad. So, you did save my number. How are you?" Qwerty and Lemmy are circling my feet and rubbing against my ankles with purrs and meows.

"Well, you know, I had the strangest dream last night. Mummy and I had gone to a restaurant. It was Drozhdy's Russian Restaurant. So vivid. I remember the steps up to the door, the lights. We sat at the counter. Mummy looked at the menu and said, 'Oh, look, they have nicotine salami. That sounds good.

We should have that.' Then the chef said there was salmonella spaghetti sauce that everyone raved about. People came back for it, even though it turned them purple. So I asked for the special for today and he said, 'The special is soup. We put children in the soup.' I asked if they were girl children or boy children? And he said they were girl children and we should have some."

I wait for him to continue.

"I just keep wondering what a dream like that could mean? I don't remember ever having such a powerful dream. Everything felt so real and alive. That entrance, the big lit-up sign saying Drozhdy's. What do you make of a dream like that? Am I trying to tell myself something, or am I losing my mind? I get to thinking how much I resent it that I didn't see you 'til you were almost two because I had to be in the war, and how much I hate these politicians not doing military service. I regret so much not being with you when you were a baby. I had a baby and I shouldn't have had to be out there in the South Pacific."

I picture Dad there in Subic Bay, his survival in question those many long hours under bombs, and how he—as anyone would—prayed to God.

"You were away longer than I thought, Dad. I didn't realize you missed my first two years. I can't imagine David or me being away from Jason. We treasured his every minute."

"And Janis. I hate to think you might not be happy. I worry that you left David, and you're all alone. You don't have a man who loves you now, and I feel sorry about that."

Drozhdy's must be David's Restaurant, I reflect to myself, and I'm the girl in the soup. The poison food—the toxic emotions—could be my divorce. Or the poison truth I spoke about what happened to my parents and me: a hard thing to swallow. Or me alone now, and in a soup. Why the vivid dream? Maybe it's the primordial soup—a rebirth beginning for us all. I hoped that having our past admitted to and forced into the open would give Dad and me some deeper last bit together. Maybe we have the start of expiation and repair.

"Well, Dad, I haven't been completely alone," I say. "You don't know much about me . . . I do have some good times. But it's been hard for me to find anyone to feel close to, the way I felt with David. I had something special there for a long time."

"Well, maybe you're not giving anyone new a chance."

"Maybe. Maybe my heart is full; I'm trying to pour water into a glass already full."

"You mean you still care about David?"

"Well, yes. I do. And he's hard to replace."

"Do you think you made a mistake leaving David?"

"Sometimes. Sometimes I do. Anyway, whatever happens, Dad, I'll be all right."

"I know. I like to think you're all right."

"I know." I fill a glass with water at the sink and watch it overflow. "I'll be all right."

"I hope so, Janis. It's important to me that you're all right."

"Don't worry." I guzzle down the water. "So . . . Tell me. Did you eat the soup?"

"The what?"

"The soup that had the girl. In the dream."

"No. I didn't eat the soup. I woke up."

"Well, that's funny. There's a play by that name: *A Girl in My Soup*."

"A what?"

"Oh. Never mind."

Love is a feeling. You can't argue with it. It's impossible to give up attachments to cherished people. I care about David. I miss my son, out living his own life, as he should. I love the Ahlenbergs, my dear, possibly clueless parents. I know my parents didn't sit down one day and say, "Let's get rid of Janis, and we can buy a summer cottage," but that's effectively what happened. Refusing help for a daughter's college education was not an uncommon thing for parents to do in the early sixties. "Education is wasted on girls," said my mother at the time. "You'll just marry and have babies." Was she talking about her own plight? Passing on her hopelessness?

I could blame the old family ignorance, the deprivation handed down by Mimay, the traditional fate of the oldest girl-child. Mum changed her mind about affording tuition for Margo and Marisol. Ironic, since they couldn't make use of it. It bespeaks the family's growing prosperity, and different parental attitudes toward individual children.

I can see how that haven on the lake must have felt earned by hard work, though it still cost money. The "cottage" clearly lifted the family to a new plane. And that had required sacrificing me. Are my folks capable of insight about their choices? Dad heard me, and he's struggling in his way. That gives me something. But he's so incapable of handling it, part of me wants to rescue him. And he may finally have a little dementia creeping in, too.

But I forge on with optimism. Their chosen investment was the cottage. At a propitious time. Elaborate mansions now staff what was an empty dirt road to the end, where my folks' basic, modest dwelling—once alone and hidden—sits so close to the water, you could be swallowed by a fish. The mansions loom high, lording over the setting and losing intimacy with the shore birds and the sounds of lapping water.

They probably denied their actions toward me, never spelled things out even with each other. What were they thinking that time I called Dad at the shop from college, desperate for five dollars to buy medicine for a bad case of gingivitis, and he told me he had to "ask Mummy"—who said no? I bought the medicine with my food money, and then actually shoplifted orange juice and canned tuna fish that week. Dad probably hung up from that call and never reflected on it. Once my mother spoke, my father canceled any further thought.

Shouldn't I just understand—not for the first time—their limitations and let it go at that? Three babies had put my parents in a situation beyond their ability to cope; then, later, they'd lived through the punishment of three teenagers losing their minds—through no fault of anyone—and the lifelong consequences of having mentally ill children. I think of my folks in all those trials, they who have always been especially baffled by complexity.

When Dad and I hang up, I grab the newspaper to read about world affairs. The cat takes his place in my lap and appears to be reading the paper too. Three o'clock is hovering, and I'm tasting that jarring tang of isolation borne by light down through the trees. I thought reuniting with my family would alter this feeling. What's happened to me? I love trees and light. Is there nothing to sustain me anymore? I have no constancy. I return from a trip or even a nice night out—which has happened a few times of late—and once I'm inside, my spirit goes clunk! Looking in the mood glass, I see Alice—small—in the voice of Grace Slick, when the mood allows song.

The actual voice is that of the steady tormentor—a figure who storms through all my mistakes, missed opportunities, false excitements, and low-return forays into the world, with no instruction how to do it better. I'm soon stumbling around. How did I just end up strewn on the bleak side of—what? Wilson Street, running past my house? I should be calling up my bracers: those internal places where you run from danger, those forests and mountain retreats of happy days, the seashores, the deserts and jungles and tundras of imagination, bountiful kitchens, the night sky. There is so much outside oneself to be small in. But the tormentor is a true "thought skunk"—brilliant term from some current self-help strategy—who tells my story as one of hopelessness, with sealed facts and figures that amount to no way out. "You've left all your pasts behind," it tells me. "There's nothing left to build on." This is the big truth! I've dropped off the social cliff with the demise of my marriage. Smoke then rises from the slammed-shut book of my life, and I'm just another body quietly rotting into oldness and aloneness. It's typical for the phone to enter right here on this note of malaise.

"Hi Janis." Margo's voice resounds. "I caught a fox trying to go after Daisy. She was in the pen. I don't think they would be friends. But I was wondering if you know if foxes eat cats. I was sitting out there and it came out from the trees. So, anyhow. If you know, give me a call. Because I have hornet spray. But I don't want to spray it if it's vegetarian. Thanks. Bye-bye. I don't know where you are but wherever it is, I love you."

Well, humor—that saving angel—has swooped in.

Mornings I wake up hopeful, hope imbued with the birth of a new, yellow day. After coffee on the deck with a visiting monarch in attendance, I have a full schedule of early patients in my office studio, out across the yard, through my lovely and very satisfying gardens.

By noon, I'm filled with work-satisfaction. Then my new neighbor, Marian, calls, canceling our plan for the evening because she has a cold. Last time she canceled, her dog had the cold. This is the sixth time she's canceled. I've been hoping against knowing better that I might have a new companion next door. I'm sorry for someone with social anxiety, but cancelations distress me. I see no future with Marian.

Luck could have gone the other way. Both new to the neighborhood, we could have been a mutual boon; we could have felt our lot in common and looked out for each other. I fight becoming blue as I consider how few people have materialized from my social efforts. I've encouraged myself to date again, thinking it's healthy. A man I met at a chamber music concert proved to be more depressed than I am. A dating site for classical music lovers yielded one handsome, ex-alcoholic, Buddhist monk, so full of himself that I had to get away. I've chosen to take on life anew, but this demands chancing disappointment.

I put my mind on my next round of patients. But by late

afternoon, when work is done, I'm facing that old sense of doom: fall headlong into comatose sleep, rise an hour later, and force myself like a drill sergeant out on that three-mile fast walk along the river in new walking shoes.

Nature restores. Cedar waxwings squeak through the air and bluebirds land on broken upright saplings. Only after the refreshment of a shower do my laments begin again about not having found new connections, and who can I blame but myself. No one ever told me I had to live my husband's life, including him. He's a good guy. It was my own doing. I tried to bring a world of my own into our relationship, but didn't have a world to bring.

I pour the wine of my evening salvation.

The porch railings around this Civil War–era house clutch like bones of a corset, keeping me unto myself, pinned in place. My only relationship right now is with myself: not quite mutual reflection. Without that mutual reflection, how does anyone know who they are? I read the Derek Wolcott poem, "Love After Love," posted in the kitchen. It's about loving oneself, being your own best friend. I read it and kiss myself in the mirror, but worry that this self-love is about being scoped down to a mandatory self-centeredness, a confinement—an iron-clad single-person self. It's not the first time I've found that I'm all I have. *Beware*, I think. *The country of Me grows larger and maybe more solipsistic every day.* Do I miss David? I don't ask myself that. Why I left is murky and complicated and not enough resolved. I only know I had to. When I did, I had to.

As for our old friends who disappeared, didn't I know people choose sides in a divorce? We'd all been so seemingly close—a chosen family—for twenty-five-plus years. I loved and felt loved by them. But *we* were loved—as a couple. The friends were his.

So, when I left, I found myself in the frightening position of knowing no one in this new town where David had recently taken a position (with my complete agreement and enthusiasm). I'd finished my Masters in Social Work (MSW), completed further institute training, and was just beginning my new profession in this new place. More than one sphere of starting over.

Too many days, the only other forms of life I see besides my patients are those that comprise the population of squirrels and chipmunks in my gardens. They're probably devouring my house from the bottom up, as Steve says those at the lake house do. But to me, they're company. This profession can be a lonely one—it's not a source of many companions—and that leaves me striking in the margins socially.

It's just hard to find soul mates. Starting over in middle age under these circumstances, when you're not well-connected, leaves you to what's available. And by this point, what's available doesn't give me much hope. So much that happens is about luck.

Driving up into the hills on the outskirts of town provides bucolic scenery and lush vistas. I stop at a pasture where alpacas roam. They're amusing creatures who look like Muppets and come to the fence to lick my flattened palms. Two of them kiss my cheeks, recapitulating a cavalcade of sweet kisses from many layers of past. I'm a less-kissed person than I once was—the thought monster steps in to point this out, and insists again on my recounting the reasons for this curbed life, this very day, and won't stop until I do.

"I don't know the whole story of what happened anymore," I respond to my imaginary tyrant. My pleas fly on breezes up into the hills. "My husband grew threatened by my personal growth, and for me the thought of striking out on my own became more and more appealing. Wondering what I would find. That's it. The simple version."

I've developed a business and made a lovely new home, with splendid gardens, and I enjoy the challenge of leading my own financial life. My work brings fulfillment. I have determination, too. Auditing courses at the university and working in a soup kitchen and as a literacy volunteer should build some niche of belonging for me. It will just require being patient and steadfast. The social dimensions will surely fall in place in time. What if it's not my fault and something larger governs—something deeply wrong with humanity, with the world? We know people are lonely in the developed world. I don't like thinking it's beyond my control.

I send myself out to the garden to weed and prune until night falls. The pampas grass is already a foot taller than me, and looks like a spewing fountain. Darkness turns the mood dramatic and gives it resonance. If the late-afternoon mood could be pictured as the bleak parking lot with the chain-link fence down by the train tracks, darkness fills in midnight blue with the boundless mystery of stars. Day is earthly detail. Night is the universe: infinity. I live in this splendid darkness now. Out in the yard, there's room to waltz around, traversing the gigantic harvest moon that has moved down and landed where I can walk right into it.

What if I had brought it all up with my folks, say, thirty years ago? I couldn't then. At least, not effectively. And am I really strengthening my connections? I believe I've made some further contact with Steve. But is my brother capable of relationships? I see I have an email from him—not a photo of his dinner but a negative rant about Ted Kennedy. Steve's political theme seems to be about getting government to stop supporting people on the dole. All those people who get something for nothing. He must see the triplets in this light. Not consciously—their impairment is significant and their need undeniable. He has in fact, researched and tried to instruct them on how to get food stamps. To no avail.

Steve, like my mother but in a manner all his own, won't let anyone in, including himself. *It hurts to love*, my thoughts continue. When hearts are broken by first loves, they remain forever fragile.

Too many layers of past to contemplate. I'm felled into a swoon on the couch; an annoyed cat crawls out from under me and I sit hunched and shawled in that unbearable late-afternoon light—bestowed from the heavens, from the Sun God—down through my beloved maples through the high window, but tinged mustard with . . . what? Time. I steep in deep molasses melancholy, then decide to phone my brother. He's my only phone possibility and he always answers.

"Do you never leave home?" I ask, knowing he'll tell me little.

"I was out last night at Betsy's Bar just up the street. There was a guy from Nevada City. That's a place I might want to live some day. Then a woman from St. Louis joined us. She works for Anheuser-Busch and was talking about some classic in-house brews."

"These are people you'll never see again. Right?"

"There'll be others. You have to make your life happen. Nothing happens if you don't get out there."

The noisy bar scene isn't comfortable for me. "I try to get out there in other ways." But I haven't developed a clear single self yet. "I don't know how I register in the eyes of 'beholders,' if I could find any."

"Men like younger women," Steve pipes up.

"Don't say that."

"It's a fact. Get used to it."

"I'm sure there are many men who—"

"If I were stranded on an island with Madeleine Albright, Janet Reno, and Britney Spears, I'd want to spend all day talking to Albright and Reno. I'd want to hang on their every word, pick their minds, and hear everything those interesting women have to say. But come night, I'm looking for Britney. That's the way it is."

"That's you—"

"It's biology!"

"You sound like some evolutionary biologist with natural selection theories..."

"You can't argue with biology."

"...locked in hunter-gatherer mores..."

"Don't even try to argue with biology."

"I thought you'd give me a little help here. Women evolved. Women embraced the pill in the fifties..."

Why don't I know not to try to get blood from a stone?

"Nature's output of fertile young women is enormous. Walk in any town or city. That's the biggest demographic you see." Steve goes on.

I should give up here.

"Get used to it."

"I have to tell you," I say, switching tacks, "I ate in a diner one night last week. I was alone. And a handsome man, facing me at another table, maybe a little younger than me, kept staring. I was actually flustered and unnerved. Neither of us got up and walked across the aisle. But I was flattered and wondering what he was thinking and what I could do to—"

"Then you went and looked in the mirror and saw you had spinach in your teeth."

Why do I talk to Steve about me? How desperate I am.

"Let me tell ya what's happening with Dad."

With that he launches into a story of my parents during the night. I give up on our conversation and listen dully. My mother moved to the little room during the night because Dad complained that she was snoring. Then she wouldn't answer his calls.

"That's Mummy," I reflect. "She'll leave you flat and check out on you. No matter how much you need her, she won't respond. And Dad is a baby."

That room—about eight feet from Mum and Dad's, across the neck of the kitchen—once had a magic when it was all mine. The room felt large then, with its vibrant Raggedy Ann and Andy motif—done by my mother in our "royal" period. Mum was a superb seamstress. A splendid bedspread with a skirt—electric blue background with bright red ribbing and two raggedy twins dressed in checks and denim, holding hands, cavorting across the meadow, red hair flying—lay like a field with matching curtains that came alive in the breeze. The pillows matched and had red ruffling around the edge. She made two stuffed dolls to match the figures on the bedspread and curtains. Those two inhabited my bed by day and slept with me and the dog and the cat at night.

Dad came in at bedtime—when the room was lit by one "bare-bum" light bulb hanging down—and read to me from my Golden Books with all the innocence of a child himself. Our favorite story was *Tootle*, the engine lost in the meadow, following the butterflies and smelling the flowers. Tootle was exactly me, a daydreamer. Dad assured me that there was plenty of room for the Tootles of the world. Then he read from the back of the book cover all the other Golden Book titles: ten titles a night. I didn't know those were titles of actual books one could own.

I had just a few golden books and one oversized book with glossy pages, called *Tommy and the Indians* (the Indians had cherry-red skin), found by my parents in a little used goods store. And *Peter Rabbit*; we read that at least once a week. *Tootle* was worth reading every night. Those were years when I was an only child. In my coloring books I made some of the children's skin that incredible Crayola color Burnt Sienna, and I gave all the children blue hair—like water. Those memories hold a happiness never to diminish. The room grew suddenly smaller when I shared it with my new baby brother—and even though he screamed through the night, I was no longer alone and life was enlarged.

Today the little room is neglected and deteriorating. The windows are irregular and have splintering, drafty frames. The faded, mostly peeling wallpaper goes several layers deep, following Raggedy Ann and Andy's flight into time. Where did those rag children go? Some faded floral motif on a white background clings to the walls in scraps, and under that are patches with green covered wagons and horses and donkeys. There is a basic, narrow bed for some lone soul and a faded wooden floor that imparts splinters to bare feet.

"So, that's what Ma did last night," Steve sums up, "left Dad alone in their room, maybe for the first time in more than half a century. If she's permanently gone to the little room, Dad'll think she's left him."

"Yeah, well I have to go," I say. "I've got a hot date waiting!"

I take myself to the movie *The Crying Game*, through which I cry.

Right on the heels of that imaginary "hot date," just when I'd thrown out any hope of meeting someone possible, a new man arrived on my doorstep. He was given my name, with my permission, by a computer instructor named Nancy who'd shown me desktop publishing for the professional newsletter I write to no one's seeming interest.

Robert looked promising—he's an engineer and a professor—but he appears to be a guarded fellow, frankly dull. Although decently accomplished, he's unable to communicate what he does. But it's hard to give up this new prospect. It's so nice to have someone. And he grows better in my eyes with wine over the course of an evening and with more wine, even better. The garnets, and pomegranates, the clarets, and cabernets all merge. Then the combination of lateness, the wine, the escape from loneliness and night-winged imagination serve to embellish the night and this partner gains my enthusiasm and generosity. Winter will be a long, howling darkness, I lament, knowing I'm not in a lasting thing. I probably don't even have a friend here. I long for someone who doesn't require the fog of alcohol.

A new relationship would help to unstick me. I feel I'm sitting, like an animal stuck in a tar deposit, in the middle of only what

I've known. But I'm not ready for a new relationship. And Robert isn't right. It's sad to admit that.

It's actually my own fine leather couch I sit on, stroking two fluffs traveling back and forth across my lap, surrounded by Jason's art from high school, for which he won prizes. One piece spent a month in the Corcoran Art Gallery in DC after touring the country, and I own that pride in my son. Things seemed to come together when my parents attended that celebration and David treated us all to dinner at Red Sage. That I avoid thinking about David and about our divorce should be remarkable. But, of course, the phone rings, and just as I'm about to cut the speaker off, my attention is hijacked.

"Hi Janis, I'm not home. I left because we get into arguments over what the people next door are doing that affects our family. I don't want people knowing our business. For instance, I had my period over the weekend, and I had my friend, AJ, come up the lake with me and I think she noticed a spot on the back of my dress. She went through my things and she kept looking at me down there and I know she's not a lesbian or anything, but she never had children herself. She had a hysterectomy at the early age of thirty-two. I guess I've told you she's got a history. But there was no one else to come up the lake with me. I hope she doesn't tell people because I don't want people knowing where my cycle is. She's someone who believes if someone was raped they shouldn't have the baby. And I don't want to be part of that kind of theology or philosophy. I'm probably being paranoid. But sometimes when someone doesn't have anything, they think you have a lot and they get jealous. Anyways . . . she seemed to appreciate going up there. But she can turn on you because she's been through a lot. And as I said before, I didn't have anyone else to come up the lake with me. I wish you would answer your phone sometimes. Just sometimes. Love you."

Margo's obsessions nudge my own aside. I wonder if her fear is caused by her own disowned sexuality, projected onto men, giving them the power to take away her control, to cause her to fragment and scatter her to pieces. Of course, I wonder if she has ever actually been raped. What is it like to think you're being stalked day and night? Occasionally I call back. That little effort sustains her. On some level she's making a connection, which not everyone does.

Today, I forgot to unplug my upstairs fax machine from my home phone line, then I was out seeing patients in my office all day. I'm just sitting down for dinner—still with Robert—just clinking my glass of wine to his and revving up my most labored imagination to feel good being with him, when sirens and lights outside the window seized the moment and we heard a loud, gruff knock.

Margo got a strange sound when she tried to phone me. The policeman knows that the sister reporting me from Rhode Island is out of her mind, yet an ambulance and a fire engine are out there streaking my property with lights.

I'm furious. I phone Margo and tell her it was my fax machine and ask her what she's so afraid of, just because my phone is out of commission for a day.

"Well..."

"Well, what? Where would I be? What's the emergency? Why did you send the police to my door?"

"Well, I thought you might..."

"Thought I might what?"

"I was afraid you might have... Well, suicide."

"Suicide?! You thought I had committed suicide! And what if I had? What were you going to do? Anyway, why would you think that?"

"Because Marisol had a dream that you committed suicide."

"You were acting on Marisol's dream?! Tell you what! I promise I'll never commit suicide. Much as I'd love to. Okay? I have a son I have to live for. When you have children, you don't have the option of killing yourself. You don't ever have to have that thought again. I promise, if I ever kill anyone, it will be someone else."

Long after that episode has blown over, phone calls come from the absent Marisol, worrying, in her mawkish, bubble-gum voice, about what happened to me. She doesn't know this crisis never existed. I tell her how angry I am about her and Margo calling the police on me, and that I'm busy with friends. But she goes on, accusingly, about Margo's nervous condition, telling me Margo "is not doing well." Taking care of Dad and Ma is too much for her, and she insists that Steve and I do something.

"What would you like us to do?"

"There's nothing in their refrigerator for them to eat."

"Would you like me to drive the five hours up there and buy groceries? I don't exactly live nearby."

She doesn't go far in conjuring what we can do, and this, Steve and I agree, is due to her laziness and slow awareness. Margo's cries into the universe elicit rage in otherwise sane people. Marisol's untimely follow-ups are infinitely annoying.

My sisters work together, merged in that "we-ness" they live. Even their names come from a set drawn from a public response. I used to sing a little jingle to the three when they were toddlers: *M and again an M and again, and an M again, make sweet sweet sweet M&M&Ms. Again and again and again.*

My sisters have reminded me about the times I played with them. I do remember teaching them songs and dance steps. I taught them to play "When You Wish Upon a Star" and "Little Dancing Doll" on the piano in the cellar. I introduced them to art as I was discovering Picasso, Joan Miró, and Van Gogh in miniature booklets I found and managed to afford in a Providence bookstore. Max and I practiced shooting an indoor bow with arrows that had suction cups. When I obtained a driver's license, I often took them all to Erisman's Ice Cream stand and then for long drives along the river. I often put Max in front to give him more of a presence (or combat his sense of absence). I took pleasure in them. I was involved then.

Max

Worry about suicide has certainly been warranted. Max has been a recluse all his adult life—much of it now spent in my parents' basement, where he's remained uncommunicative and under the radar. But occasionally he's taken actions that would have glaring meaning even to the casual observer. He's brought his belongings, piece by piece, to the end of the driveway to await trash pickup: clothing, notebooks, towels, blankets. My mother salvaged his high school yearbook, a lava lamp from the late sixties, books on world explorers, sneakers, skates, a camouflage jacket, the stool he made in his high school shop class, and letters he never sent to a girl who had rejected him. She also retrieved family photograph albums he'd jettisoned, as if he were killing us all off. She rescued anything salvageable, but after that incident, the whole family feared that Max intended to end his badly discouraged life.

Max's move from the little room to the cellar is understandable. It's the only imaginable way to have privacy in our parents' house, even if it is in a barely habitable place, the site of that defunct coal bin. The whole cellar is a stone and concrete spider haven, sooted with 1940s coal dust.

But Max is not withdrawn the way he used to be. He now emerges from below to meet up with his friend, Bart, to go bicycling. This friendship is a long story.

Already on disability in his early twenties, Max lived in a superb historic New England mansion that the owner had converted to apartments. For years, he seemed to live there quietly and comfortably, keeping completely to himself. David and I visited once. He showed us his pot "plantation" in the cupola, said he smoked all day and watched C-SPAN. He knew every congressman and every detail of congressional activity and could speak intelligently on politics and current affairs. But he didn't go out or talk to anyone. He saved chores like going to the Laundromat and grocery shopping for the wee hours, when few others used those twenty-four-hour concessions. Then one day he turned up in a woman's bedroom closet in another apartment. When she screamed, he said, "Please, I won't hurt you. I do this all the time." He was jailed, then hospitalized, expelled from his living situation, and mandated by probation to live with my parents, where he has remained. Once in the system again, however, Max was put on lithium, and was found employment in an antique furniture refinishing business, where he met Bart.

Max and Bart worked side-by-side in a big, gruff barn full of pragmatic wood designs and the smell of linseed oil. The shop was full of people with various roles, unlike any environment Max had known. He enjoyed that job. It was an easy place and the work had immediate satisfaction: bringing out the gleam in mostly natural wood, sometimes securing hinges, filling in nicks and scars, and sanding wood surfaces to a smooth finish. The furniture was mostly American antique, but there were some European pieces, and Max managed to bring a couple of those home, hopefully through an honest arrangement with his employers. Six months into the job, he and Bart had a firm friendship.

Bart was a few years younger than Max, a surprisingly slick guy with a high turnover of girlfriends. He was handsome; his mother had been a Spanish beauty queen and his father a Norwegian businessman. Bart was estranged from his parents and on his own, but rumor had it that he would one day inherit wealth.

It was hard to understand Bart's interest in Max. But he had a custom-built bike—a knockout, a perfect expression of himself—and he got Max to take up biking. He also moved a lot, whether because of his drug dealing, running out on debt, or maybe the plethora of girlfriends.

Then came the fateful day when Max sold some Dilaudid to a fellow employee on the worksite, a young woman with the poor judgment to use right there on the spot. In her drugged delirium, with her employers shoring her up on either side, she revealed how she'd come by her state of mind and who had helped her procure the substance in question. Max was promptly fired.

"Nuttin'," he said to my mother when he scuffed in the back door early and went off to his room (he was still using the little room then). But he didn't go to work the next day.

Mum got nothing out of Max, so she phoned the Eggleses, the mom-and-pop owners of the business, and Mrs. Eggles told her in no uncertain terms what had occurred. My mother was shocked to hear what Max had done. She asked Mrs. Eggles if Bart knew anything about this.

"Oh, he most certainly does," said Max's former boss. "We let him go too." She commiserated with my mother about how bad this was for Max, and implied that it might not have been Max's own motivation that created the situation and how they regretted that they had no choice but to fire him, because they liked him. He was a good worker and a sweet man, and they hated to see him go.

From then on, Max kept almost completely to himself, especially when he moved to the cellar. He only came upstairs for food and to shower.

More recently, though, he's been coming up to help my father, sometimes to help him bathe. He's also done jobs around the house. He's done some landscaping and scraped much of the flaked-paint siding off the house—but he quit short of repainting, so the house now stands like a poor old man, stripped naked.

After losing their jobs, Max and Bart started spending their long free days together. Soon Max owned a mountain bike, too, and went out for whole days with Bart. The bicycling seemed a miraculously healthy development. Max seemed to be emerging. It was easy to become hopeful.

Steve, however, didn't let the subject of possible exploitation go. He sat Max down one day beneath the giant hemlocks in the backyard, against which Max looked like a helpless child. Max insisted that he did no drug running for Bart. He got the drugs from Bart, but he sold for his own profit. Maybe that's how he paid for his bike.

Of course, we continue to wonder. Concerned that this job loss might leave Max depressed, I asked my mother during one of our rare telephone conversations—I called her—how Max was doing.

"Oh, he's fine," she said, then added, "but he does some strange things."

"Like what?"

"Well, when I paid the bills last month, I asked him to mail them. Then I started receiving late notices from the phone company, the electric, the gas. So I said, 'Max did you mail those envelopes I gave you a few weeks ago?' He said yes, but when I asked where, he said, 'It was a green mailbox.'"

Is it possible that Max has never noticed that US mail-collection boxes have been a deep, solid blue for decades?

Nevertheless, Max is clearly not a recluse anymore. On occasion, he comes up out of the cellar and goes into town to have a sub sandwich at the diner. This has to be a new luxury, given that he's living only on disability. But he's getting out, after spending so long untouched by daylight. And he not only goes biking, Margo's messages tell me, he has also advertised himself on Craigslist and is doing Mr. Fix-It jobs for people in their homes. He's installed toilets and built closets and replaced kitchen counters. He is paid poorly, because he's unable to demand a good price. But one businessman gave him a fair wage for a project he was satisfied with.

I've learned from Dad that for every three or four jobs Max does well, there's one he screws up. He hung someone's front door upside down, having planed what he thought was the bottom, which was actually the top. The cost of a new door came out of his pay, and ultimately someone else was hired to take over the job. My father says he lives in fear that Max will get into serious trouble.

"For what?" I ask.

Dad says Max does electrical work, for which he's not licensed. And some of the stories of his work are frightening. He's afraid Max will be sued.

"But he doesn't own anything," I say. "What would they get? His bicycle?"

I learn that in Max's quiet, out-of-sight life, he's been taking correspondence courses and has learned web design. Typically, he managed to take the most expensive courses possible, and has incurred deep debt because of it. He claims to have a natural gift for computer technology. He becomes relatively effusive when he talks about it. However, he is now in debt for over $40,000, and won't engage in discussion about why he chose the most costly route. Instead, he's talking about declaring bankruptcy.

Dad starts snorting and blubbering and weeping in his recliner.

"Dad, what's wrong?" I ask.

"He's declaring bankruptcy."

"But why are you sitting there crying?"

"If my own son is declaring bankruptcy . . . then . . . I . . . I must not have been a good father."

Steve reasoned with Max about the high cost of these courses and gave him all kinds of alternative possibilities. But Max does what he's going to do. Now he can't be talked out of declaring bankruptcy. He goes right ahead and hires a lawyer—which adds to his debt—and discovers that the $40,000, because it's for education, does not have bankruptcy protection. So, Max has found himself in debt for life.

I try talking with him about how he defeats himself. I tactfully bring up an event my parents cite as the beginning of his mental illness. He was about sixteen, competing in a swim meet and inches from being the winner, when he stopped to look back and lost to the guy behind him. "He withdrew from the world after that," says my mother.

"Someone should have told you not to look back," I tell Max. "Any kid might not know. And anyone would be tempted. But you don't want to go on defeating yourself."

"Yeah," he responds in his monotone.

Max has told me he feels trapped, living in my parents' home all these years. Since his arrest when he was twenty-two, he has never lived on his own. He longs for a place he can call his own home one day.

In any case, he rides off with Bart on his mountain bike, through back roads and along forest trails, all day long. He's covered the grounds of McLean—where, he tells me, he felt most happy and free, even though he was institutionalized there. His bike-riding seems healthy and independent for someone who's been so locked in. While we worry that Bart has questionable motivation, it's good that Max has a friend. We try not to meddle.

Where Does Love Live?

When I lived in my parents' home, I didn't imagine a future anywhere else. But I've since lived in too many places to count. I shared probably four apartments with roommates in Boston. David and I lived in five places together. I've actually moved three times, following our separation, to finally be where I am now. But my formative years were spent on Eden Avenue.

The family bathroom—even when it served only four people—was always in use. No matter how badly you had to go, or how hard you begged—*Please, Dad, please*—my father seemed to finish his entire *Popular Mechanics* in there. When he finally emerged, I'd say truthfully that I was never so glad to see anyone in my life. An odd vision of affection, a family amusement: Dad in the grip of the human body condition.

In my dream this morning, I'm bathing in our Catskill stream, as David and I did when we went to the mountains, since our basic cabin had no tub or shower. David is fishing nearby, but his back is turned and only I am talking. I soap up and shampoo, but feel it's disrespectful to pee in that pure mountain water and so head up to the cabin, in sandals, wrapped in a towel. Suddenly I'm about ten, outside our family bathroom, pleading to get in. In real life, my mother always called from outside the bathroom door, "Horace, did you die in there?" In my dream, a voice says, "Someone died in there."

"That's a joke," I pronounce out loud as I wake up.

Before I ever knew otherwise, our family bathroom was a cozy place with watery echoes and loving light, the scene of my first remembered baths. There is something eternal about a mother immersing her child in warm wetness that repeats the most primal womb-comfort. Mum would lift me from the tub, swaddle me in a towel, stand me on the toilet seat, and pat me all over with a big, soft-smelling powder puff. Each pat that touched my skin defined me as Mummy's child: "Everything I pat is you."

Steve joined me in the tub when he was less than a year old. My mother stood in wait with the towel for each of us in turn. I remember the hush of her fingertips against cloth—like breath itself—and that bunny-looking thing hopping all over our clean child flesh, puffing clouds.

One night in the midst of our pleasures, Steve and I, both standing on the toilet seat, were told to watch out the window for my father to cut through the dark with headlights of the new car he was driving home. Once we were clothed in clean pajamas, we were carried out to sit in the leather-smelling backseat of the new vehicle. That night my mother made broiled sirloin, a cheese soufflé, and broccoli with Hollandaise, along with homemade corn and banana fritters and melted butter and syrup served in tiny, unfamiliar pots warmed over miniature candles on the table.

But our bathroom later became a source of shame. The tub was that typical ball-claw-foot affair—porcelain-coated cast iron—and it became dated as a suburban world grew up with modern molded bathtubs (not anywhere around us, but we saw it in magazines and on TV). What makes a child's world so possibly joyous is not yet knowing what else exists. One Sunday we tasted that suburban experience, and it changed us forever.

The four of us took a long drive that afternoon to a modern development to view something billed as a "split-level ranch home" that was on display to the public. The house was like an open field inside. It had two bathrooms—something not imagined in 1955 rural America—and that meant two bathtubs, two molded fiberglass tubs, fitted neatly against the walls. Those tubs had showers above, coming out of the wall. Dad said he'd taken showers in the Navy. But we never had. I tried to imagine this height of luxury, to say nothing of the four bedrooms, all just one step up from the living room-dining room floor that had the kitchen.

We imagined all the way home what life would be like in that house. My mother thought the dining room was a dream. Since the kitchen had a counter with tall stools, we could have breakfast there. The kitchen table could become a permanent base for her sewing. Meals could be enjoyed on one always-cleared dining table. "In the kitchen you eat," I reflected from the backseat. "In the dining room you dine." That set the picture of elegance Mum and I loved. She said she'd put a pot of zinnias in the middle of that dining room table for us all to sit around. My father couldn't get over bedrooms just one step up from the TV in the living room. He'd be able to hear the ball game throughout the house. I imagined music spreading like breath, me roller skating end-to-end, Steve running and shooting his cap gun. In our present home, our sounds bumped and crashed like brawlers against the solid walls. In the ranch home, soft notes would dip and sweep and flutter down.

"Two bathrooms" became the name of our dream. Not a dream of owning—just a property for our imagination. It wasn't our way to want things. It's not that we were a poor family then, in our "just us" period. We always had a reasonably new car and those two-week vacations, most years out on Cape Cod. When the family down the street got a TV, we had a place to watch *I Remember Mama* at eight o'clock on Friday nights and *Milton Berle* on Tuesdays. It took another year or two for us to consider owning a TV and having *The Lone Ranger* to ourselves. So the modern home was just something to think about. A game to play. We designed wallpaper, color schemes, and kitchen tiles. Steve thought of an electric train set in the spare bedroom. Dad couldn't stop remarking on the attached garage. This picture was happiness. We were all made expansive by possibility. Dad whistled "Home on the Range" for days after our house tour. "If everyone starts having attached garages," he'd say, "we're looking at a changed world."

I think of us all so simply content then. Steve and me, Santa Claus, Easter Bunny, Tooth Fairy, and all. Not out from under God yet.

Until I was four, my parents and I lived in our "first house"—my father's parents' house, a saltbox with three small rooms inside—just behind this present house. We still see it from the Eden Avenue kitchen window. My folks and I slept in the attic under the eaves. My crib was just inside the door, against the wall. My first memory is in that room. One night under an overhead light, my mother cradled me in her arms before the mirror over the dresser. My father sat on the bed in his sailor uniform. Mummy's framed photo-portrait was on the bureau in front of the mirror. Her touch, her heartbeat, her voice are all one in that memory. She sang "Rock-a-Bye Baby," as she always did, followed by what's known simply as Brahms' "Lullaby," as if the two were one continuous song. Whether this is a true or a screen memory, it's a vivid one. And now my father tells me he saw me at ten months, then again at two. This could have taken place during one of those returns.

A slightly later recall must be the universal most everyone can locate, if they remember early life: that beat of one's own blood inside the ears. I'd awakened sweaty from a summer afternoon nap in my crib in that attic-bedroom. Tops of trees filled the windows along the far side of my parents' bed. Suddenly I heard that wash and rinse, that charge of inner self. I knew I would never forget this moment, the pumping and churning inside—the location of my inner being, that one who was looking out. Then Nana Dagmar's footsteps sounded on the stairs and she appeared through the door to take me.

That house sat on the tarred road that teed into a dirt road at our corner, as if the town ended with us and the magic of wilderness began. We teetered on the verge of meadows leading up to forests and hills and Langley Brook, a long, wild stream that trilled and plunged through, accompanied by a breeze that sometimes spoke; the water and the air gurgled and hummed, or keened a mournful melody, or deliriously howled. Sometimes they sang "Lullaby of Broadway" into the sparkling night. Birds flew in from that glory beyond and sketched arabesques and bows on our airspace. Wild turkeys came and gawked at us, then took to their clumsy flight.

Many summer mornings, while everyone slept, I dragged my blue plaid rocking chair out into the road and sat facing the sunrise and Langley Brook beyond and the sawmill beyond that where my grandfather went to work. Then, with full-throated exuberance, I sang every song I knew. I started with "Oh Where, Oh Where Has My Little Dog Gone" and ended with "You Can't Be True, Dear." I was always singing in those days.

Eventually, my father came out to take me inside, where coffee was percolating in a shapely silver vessel that was plugged into the wall. The machine had an orange light and a graceful glass bulb on top where the coffee bubbled and pulsed. It was a droll symbol of our lush, young happiness. But a shadow already loomed.

The few neighborhood kids typically played in the road—baseball, jump rope, tag. We were safe playing there, as it was rare for cars to come to that end of town. One girl we played with was Peggy Vickry, who lived across the dirt road from us. She was my hopscotch friend. She was six when I was four and seemed impossibly grown up. But she was my first tragedy—the reason that, at four, I learned all was not always right. One night Mrs. Vickry shot and killed her six-year-old daughter. She also killed herself. Five-year-old Martha came over to tell me the news the next morning. She said Mrs. Lessbloom and Mrs. Bemis had gone over and peeked in the windows and saw Peggy's blood all over the kitchen floor.

My mother confirmed that it was true, but said, "Peggy was sick anyway. She had kidney trouble."

I knew Mummy didn't think a mother should kill her child just because the child was sick. After all, Mum had my doll, Pretty, seated—the picture of contentment—at her doll-table in the kitchen, wearing the yellow party dress with butterflies Mum had hand-made. The table itself had an assortment of decals—rows of flowers, garden worms with hats, and watering cans—all Mum's doing. My mother had just not thought deeply about Peggy.

Mummy was eternal to me then. Sustaining as the air. So I chose to brush away that puzzling moment like a bug that lands suddenly on a bare arm.

But where was I to go with my Peggy-love? Dad worked way out of town and didn't tune into these neighborhood happenings. Day after day, I sought Peggy in the sky. I thought if I looked hard enough, she'd step out on some cloud balcony in her braids and white knee socks and scatter petals from a basket; her braids would gleam in the sun and her smile would hold forever. Years later, I tried the neighbors for an explanation. Their faces snapped shut like curtains over a window. They said I was too sensitive and to leave it alone.

Mr. Vickry walked the dirt road past our yard with his head down forever after that day, lunch box in hand, to and from his work at the pumping station (a water-treatment plant). The pumping station pumped its sound out every day like a giant heart beating in the air, speaking for those inarticulate men. Then we moved to Eden Avenue, one street over but still beside the same dirt road. I thought we moved because Peggy died. Now we had our own apple tree on the dirt-road side of the house, which I climbed to lie—like a caterpillar, but face-up—on its most horizontal limb and watch its topmost curly branches crawling at the sky. When Mr. Vickry passed by at the end of his workday, I called down to him from my high perch. But he never looked up. I climbed down a few times to show him I was there. "Hello Mr. Vickry," I'd sing out. But he never answered. He walked with his head down and his lunch box traveled a straight line over that yellow road, and my heart pressed after him.

"Poor thing," my mother said of Mr. Vickry.

He had always raised pigeons, and I was glad to see that he continued to do so.

I wanted to love Mummy more than anything in the world. So when our family, including my grandparents, moved to Eden Avenue—them upstairs, us down—I watched her outside planting. How she worked, setting roots and bulbs and leafy things in place, working her garden tools with meaning and determination, her baggy pedal-pushers billowing and deflating in the breeze. The plants grew like spirits. Hummingbirds flew straight to Mummy's trumpet vines, as if she'd beckoned them, and I restored my mother to a place I'd try never to shake her from again. Her elegant morning glories opened up every morning; her Chinese lanterns tried to spread all over the yard; her gardenia in the mossy stone pot on the pedestal in the living room had an angel presence. All seemed to thrive on something wonderful about Mummy. Some power of high command, some life-light.

It's that same sun we all live under now, all in our separate abodes. The "rosy fingers" slip in at my present-day window and open my eyes. The light of day uplifts. I love to rise in the morning, as if that sunshine is my mother and the song we sang together. I was her sunshine and she was mine. She was my light. If also my dark.

Who was she—this "Mummy"—whose body was my original dwelling and through whom I felt my way into the world? When Mummy was mine alone, when the backyard of our Eden Avenue home seemed large, I recall her out among the clotheslines—fixing drenched cloth characters of just us three—as if assembling a family portrait to blow in the wind or freeze and sparkle in the sun. She appeared in pieces among those colored cloth-shapes: glossy hair and glowing skin peekabooed through that forest of wet sleeves and flapping towels. I could see her feet, wearing comfortable loafers; her neat slacks; and her pretty blouse. Bedsheets, bellied by exuberant breezes, jigged merrily at her; pant legs embraced her. Her glowing cigarette appeared and disappeared, as if lighting the way. Wisps of smoke curled and stretched like luxuriating cats into nothing.

I remember chasing among the fresh-smelling laundry rows, trying to find her. "Finding Mummy." That was what I named the game. She didn't make it easy. Mummy didn't like to be caught hiding. For me, there was no one at the end of the maze. A little gray hang of smoke faded to invisible, and it seemed as if grand mists had shrouded my mother away.

Mummy had gone inside to sit with her *Reader's Digest* open on her lap, her feet up on the hassock. She didn't like the game, she told me, and she was too busy. I knew she could not bear to be found—even in play. For her that would mean submitting. Submitting would be a death. Mummy could never let herself be caught unaware. But I—and I think Steve, too—never stopped seeking.

In the master bath of our last house, David and I had a glass-walled shower with several shower heads and on the other side of the room, a Jacuzzi. The house was a grandiose architectural wonder on a cul-de-sac circle on the edge of this university town.

The grandiosity was mine. David would have liked a more modest place. But even to me, the grandiose house never felt right. It was aesthetically pleasing—with our eclectic variety of modern pieces and French antiques surrounded by glass, under skylights—but cold in feeling. It was so spacious inside that sometimes we couldn't find each other. By then, probably, we didn't want to. A powerful estrangement had overtaken us and when Jason wasn't there, we argued and withdrew from one another. David found new colleague-friends and disappeared on Saturday mornings. I embarked on my career. That house is gone from us now and I own my own small Civil War–era house with the separate converted garage-studio office. I bear all those homes inside. Actually, heart is the home, I must believe.

Our thirty-years-long marriage contained a deeply shared sense of home. I can't say when the clouds started rolling in. I think there is nothing like the fulfillment of a long, committed partnership, of growing together and raising a child. But our baby grew up and David and I have parted. Maybe a mutual action. Our bond exploded and we fell together—red-faced and pointing fingers—into the black hole of anger and blame. When the long, drawn-out tempest was done, there was nothing in the spot that had been so fully inhabited. Change was happening. Our son grew up. And we had moved to this university town—and this home didn't last.

On Thursday nights I leave the parking permit to our local train station on my back porch. I leave it under the sad-eyed wooden turtle, with a note asking David to knock and come in to say hello, as he sometimes used to do. But at midnight, when I head up to bed, he still hasn't come, and when I check at six thirty the next morning, the permit is gone. We don't see each other. We don't know each other anymore.

I don't spend time wondering why. I've restricted that faculty concerning David. I know he has a new woman, so I should get on with my life. Yet I live two miles away and don't admit I'm always looking over my shoulder. How often do I drive past his house without owning that I've gone out of my way to do so?

During our marriage, when I managed to find friends, they weren't of our regular circle. While it was clear that our regular friends liked me, I knew that they were David's friends. So I sought people outside our usual realm. Yet I didn't really need or want anyone outside us and our small circle. I was living a hermetic life. In time, I hardly went out. David had become everything to me. He was nurturing and protective and encouraged my writing. He had rescued me in the first place—one of the handful of young-love plots. I never knew why he chose me. He could have had a girl from that privileged realm he'd earned his way into. But he wanted me, who'd inhabited the workplace at too early an age and lost my youth to low wages and exploitation. I loved the way he loved me. I loved him in all kinds of ways: his voice, his quick mind, the way he handled himself—and me. I cherished that surprised humility with which he enjoyed his growing success. He did more than well enough for both of us. And so I collapsed into the bosom of the first security I'd known in a long time. Truly, the sense of home.

Following the year we lived in England, where, encouraged by David, I spent most days writing in the university library, we returned to New York. In time I hardly went out; instead, I stayed home writing (seven of my stories and five poems were published in literary magazines and won some recognition) and reading. I stayed in our Park Avenue apartment and ordered in all day. I began a small career of ghost writing—a perfect job for who I was then. I was paid well, but received no recognition—perfect for who I was then, too. Mostly I looked forward to evenings with my husband. Sad to face this now. Throughout the day, the groceries arrived, then the videos, the dry-cleaning, the wine for dinner. Sometimes I wondered what David thought about the way I was living—in fear of life. It was David's cousin Kevin who called me on my behavior when visiting for a time. "You haven't been out all day," he said, and then cut into my protests with, "I think you do this every day."

I had stepped out of my own life and into my husband's. Had my shyness never ended? In general, in our group, the women of the couples played to the men. The men were successful. The women, though they'd had the best opportunities and educations, didn't take themselves seriously enough. That was the general conditioning of our generation. I came to resent the husband-focused format and the lack of sisterhood, and that resentment ultimately developed into one of mine and David's complicated quarrels. Some of the men in our group had known

David since childhood and adolescence. Some were his colleagues. Over time—realizing success in the career he loved—he gained considerable respect and fame. He was idealized by many, including me. Within our circle, he was the kingpin, the center of the club; he drew loyalty from others. It was his society, and that's part of the reason I finally left.

When we were with friends, I felt put on hold, while David gave himself fully to them. That meant feeling cut off from my husband, having to wait for later. Even the dogs and cats and parrots of our friends were addressed more than me when we went out. We didn't seem represented as a couple. I tried many ploys to master the situation, each with more determination. Some of these became pathetic. I couldn't break the spell. For years I thought this experience must be about my own insecurity. He thought the same. Ultimately, I couldn't make myself understood. Confusion turned to anger. Marital therapists scolded me, not him. Finally, both of us were overwhelmed by mutual hostility, and I left because he wouldn't.

And now? I've engaged some painters to paint my own home. This home is now my focus. Sometime soon I'll face the fact that Robert and I are going nowhere, and then I'll be alone again, with only myself and the cats to love. Time worms along, hauling in each new dawn, that incomparable gift. Then small worthy and unworthy events start filling the day. I feel blessed when a house finch's nest with eggs establishes itself on my front door in the artificial-flower wreath I got from that beautiful company, Smith and Hawken, that never would have gone out of business in a right world. The newspaper thumps on the porch; a promising-looking invitation in the mail asks me to a financial presentation dinner from some stranger who wants my money and is not getting it. If anything in my mail ever looks interesting, I know it isn't. The "nothing happens" theme of my early life has returned. The Stones are singing about no satisfaction as I walk in with the unsatisfying mail.

Dank shadows will soon be pressing across the yard. Where is the life I'm not living? Where are you after you've vanished into thin air?

Maybe the truth is that on my own again, I won't be able to enlarge my life. Maybe there's a lock on it. Some witch sat at my cradle at birth and set the curse of small life—"a life so miniscule," the curse said, "it will wear like a cage." And now, as punishment for leaving my marriage, I'm yoked again to that original feeling that "nothing happens." I've reentered the world of the lonely—where David first found me.

But I am not that shy, inadequate person anymore. I'm not so fundamentally bewildered. I enjoy my profession. In that, I feel whole. I know my expertise and I'm creative in my work. I'm entering the world more fully. I've volunteered to do a fundraiser for The Sierra Club in my home. I'll be making lasagna for about one hundred guests. A woman named Carolyn will cook with me. Someone named Jeanette will arrive early with salad. Others will bring wine, beer, and soda. Another lovely woman, also named Carolyn, is bringing homemade cookies.

An urgent phone message from Margo hardly interrupts.

"Max is drilling up the driveway. Ma and Dad can't stop him." (I can hear my father hollering in the background.) "He's just drilling it up and throwing the broken concrete in the yard and on the road. Steve is very upset but he won't talk to Max because he thinks he steals. And you don't talk to him either. Unless you do, there's no one to tell him to stop drilling up the driveway."

The driveway will be back to cinders, as I knew our driveway when that was the place I called home.

But the phone calls take me far from any home base. They are from some disturbed Neverland that can't be embraced or understood. A source of amusement, or pathos. Steve and I call these Margo's little bouts of diarrhea of the mind, discharged into our telephones. Her messy disturbances. And we are obliged to clean them up. It's like changing diapers forever.

Margo has been in worse states.

Margo

Just as David and I were separating, before my September and May visits began, I visited my parents on the lake. My parents were still whole then—as whole as they'd ever been—and were living in the cottage in the fall and spring, traveling all winter in their trailer, then renting out the lake property and living back at Eden Avenue for the summer.

Margo, meanwhile, was living not far from them, in a tragic state of poverty. What I remember most is what Margo's state of mind was like then. Steve was there, too, and we took on the problem—an endeavor that didn't allow for much meaningful contact between us.

We found her in a trailer park, which more resembled a pioneer camp set up in a molasses-colored clearing below high-headed conifers thick enough to hide the sky. About six rusted trailers made something of a circle, like a wagon train, among gigantic tree roots. Smoke curls spewed up into low, pewter-colored clouds. The old forest floor was scarred mud; the air was thick with the smell of sap and scrap fires.

Margo was living not in a trailer but in a teetering, almost vertical structure that, if it had had laces, would have resembled the old woman's fairy-tale shoe. We found her on the floor inside on all fours, looking for her cat. The cat was ill and trying to hide, and Margo was consumed by a mission to cure it. There were dirty dishes and clothes strewn everywhere and no place to sit and barely room to stand. Steve had to bend to keep from bumping his head.

She didn't want to talk and soon just wanted us out: "Take your godless souls to the mall," she lashed out—so unlike Margo the telephone messenger, who always says, "I love you."

Steve and I visited her again a few months later. She'd been forced to move into a single-room apartment not far away from the trailer park. My parents had said she was doing badly, and we'd agreed to go to her. They weren't too old to go themselves, but they were weary.

Margo's new space—once a porch, now paneled and windowed—contained a stove and refrigerator, a couch, and a tiny bathroom, all in about one hundred square feet. The cat was still ill, and Margo was obsessed.

I didn't fully understand about Margo then. Her undone spells seemed intermittent. She'd always been more sane on the phone, although I recalled one phone exchange we'd had when she was in her early twenties, living outside Boston. She had called—and I had answered, which I did then—to tell me that there were men trying to break into her apartment. She was panicked.

"There are no men trying to break into your apartment," I said, definitively.

"Are you sure?" she asked after a stunned silence.

"I promise you."

"You're sure . . ."

"I'm positive. There are no men breaking in."

"No men . . . You're sure there are no men breaking in."

"No men." Long pause. "You wish there were," I ventured.

And she burst out laughing. We laughed together. I felt she'd been pulled back from the edge.

I was not prepared now for the level of disarray in her living situation. A pot of oatmeal on the stove had turned to mold and fungus. Her mail and bills were all over the floor and two small table tops were strewn with forgotten snack food, spattered milk, and an open can of rotting tuna. She'd taken the cat to many veterinarians and alienated them all. The last had a restraining order against her. She'd developed a crush on him. His office building was blue, and since her cat's name was Blue, she'd assumed a kind of kismet. I don't know how she paid veterinarian bills.

Our intention was first to find out if she was on her Stelazine. She was not. It took hours to get a plan afoot to take her to the pharmacy. She had to get the meds herself, as she distrusted us; she thought we might poison her medicine. But the plan kept getting sidetracked.

"Look," I finally said. "We have to take care of this. We're not here for long."

Well, no, she had no intention of going.

"Why?"

"Because," she said to Steve. "You're going to kill my cat."

There was no dissuading her. Only she could get the medicine; she wouldn't leave her cat alone; she wouldn't leave Steve with the cat; she wouldn't go with Steve in the car without me. Max actually made the three-hour drive up that day, and he stayed with the cat. Margo climbed into the backseat. Steve drove. I was the front passenger.

As Steve pulled out from the first stop sign, Margo began screaming that we were going to crash, though the oncoming cars were distant.

"Calm down, Margo," I commanded. "Steve drives well and makes good judgments." But soon she was screaming at every turn, as if he were driving the Shelby GT 390 in the chase scene from *Bullitt*.

"Margo, stop it," I shouted over her. "Steve's a safe driver."

"We're all going to be killed," she screamed at the next stop sign, sobbing.

"Margo," I yelled again. "Stop it. Right now. Stop. Just admit that it's you who want us killed. You want to kill us all. And stop this fuss."

That settled her into silence.

I felt enormous pity at her permanent state of fear and distrust, her sense of constant danger. Her medication helped. But by summer I learned that she was appearing every few days at my parents' door at Eden with her deteriorating pet in a baby bunting. Every time she became overwhelming and they forced her to leave, and she only sprang back like stuck chewing gum. She felt she belonged under their roof more than she did in that tiny place paid for by HUD. Finally, I suggested that since she couldn't be persuaded to leave, maybe she could stay. She was going to be there anyway. "The poor thing," my mother said. I made a case for her. HUD agreed to pay toward the apartment upstairs.

My father phoned me. I phoned back. She was invading their territory and plaguing them all day long. They couldn't keep her out. Dad finally agreed to let Steve get a locksmith to put new locks for both doors to their quarters on the first floor. He did this from California. One door opened to the kitchen, and one opened to the front-house end of the living room. That was accomplished. Then, inexplicably, they gave her the new keys.

Otherwise, it worked well. She had the two upstairs rooms where my grandparents had lived, that had then become Steve's and my bedrooms and later, I gather, the triplets' rooms. Max put a bathroom in what we called the green-stamps room. He set up a kitchen in what had been my room. He put in a sink and a stove, and then a fire escape from her bedroom (once Steve's) down the side of the house, which HUD required; they inspected, and approved. Margo promptly bought a table and chairs at a yard sale and a refrigerator from Sears, which Max set up in her kitchen, too. I'd already had the idea of her cooking for them, becoming the family chef. But just then, she was too out of commission.

The cat grew sicker. She nursed it with insane love. She kept it in her room, allowed no one in, and conducted private rituals with church music. She appeared to have stopped eating. And then one day there was a wail in the early dawn.

No one was allowed to go to her. My parents and sometimes even Marisol took turns standing outside her locked bedroom door, pleading with her to accept reality. Even Marisol's now husband, Fred, came, and even Fred's potential kidney donor, Nestor; all stood at one time or another trying to help her understand that her cat was dead. But if no one could go to her during the whole course of the cat's illness, clearly no one was going to help her part with the cat's body.

My mother threatened to break down her door and take it from her. She felt terrible for Margo, but she warned that the body was going to rot and smell. My father went up there, offering to help with the burial, and sang a Swedish song his mother used to sing that he said was "guaranteed to get any cat to heaven." No one knew where the body was: with her in her bed, in an opened bureau drawer, bedded in her closet? Margo opened the door a crack one day and promised my mother that the body wouldn't rot and wouldn't smell. She had her reason, which we all assumed must be that the cat was now risen, or sainted.

"Hope she didn't eat it," Steve offered.

My mother snuck up there later on, when she was sure Margo was asleep, snooped through the other areas, and finally located the corpse, swaddled in its baby blue bunting in the freezer of the new refrigerator.

This stopped everyone in their tracks for a while. It was decided that we would say nothing.

At first Margo didn't come down, even when invited. But days later, with hair streaming wet from a shower, she appeared in my parents' kitchen one morning. She proceeded to toast two frozen waffles in my mother's kitchen, spread them with peanut butter, and sit eating in silence. Later she went out in the garden and buried the cat in Max's strawberry patch.

After that she took on the job of cooking for everyone, which has continued to this day.

Who are they? These sisters. So caught up in delusions and paranoias that they can barely function. And if I parse my feeling that might be some basic form of love, I get attachment because of familiarity, the strength of blood relations, and genuine sorrow over a tragedy that is no one's fault. They're here. I love them because they're here.

Bad Times with Mum and Dad

Shortly following the Margo episode, I visited my parents once again on the lake and had an interaction with Mum that echoed our whole troubled relationship, reminding me why we'd become estranged in the first place. I have a naive blind spot that sets me up for what shouldn't be surprises.

On that visit, it was just my parents and me. At my folks' suggestion, we first got into the car and followed the path of a recent tornado. My parents have always been storm chasers. This was an adventure. In one place, the twister had eaten up half a house and spit out what looked like a beavers' nest of splinters. Couches, mattresses, and a television were all scattered nearby, as if shaken out of a cracker box. The other half of the house remained solid and untouched. "A house divided," my mother said. We stood there, amazed and awed.

Back at the cottage, we had dinner and my father went to bed. Then I had that moment with Mum, which still burns like I've touched a hot stove.

She and I sat side-by-side in the Adirondack chairs on the deck, small against the still-visible titanic spread of water before us in twilight and the start of evening loon sounds. I was generally nervous because I was newly on my own, trying to make it in my start-up business, after having been a dependent wife for twenty-seven years. I told my mother how insecure I was about surviving. Perhaps the serene lake invited that openness.

I gradually realized my mother had withdrawn into a smoldering silence.

My breath stopped and the lake went hard before my eyes. "What?" I asked.

"I wish these kids had the problems you do," she said.

"What? What kids?" I responded, feeling my fury rise. The horizon shuddered. "These forty-year-old triplets?"

"They don't have a pot to piss in and they never will," she spat out.

"But we're not talking about them. We're talking about me."

"You don't care about them. They've got no one but us."

"They're *all* you care about. You can't admit I exist."

"And you hate them. You've always hated them."

"And that's because of you. From the day they were born, you've thrown them in my face every time I tried to speak. I never had a voice again in this family. You've always stuck them right between you and me, so I can't be heard or seen. It's your fault and all my hate should have gone to you."

Typically, Mum picked herself up, said, "I don't have to listen to this," went off to her room, and slammed the door.

Alone in the living room, I sat for a while, and then moved out on the deck to gaze at the stars. When did my mother's hatred of me begin? And why? Way before the triplets; that event only solidified and finalized it. Did she fault me for her unplanned pregnancy? In her generation, women's lives, in general, didn't go in many directions. Women had no choices then; it was largely marriage and motherhood. I can only guess. I'll probably never know. I got up before dawn and left in the dark.

On my drive home, I deeply felt my mother's hate. I've also felt her love, that intermittent early childhood love. I am made of both. I both hate and love my mother.

My hate for Mum has long standing. For many of my early years, I kept a diary that contained the awful moments I'd had with her. I kept it locked with a tiny golden key. I hid this record of fury and torment under my bed. But I killed it one day when it became too much. I was twelve; this was just prior to the births. "No kid should ever have felt like this," I said to myself one day, and I took the diary out to the trash barrel in the backyard, where I tore the pages out and burned them, one by one. Each page began: "I still hate my mother" or "I hate my mother more today than yesterday." It was too large a hate for a kid.

The other part—the love—has thrived, because it's also true. But the hate, when it died, deadened me. Some part at my center doesn't feel, stays numb and detached and forever feels unreal.

Steve tells me of a similar bad time with Dad.

"They hold it against you if you've had any accomplishment in life," he pronounces.

"Because the others can't?"

"That's right. You only exist in this family if you never move outside their orbit. Being handicapped is an asset here."

"They can all live together in their bubble."

Steve tells me that at the height of his business success, when he'd made a few charismatic television appearances where he explained his work with both landlords and tenants in Los Angeles, my father could only say, "Well, you do all right. But these three, they could never do what you do. They've got nothing." No matter how Steve tried to impress my father with his success, Dad could only harp on the three. Steve says he was so angry at my father's refusal to see him that he went out, jumped in his motorboat, forgot to unchain it, and took off with such fury that a piece of the dock came with him and he did several hundred dollars' worth of damage to his boat.

Do my parents feel they lost us to the world? And now just not recognize us anymore?

Dad's first response to my wish to go to college was to tell the story of a man at the shop whose son went to college. "And you know what happened? That kid never came home anymore. He never wanted to bring anyone home because he was ashamed of their couch."

My eyes flew to our sorry couch, full of years and Dad's permanently imprinted reclining shape at the end of his workdays. I felt Dad's fear of losing me. But I was no longer of that couch. I'd not then known a world much larger than our living room. But I was no longer of that living room.

A few days after the couch conversation, my father knocked on the door to my room (upstairs by then).

"What I want to tell you is," he began, "I know you want to go to college and I see you studying. I'm glad you want to better yourself."

It was just after my junior year, and I'd arranged with our new guidance counselor to spend the summer learning those academic subjects I'd done so poorly in my freshman year so I could take second-year courses in my senior year.

"I'll try to help you as much as I can," Dad said. "You're doing a good thing and I'm proud a ya."

Mum was at her most cruel. "College? And who's going to pay for it? These kids are not going without shoes just so *you*"—the word twisted ugly—"can go to college."

White-hot anger paralyzed me when I heard those hard New England knuckles in her voice. Mum was not going with me in my life, and Dad could help only so much. I'd be going it alone. Paying my own way forward was going to be formidable.

"I could see helping you if you were a boy." She left me with that.

Encouragement had come from my English teacher, Mrs. Morning, who'd taken me aside toward the end of my junior year and said, "You have to go to college." I'd already been panicked about the future. "I don't know how you'll do it," she said. "You're so unfinished. But you've got to go for higher education." She got me out of typing-accounting-shorthand courses and into the academic curriculum. She was too overwhelmed with large classes in our small school to help me more, but she said my paper on Heathcliff was the best thing she'd seen by a high school student.

It was a tap, a touch, enough to launch me. But "unfinished" stayed with me.

Can I ever forget these scalding exchanges with Mum? She refused to help even with my college application fees—ten dollars each. I took on a lot of extra babysitting. In that fifty-cents-an-hour era, I just made the deadline with twenty dollars, enough to apply to two colleges. I got into Northeastern. Besides Rhode Island College (and, of course, MIT, which was for geniuses), I didn't know what other colleges existed.

But I don't forget that it was the best of our parents that made it possible for Steve and me to do well in life.

Or was it just our own talents? Steve's financial success grew considerably beyond his retirement in middle age because he is a savvy investor. I believe he now has more money than he'll ever need. And I, by any standards—even with my late, slow start—am doing well as a therapist. I help people, I support myself, and I'm fulfilled. Sometimes even inspired.

The three didn't survive like we did. Whatever made for their mental illness, it has kept them infantile; they, unlike us, took up residence within my parents' limitations (and their own, maybe excepting Max) and never moved beyond them. Did my folks play a part in keeping them arrested as a way of keeping them home? To take care of them in their old age?

They did seem to love their older children less when we became citizens of a greater world. Yet they instilled in us the ability to play, a quality that has lent success to my profession and to raising a child of my own. To play is a realized way to live. Play is full of humor—the highest defense—and saving grace.

Could my parents comprehend what I do all day? Their family therapy in the past was because of florid mental illness and would have been about managing the situation, different from the in-depth work I do. I've worked with more neurotic, garden-variety suffering, but more and more often, my work goes beyond that. In each treatment, I also feel the expansion and evolution of myself in tandem with my patient.

With child patients, the subject of a brother or sister often provides the easy point of access. Sibling rivalry is one of the most fundamental motivations. One has to wonder what purpose this has served the overall human condition. I think a negative equivalent of sibling rivalry has caused much of the world's strife. Positive bonding makes for our immense progress as a species. And differentiation is key. In my office, stories of siblings are often about fairness and favoritism. Any opportunity to see the world through one child's eyes gives me material to work with. And my clients all warm to the subject of their family's other children. The truth doesn't matter; the story told about a sibling can provide a way into my child-patient's inner life.

Couples are another story. Overall I try to increase their empathy for one another, if possible. Empathy and generosity can go a long way. My practice right now, however, has a number of storming couples. How I sometimes wish I could just tell them what I know from experience: Divorce hurts. Even a divorce that should be.

After a full few days of helping warring partners see one another in a kinder light (with varying degrees of success) and taking care of extreme anxiety levels, I find myself envious of what I do for them, that no one did for me and David.

Tonight, as darkness falls, my patient, a large man, gets up out of his chair, takes two swift, giant steps across the room and physically attacks his small wife. He has his hands around her throat.

I fly out of my chair and manage to pry them apart. "Stop it," I order him. His grip is tight. I put my hand on the middle of his chest and push him away. He immediately breaks out of a trance and becomes the picture of equanimity. He walks back and takes his seat, straightening his tie with a weird little smile that lacks happiness. The tie, I noticed before, has puppies and balloons on it, and his socks bear other cartoon characters. He wears a good jacket and respectable trousers, but with Keds sneakers—á la 1956—and his hair forms a curly cloud like that of Clarabel the clown or Harpo Marx. He is an accomplished mathematician.

His wife, a neat woman who wears her hair tidily pulled back, is gasping for breath. She has a bottle of water. She takes a sip as I help her sit back in her seat.

"I'm okay," she insists. "Really, I just need water."

"What just happened?" I sit down and look searchingly at the man and at his wife, from one to the other. They insist this has never happened before. The fact is, my interruption broke the spell and any chance of getting to the motivation was thus lost. But, of course, I had to stop it.

"If it just came out of the blue," I say, "that worries me. What else comes out of the blue?" Both promise that safety will prevail. We talk it through and they agree to continue therapy and to feel appropriate concern and need to explore the event.

After they leave, my workday is done. I'm so thoroughly shaken, I run back across the yard to the house, which has Robert inside it. He's making margaritas. Fully knowing better, I throw myself into his arms, tell him what's happened, and ask him to please hold me. But Robert is a strange duck; he doesn't react in a comforting way.

Were I not so shaken and in need, I wouldn't have asked for what this person can't give. Robert doesn't have these capabilities. I know this.

I accept the perfect margarita on which he prides himself. I don't try to choose disappointing people, but I wonder why that's all that comes my way. *Because you no longer live in a well-connected world, as you did with your husband,* yackety-yacks the thought-skunk. *Yet, so much better having someone here than having no one*, I lament. What a predicament.

Robert and I take our drinks into the living room and watch the news.

I resolve to return to the dating site. I'm sad and jealous that David has someone new, even knowing it's probably good for him. He's moving on with his life, as he should.

Robert goes home, and I go to bed. Throughout my sleep alone, some night creature bounds overhead in the attic all night long and I have dreams of Godzillas up there bowling with fireballs. I wake up a few times with cats on my head, pull the covers over us, and wish for time to stop.

Marisol

Four phone messages from Marisol await me in the morning. She wants me to "come home" and take care of my parents, as Margo has fled to the monastery again.

I don't hear much from Marisol. She is a less-seen presence in the family, even though she feels she must always visit when I do. I only have clues here and there.

On one of my first spring weekend visits to Eden Avenue, sitting in my parents' living room, I was sorting through family photographs I'd emptied out of the greasy brown shopping bag Margo keeps in her attic closet. I came across a magazine with a *Playboy*-type centerfold picturing one of the most beautiful women imaginable, sprawled across two pages, in a nightie. I stared for a while and then realized it was Marisol.

She had told me during a Thanksgiving visit to my new home just following my divorce that she'd had a modeling career. Jason was spending his college junior year in Nepal, so he wasn't home. Mum and Dad and Marisol and Max had all come to have Thanksgiving with me. Margo had stayed home, having had some fit or conniption no longer lodged in the memory of anyone.

That trip shouldn't have been made. It was 1999, two years after Dad's stroke, and no one realized he wasn't up to it. He'd had diarrhea on the drive there; they'd made many rest stops along the way, where Max had taken him to the men's room and cleaned him up and changed his clothes. My washing machine was busy all weekend. But as soon as Dad settled in the living room, Qwerty and Lemmy were all over him, and he loved it. All seemed well. I made and served a beautiful Thanksgiving dinner.

The next day, Marisol and I took a long walk along the local waterway. That's when she told me about her modeling career. I assumed delusion and distortion. But she also said she'd been required to have plastic surgery to her chin, to make the jawline perfect. That made me think there might be some truth about an oddball modeling career that couldn't have amounted to much. Marisol was quite overweight now.

We went on to talk about her surgical history. At puberty, she'd been discovered to be missing a uterus. Several operations had been performed to build in that female apparatus, but she would always be missing ovaries, they'd said, and she would never produce children.

I was no longer in the family when Marisol had to face this trauma. Her pain was still visible. This sad fact, I thought, could play into many of my sisters' imaginings and delusions. Marisol told me she had vowed back then to some day adopt a child. I felt the fervency of her desire. Fred was not in the picture yet.

When we returned from our walk at about three o'clock, I announced that I planned to serve our dinner of Thanksgiving leftovers as soon as I took a shower and changed clothes. When I came downstairs, I found that Marisol had put all the unheated leftovers out on the dining table and they'd all eaten. The food was slopped all over the table and the floor as if a mob had descended. There had been no grace or thought. My parents were obviously missing enough pieces by then to have said nothing and had no reaction. Max had stared into space the whole two days and was unfazed even when the cat knocked a stack of pots and pans onto the floor nearby and made a thunderous sound.

I was stunned and irate. After feeling such sympathy and empathy for Marisol, I wondered what this meant about her.

Her lack of manners and good sense made her seem seriously handicapped—and just lacking class.

When, in the Eden Avenue living room a few years later, I came across this photo spread from her modeling era, I remembered a key piece of information I'd heard about Marisol years earlier: the fact that she'd dated a high-level official in the state office. I don't know how she met him, or how that relationship went. I imagine that sparkling girl in the magazine sitting at a table in a restaurant, maybe Loche-Ober in Boston, dripping pearl earrings, silken hair swirled up like a sand castle, and eyelids dabbed with candlelight, while waiters lifted silver covers from platters of splendid cuisine. This man across the table would have had eyes filled with her beauty and probably ignored it if she never said one sensible thing and gobbled up her dinner and dessert in a gulp. Where would they have ended the evening?

"Marisol, this is you?!" I said with total surprise that day, the magazine open in my hands. We were all sitting in line in the living room.

"Oh, I can't even look at that picture, Janis," she said. "I can't think about those days. I was so sick then."

My heart and my imagination stopped still. Maybe one day I'll understand how sick that was. I'd like to know how it feels to be Marisol. But our visits now are too chaotic, too focused on Mum and Dad.

Marisol was able to move out on her own, and she now lives in my parents' "out-of-sight-out-of-mind" perspective—a perspective I know all too well. She was able to marry a second time. Fred, whom she met through a Christian dating service, is six foot five and never removes the wooden cross the size of a baby that he hangs around his neck. His manner is gentle and kind and they appear to be a good match.

With the help of Fred's father, the newlyweds purchased a small home. I know nothing about this home, but an image forms in my mind of a dwelling down along what was once an abandoned stretch and is now a rail trail. I'll have to embroider what I know about Marisol with my own imagination. The house I conjure is one of three that are actually there. It looks like a fisherman's hut, sitting on a sliver of land between the river and the road. I picture an added-on living room at the back with a picture window facing the widest part of the river. Both river and track road once served the old wool mill and run parallel all the way out to Lake Crockett. The rails and ties of the track have long since been removed and heavy brush grows in along both sides like mutton-chop sideburns. Few people drive here other than fishermen, local drunks, and high school kids who come on late weekend nights.

A place so far out on the edge of town has natural beauty, but it also embodies the despair of the marginalized and bears an air of danger. Suicides happen in these woods and strange, unpredictable people turn up. The road itself is subject to forces that distort its run. The river, in varying states of ire, runs over its banks and leaves puddles that strand fish and drown small animals. The stretch might be steeped in the overflow for days if the river goes sluggish before drawing back. The pits and troughs and swellings, meanwhile, are permanent, and an intermittent cover of creeping vegetation lies so heavy and dramatic that the road vacillates between being and not being.

This is where my mind puts them. Theirs would be the first of the three small houses strung along this old track leading up to Anders Bridge, beyond which the road almost disappears into wilderness. The three structures sit like wise old women wrapped in shawls and contemplating the river. Each poor house has a splendid view of the fat, fertile belly of the river and all day they witness ospreys, blue herons, egrets, and occasional shearwaters, who live on jumping fish.

I know that in fact Marisol and Fred had an awkward dog who got lost one night out on the frozen river and was found and returned by a stranger. I picture this scenario. As if drawn to the magnetism of a happy new couple, this stray dog would have arrived one day—hound-like, with great, sympathetic eyes and ears so long and floppy and legs so short that the ears frequently got under its feet.

I've made up the rest of this story. They take her in and name her Giddy, because she often hosts—as if her body were a transport—a population of invisible things that make her scratch so hard she has the look of being tickled and falling over laughing. All live happily and seemingly without event.

Then one night, long after dark, they forget to let the dog in before they go to bed. It's a cold winter night. Weighted snow plops and sizzles on Giddy's warm body as she burrows around holes and openings in the foundation of the house, trying to dig her way inside. Finally, she hangs one of her unmanageable ears into the sprung opening of a cellar window. There is a sudden clamp. A mousetrap bites and hangs on to the dog's inconvenient ear. Poor Giddy is moved, instinctively, to take flight toward the open river and, once entered on the great spread of snow on ice, becomes somehow entranced and compelled to keep going.

The river is wide and generous, as if the moon has poured a spread of milk. The mousetrap dangles like an earring on a señorita, and Giddy follows the drive to take one step after another until she reaches her destination, seats herself on the snowscape out under the unimpeded universe above, and fastens her nose to the North Star.

I fancy her (ear numb by now) the picture of contentment—waiting and contemplating the full moon as if it were a hearth. But nose pointed north has her rear headed downriver. The ice, under the innocent snow, is imperceptibly moving. Giddy just sits. She may look calmly expectant—a kind of take-what-comes attitude shaped by her life so far—and she may or may not notice that the setting changes. The river has felt called upon to swell its bosom to the rising call of a new day. Soon the ice begins separating soundlessly, not breaking or gnashing but unfolding like fingers softly letting go. And soon Giddy is ferried down under Anders Bridge in a serene flow on an ice pillow all her own. As I picture her moving soundlessly—her mind a comfortable and even shade of blue—she doesn't even utter a dog sigh, so calm is her acceptance of what destiny might await. Giddy just looks the way she always does, like someone born to trust.

The person who finally does find Giddy is Nestor B., encamped in his van on the edge of the river, down an old wash. (One Nestor B. did actually enter Fred and Marisol's domain.) He wakes to see the creature being ferried along like a figment on a cloud. Most everything in Nestor's life has looked like a figment. But seeing those ears, he is moved to rescue her by bamboo pole and lasso and an ice fishing hook that he digs into her ice floe. He captures her at a small brink, and soon shares his beans and hot dogs over the campfire with his new friend. He removes the mousetrap that failed to trap her at home, cleans the modest wound, and assumes her to be a gift from on high. Anything that ever comes to Nestor comes by miracle. And so for a week or so, Giddy and Nestor are a happy pair, romping in the snow. Giddy accompanies Nestor as he fishes and gathers wood for the fire, curls up with him in the van by night, and occasionally drives with him into town to collect his unemployment check and stock up on life supplies. He calls her *mi amor*.

One day Marisol encounters Giddy and Nestor in the laundromat. She recognizes Giddy and runs to embrace her—thanking Nestor, assuming him to be the dog's savior. Nestor understands the woman to be the dog's owner, glad to have its return. By late afternoon—and this part actually happened—Nestor is residing in Fred and Marisol's living room and has accepted being read to from the Bible, feeling the full force of salvation, as if he's been restored to lost kin. Within days, he's had a total-immersion baptism and promised Fred one of his healthy kidneys, as soon as Fred is able to schedule the transplant he needs. They all get on well. Nestor finds a janitor position in the office-complex reincarnation of the wool mill.

The rest of this story is true. In time, Marisol and Fred took in a young "foster child," Joshua, who, at age two, had already been in four other foster homes. His father had been released from jail because he was dying of pancreatic cancer, and his mother was incapable of caring for her children. Fred and Marisol had wanted a child badly. The first plan, put together by Margo and Marisol, was for Margo to produce Fred's baby by artificial insemination. They had appointments with fertility centers all over the state. No center would accommodate them. They were told that they were too old. So Fred and Marisol were happy to have Joshua; they offered immediate, straight-up, uncomplicated love.

Even at two, Joshua seemed to understand that good fortune, or at least safety, had finally found him. He woke up every morning and wrapped his arms around his new mother's thigh and stuck like an octopus. The couple adored him, and after Fred finally did get a new kidney (not Nestor's), they set about adopting the child. This meant a committee of state social workers was to frequent their home unannounced over the next few weeks to assess their capability for parenthood.

In keeping with their profound inability to maintain order—and tendency toward excessive hoarding—the place was always in a state of disarray. It matched the state of things with Margo, Max, and my parents. But knowing this committee would decide their family fate, Marisol was moved to begin the impossible job of cleaning. She spent days mopping and sponging up soup and grease everywhere, sweeping dirty clothes and junk food wrappers out of the living room and bedroom, scrubbing the kitchen cabinets until they gleamed. The kitchen chairs were replaced around the table and couch cushions cleaned and put back on the couch. One woeful middle of the night—toward deadline—she fell, exhausted, on her knees to polish the doorknobs. At any other point in her life, Marisol would have been incapable of cleaning at all.

But they won. Marisol and Fred became proud parents. This determined woman created the family she always wanted, including a child to whom she could give all that saved-up love. I offered guidance and advice, if wanted, and several phone conversations followed. Having a family, people belonging to one another, is a profound way to be not alone.

Nestor saw he'd lost his purpose there. After receiving the Lord, no longer so alone himself, one day, when no one was paying attention, Nestor slipped away in his van.

Family Trust

Following my Godzilla night and Marisol messages, I drive into town and run into Natasha, the artist. She expresses an interest in seeing my historic house and my gardens, which have gained something of a reputation. Since she'll come after five o'clock, I invite her to dinner. She's someone with a lot of pizzazz and I think she'll be interesting.

I make wild salmon and a colorful salad. It's been so long since I've cooked for anyone—except myself and Robert—that I'm thrilled.

After a garden tour, Natasha and I arrive in the kitchen. But as I take the salmon from the oven, a look of panic crosses her face, she hunches her shoulders and shrinks back as if she fears I've poisoned our dinner, and then she produces from her pocketbook . . . a baked potato.

I'm quick to realize that I'm in la-la land. I suspect she's not going to eat the salmon or the salad. When we sit down at the table, she places the potato on the plate in front of her and brings her hands to her lap beneath the table, where they stay. She's not going to eat the potato, either. She's going to sit and look at it.

My patients are the sanest people I know.

I set about renewing and redoubling all social efforts. I'm working with a professional organization to which I belong, trying to secure a mental health carve-out with local businesses outside the dawning HMO system of "managed care." Writing our newsletter has proven an isolating and rather thankless pursuit. I've also joined an environmental effort to save some local wetlands. It is a local town-committee project of turning a grand old family nursery into public lands with hiking trails; it's worthy and interesting, but soon over.

Otherwise, I'm not geared this way. I was miserable doing the Christmas bird count this past winter with the trails people: out there at 7:00 a.m. on a freezing December day. The birds were hard to see against a socked-in sky and I get no thrill out of counting and listing, even for the worthy purpose of elucidating winter bird patterns. Such missions are taken very seriously, and I was out of step and possibly frowned upon.

My attempts at finding solidarity have failed.

I've always been a sorry "joiner." Girl Scouts and the 4-H Club in my town were boring and uninspired. A college sorority had endless meetings to discuss bylaws, and I was working too many part-time jobs. Now it's hard to locate the right groups, and all these failures play into my present desolation. Almost seven years have passed since David and I separated. But it's a slow process trying to build a new life, a new self; there is little immediate gratification and only gradually educated judgment. And he's still always on the bottom layer of my mind, and turns up in all my dreams. I'm not letting go and I'm not admitting it.

I've read that introverts are having a vogue.

I set about finding other ways to enlarge my social terrain, and am interrupted by the voice of highest catastrophe and alarm sounding out over the speaker: "Call back right away. Max is doing a website for prostitutes!"

An email from Steve tells me Max is designing a website for an escort agency called Lip Service.

Margo emails us both that we need to do something right away.

"Max is running a business," Steve replies, "and he owes service to whoever comes his way."

She goes on. Mum has been diagnosed with Alzheimer's and it's getting worse. She is moving furniture up against the back door at night with some vague fear of break-ins, which never happen there, where no one locks doors. I learn that David has come through for my mother, as he did with my father, and gotten her to a colleague and friend who is chief of neurology at Mass General. He and I are generous in the little we see of each other.

I call to tell him how grateful I am. I think he's glad to hear from me. We tell each other how fine we are and fall into business mode. *Oh, David*, I think. *Remember?*

After Thanksgiving, I learn my mother is refusing to take her medications. I call and tell her she has to do so. Mum does what I tell her these days, so it's worth my effort. Then I learn that she's lost their will and trust documents. They think she put them out in the sun porch among all the piles of debris.

I have reason to be outraged. I had made a special trip last winter to an Office Max—some fifteen miles away—to buy a huge hard-plastic file bin for my parents' important papers. Coming back, I got caught in a sudden, driving snowstorm and was run off the road by a sadistic snowplow driver. I was shaking with terror as I spun my wheels back up the icy embankment to join the line of traffic.

I returned from that dangerous excursion, unnerved and still shaking, with this hard-won treasure. I gathered them all in the living room—including Marisol and Fred—and lectured them about the importance of keeping *especially* the will and trust documents in one place. No one was to go near this bin. Ever! Upon pain of death!

The bin was placed securely with its tight cover right by Dad, on the far left side of his recliner. I made it clear that Dad—the sole owner of sanity and rationality—was the guardian of this receptacle and all important papers would be filed there on this day by me. "Remember, Dad," I said. "You are the common sense here. There is no one but you. Guard this file bin at all costs." He agreed, face serious, and I got everyone to actively voice assent. I opened a bottle of wine and Mum and I toasted this accomplishment and also toasted Joshua—the new little family member.

Thinking I'd taken care of that situation once and for all, I dusted off my hands.

But later a strange drama took place between Dad and me. I talked about the impossibility of meeting good men, and even roundly condemned men for preferring younger women. Dad piped up to—of all things—defend the men. I poured more wine. Dad began shouting. After more wine I actually began to cry. I can hear myself this minute, repeating over and over that "young things are going to steal all the love." My father continued shouting back. I fell into bed in the little room and into merciful sleep—only to learn the next day that Margo had phoned and reported the incident to Marisol and Steve, including my refrain about the young things stealing all the love.

I woke that morning and stared at the ceiling, swirling above my head. The young things—I repeated—the young things. Those young things had already stolen all the love. That happened a long time ago. When I was twelve.

Margo entered the living room as I sat nursing a cup of coffee like it was medicine. "Dad gets upset," she said, "when you talk about these things. Because he knows he can't do anything about it. That's why he was shouting."

A good point. If we ignore the symbolism of the whole communication. Right she is. Perspicacious. Insightful on the front level.

I returned home to a phone message from her. "Take care of yourself. That's what prayer lines are for. Oral Roberts ministry in Tulsa Oklahoma—918-495-7777—is a twenty-four-hour hotline. They sometimes have a waiting time."

The story of the lost documents emerges more fully. It seems that for Thanksgiving, Margo decided to brine the turkey the way Steve does, and she chose for the brining vessel that very file bin. No amount of insistence on Dad's part could stop her. She removed the documents, put them on the kitchen table among picture frames and vacuum cleaner parts, and told my mother not to lose them—which my mother promptly did.

I understand they're looking everywhere. Mum pads around in her slippers, patiently looking. She returns to my father—like a little wind-up doll—to be reminded what she's about, then pads away again. Margo accepts no responsibility for losing the papers. Again I have to know the feeling of wanting to kill someone. If those papers are found, they'll be placed inside a now gritty and grease-lined box, cleaned as best as possible by Mum in her present state. How I'm wishing there were something going on that was more personally important to me.

It's almost Christmas. I've just had my last evening out with Robert. I return relieved, and enter through the back door alone to see the phone light blinking in the dark kitchen. I play the message from Steve.

"Family's all fucked up again. Ma was dragged out in the middle of the night by policemen and firemen because she was talking funny. Margo threatened to call her lawyer if they didn't take Ma straight to the emergency room. Ambulance comes. Fire truck comes. They wouldn't listen to Dad telling them she just had too much wine. He kept shouting, 'Please, she's just drunk!' but no one paid attention."

He goes on to tell the story of the police getting Mum into her coat and her boots. Then the emergency room called my father to say they were doing a CAT scan. Dad could hear Margo yelling, telling the hospital staff what to do. In the midst of it all, Max came upstairs to use the bathroom, walked past their room, looked in, and said, "Where's Ma?" Dad told him she's gone to the emergency room. Max said "Oh!" then went on about his business and back down to the cellar. When they came home—after midnight—my mother went straight to bed and fell asleep. Margo went on to call the police on the Bagnewskis, across the street, who were having a party. There were cars parked all over the road, she complained. The police and the fire engines all returned and explained patiently to Margo that the people were parked legally and the noise level was acceptable. Next day, Margo acted as if nothing happened.

Steve rounds up, saying that when my father woke up this morning, he said to my mother, "I can't believe you had to go to the emergency room in the middle of the night." He sounded like he was just about crying.

And Mum said, "I did?"

This is a pivotal realization, how far gone my mother is, and also the extent of Margo's troublemaking.

My father chalks up the whole event to experience.

"Yeah, life is getting so different, since my stroke," he muses. "I can't do anything for myself anymore. But I have a man who's going to come and bathe me and take care of me. He's coming tomorrow. He's a black man. I'm so glad to have a man. I hate having women bathing me. He's coming tomorrow. Yeah, he's a black man."

There were only white people in this town when I was growing up. I wonder how much the population has changed. I see a Brazilian and a Thai restaurant on Main Street. I wonder if a better mix of people would help what I knew as an alcoholism problem here, when I was growing up.

My father, getting from his bed to his chair in the living room—through the kitchen, whether on his feet with his walker, or in his wheelchair—looks like someone climbing Annapurna. It's with greatest difficulty that he gets to his commode.

"Christ, I gutta take my life in my hands just to take a shit."

Christmas Presence

Dad thought he might not be here for Christmas. He thinks he might die this year because the Red Sox won the World Series. It's 2004. The last time they won the World Series was the year he was born—1918, the days of Babe Ruth and Carl Mays.

Jason will be with David this Christmas. That leaves me spending the holiday with my parents. I have no other offers.

So Dad was born in a lucky year, and he met an interesting curveball in his journey when he met Viki and JW, his employers. His career in machines was exactly what he enjoyed. I was in fourth grade when he attended night school and spent late nights at the kitchen table doing homework with his slide rule set out on the checkered oilcloth. I don't believe he enjoyed the education part; in fact, he probably didn't complete the degree. He'd not been conditioned to school or homework. I could hear his concentrated breathing and cursing from my bed in the little room as Steve, a toddler in his crib, chewed his way through his blanket. Then, just before the triplets, my father's car accident ended his education. But the shop grew and my father remained with JW and Viki until he retired at sixty-five, bought the Airstream, and set off to see the country with my mother. Their RV years overlapped with my happy years with David, the years before we hit the whitewater rapids of middle age.

So, another holiday threatens. Christmas Eve was so full and rich for some twenty-five years, when I gave parties for my own family and friends; now it's fraught with dread of being alone and eaten alive by raw emotion. I pack the car and head north, reflecting on how I age, my life pares down and my cynicism grows. I'm still recovering from last time. But returning to Mum and Dad feels comforting. I'm lucky they're still here.

The three will be there. Steve won't. He only comes in September and May—and only to the lake house.

I have to pull off the road twice on my way to Mum and Dad's to go unconscious for twenty minutes. I'm sure I must have narcolepsy. Then I hit hard traffic, miss my last turnoff, and go practically all the way to the coast.

I call the house, and Margo guides my return over a complexity of back roads. I'm impressed with her knowledge of territory and sense of direction. What a good mind for spatial relations, in spite of what I've been reading about the dearth of synaptic connectivity in schizophrenia that can leave someone so sadly deranged. She has a detailed knowledge of a terrain some twenty miles from them: "Watch the intersection," she counsels, "that has a fire station on the left and a white house on the right with a statue of the Virgin Mary. Take the road that slants between them, not the one to the left of the house. Then an immediate right you can hardly see because of a big sign and the second left where there's a set of swings in the front yard."

I wanted to get there before Dad got exhausted. But it's after ten.

Strange to be back again so soon. Nice to have somewhere to go.

The back porch is still a veritable wall of cigarette smoke; the taste and smell forces me to hold my breath. Mum's splendid array of prize-worthy African violets survive there and several Christmas cactuses are in full bloom for the holiday. A robust

Tibouchina, not the least bit gangly, jumps out at me. All are lined under the porch window like a welcoming committee, and look like they've been groomed by an expert horticulturist.

Mum hugs me at the door. I'm surprised by her affection. She looks especially twinkly and glad to see me. She guides me by the shoulder, pressing me toward the living room, and there sits my father upright in his recliner, proud and pleased as a newly hatched duckling.

"What a great surprise, Dad," I exclaim. He usually can't make it past seven or eight.

"You look terrific," I say. "Look at your hair. You look like you've been to the beauty parlor." His straight, blondish hair falls over his forehead the same way it does in all his childhood photos. My father is one of those people whose looks don't change. He's looked like himself all his life. Even his portrait at a year old—somewhere in the attic in an oval frame—is clearly him.

"Yeah. Max cut my hair for me."

"Didn't he do a good job?" my mother chimes in.

"He cut my nails, too. My toenails and fingernails."

I know that Max regularly clips my father's hair and nails, carefully and quietly. I'm touched by how Max takes care of Dad.

We talk about Max. He's certainly finding work in website design. His present life actually involves his leaving the house.

I go down to the basement to talk with Max about his new job. He lights up, glad to see me, motions me to sit down on a large leather sectional sofa that's quite elegant—incongruous with this setting. He also has a sophisticated-looking computer setup and tells me that he spends all his time on it. He is indeed doing website design for the escort service. He shows me the site. "Lip Service" features girls in thongs slinky-dancing around poles against a ruby and black glitter-spangled background. Each one moves forward to press her lips against the screen and "suck in" the viewer.

"You're going to be paid for this?"

"I've been paid. It's done. It's up and running."

"Max, who hired you? Who do you interact with? And the girls? Are the girls minors?"

"No. They're not minors. They have a manager. He contacted me."

"That's called a pimp, Max. You're dealing with a pimp. I'm not saying you shouldn't, but just know you're dealing with a criminal element. He pays you?"

"Well, I probably shouldn't say, but first he set me up with Ginger."

My imagination takes flight. Steve and I are pretty sure that Max has never had sex. If he is being given the opportunity, that would be a good thing. "So, that's how you got paid?"

"Yeah."

"And I guess you keep up the site and add to it and monitor it and all that?"

"Yeah."

"And you get paid with Ginger or Rhubarb, or someone..."

"Nah. I said I want the money."

"And he gave it to you?"

"Yeah. He pays me good. And he pays right away; he doesn't make me wait."

On Christmas Eve at about four o'clock, there's a sudden, loud commotion in the living room. Margo is in high bossy gear, announcing that problems are not to be talked about on Christmas. Max is sitting in the far corner, Mum on the couch, Dad in his recliner. Margo huffs out of the room, as if her pronouncement has put a firm stop to whatever is going on.

"What's the problem?" I ask Mum.

"Max has just told us," she says practically in a whisper, "that he made a big charge on our credit card. It's for a flight to China."

"What?" I exclaim. "Max? China?" This man who lives in the airless basement, who's hardly gone out for twenty-five years except for that one work spell and bicycling. "You did?"

"Y-e-e-a-a-h," says Max.

"This makes no sense. I can't believe you'd do such a thing." I'm assuming he is resorting to escape because he's feeling hopeless and irrational about his present life.

"I know. I couldn't believe it either. That's why I told," he says, like a child.

"Why China? You hardly leave the house. Dad, you could stop payment on that right now."

My father gets on the phone. But this $1,700 charge for air travel cannot be reversed. My father is told that this is a family matter. In the meantime, Max leaves the room.

Mum gets up and marches straight to the door to the cellar. "Max," she calls downstairs like the person she used to be, "bring my credit card up here right now." I see that when my mother has a lucid moment, she can still be effective.

Max brings up the credit card, slaps it down in front of her on the coffee table, and leaves.

Mum and Dad and I try to determine a course of action. They call Max back into the living room. Margo comes storming in behind him and can't be stopped from taking over the whole discussion. Her gist is that while it was wrong of him to steal the credit card, none of us can appreciate how important it is that he has finally found the love of his life on a website, and that this true love lives in China. (There's a woodpecker in my head, hammering about the futility of it all). Apparently they've developed their relationship over many months by email and cell phone (he bought his Chinese lady a cell phone too, courtesy of Mum and Dad), and Max is planning a marriage.

I try with less-than-perfect patience to tell her that the romance is another issue and right now we have to deal with the stealing of $1,700. This sends Margo on another tirade, of the kind that provokes a psychotic rage response in anyone around her, including me. I find myself screaming over her shrill raving.

This time she rounds up with, "You don't care that we don't have lives here. All you care about is yourself. Your life is okay. Aren't we allowed to have lives like other people?"

"That, Margo, is another subject," I say, toning down. It's true that they don't have lives.

But Dad continues to jump on Margo. Both bawl rage.

Finally, Dad says in a loud but normal voice, "Max, I don't want any Chinese women living in the cellar. I only want family living in the cellar. Do you understand?"

"Where's the wine?" I ask, despairing.

Later, when only Mum and I are left in the living room, I try to explain that Max would love to want a girlfriend. But it's more about wanting to want one. Otherwise, why would he be proposing marriage to a stranger on the other side of the planet?

"He's tried around here," my mother reasons. "But no luck. He's had a lot of rejection."

"But going to the other side of the earth is not the rational answer. There are hundreds of thousands of women around here who he hasn't tried to know. I believe he doesn't really want to go; that's why he came in and made this announcement. With hostile timing, to be sure."

"Yeah," says Steve, comfortable on his phone out West. "He took a shit on your Christmas Eve."

"He wants to be saved from going to China," I tell my mother. "He wants to be rescued. Much as he'd love to love someone, much as he wants to want someone, he can't."

"I think I see what you're saying," says Mum. "I'll have to sleep on that one."

With this, she takes herself to bed. The whole episode will be forever lost to her. Futile conversation, too.

Christmas day centers on dinner. Margo has set up a tall Christmas tree—its lighted top star almost touches the ceiling—like the one in all our childhoods, with bubbles rising in the clear-glass candle stems of Mum's amazing Italian bubble lights. Gone are the days when Mum put her all into Christmas, buying presents we couldn't afford, making up for the Christmases missing from her own childhood.

Marisol and Fred arrive with Joshua, bearing bags and trays and casserole dishes to cover every surface of the kitchen. My sisters scream at one another for the next few hours. It appears to be bickering. I begin sipping wine and settle in the living room with my feet up. Joshua sits on my lap for a while. Max emerges from the basement when dinner is served, takes a plate of food, and quickly retreats. I can't imagine he'll follow through on his plan to go to China. I am wrong about Max.

"He's been Theodore Kaczynski all this time," says Steve, "then suddenly he flies off to China."

He's gone to Guilin, a city surrounded by otherworldly-looking karst peaks along the serene Li River, to visit the woman from the dating website and to live for a month among exotic banyan trees and dreamy scenery. He—my unknowing parents—not only bought her a cell phone and paid the monthly bills, but he has also had long conversations with her for months. Max conversed!!! In what language? This is all progress, despite the illogic of finding life so far from home. He imagines he's found acceptance.

What's it like to be Max? To feel foreign, even in your own country, and have no concept of making sense to others? Could this "Lili" actually return with him and live in the cellar too, and be another burden for the Ahlenbergs? And what if a baby happens? Or two? Or three?!

In the meantime, Max designs a fantastic website of his trip and sends us digital photos of himself in sumptuous Chinese-emperor robes and hats, standing before famous pagodas. He uses money wired by Margo and Marisol, who are invested in his dream. It's never clear where they get money. He buys a bicycle and a radio at a Walmart in Guilin. He tours the city's parks and looks initially happy. In between sightseeing, he spends time on Lili's computer while she works in the local hospital all day.

I learn that some of Max's website design courses did indeed require his presence in a classroom. Some emergence from the basement and regular appearances in society preceded the China trip. But true to form, he's put himself in heavy debt. His going to China might be relatively good news, given the once-constant fear that he'd do away with himself. Is it possible he'll stay there?

The daily diary on his website for that month suggests, however, that he's done some very non-endearing things. He went to the home of Lili's parents on many occasions, vomited after eating their food—I gather it was very strange to him—and got so falling-down drunk that her brothers had to carry him home. Between contacts with Lili—the most intimate seems to be when she came to his room to take a shower, and he went to bed and drew the covers over his head—he has spent much time alone. Lili made it clear suddenly one day that she has another boyfriend, and this "Lewis" (American?) was rubbed in Max's face when flowers arrived for her. Max did one good getting even when he erased all the photos of Lili and Lewis together on her computer. Max had sent her a digital camera too—courtesy of unknowing Mum and Dad. When not with Lili, on her computer, or on his bicycle, I picture Max sitting in his hotel room and staring at the TV or the walls.

"Getting there was on stolen money," Steve points out. "The bicycle was on borrowed money. The rest was on charity by Margo and Marisol. This is how Max gets along. He has to beg, borrow, and steal."

Max definitely has our admiration.

But Max is back in his cave six weeks later, undiscouraged. He's had the adventure of his life.

The Ramp

It's May. I'm here at Eden, planning to follow with a visit to Steve again at the lake. It's late, following a long, weary drive. The town is dark. I wonder if David would marvel to see me, in this stage of life, back with my estranged family. He last knew my parents when they visited on their RV travels and we all had such fun. I wish he could see me at this midnight hour—this delicate hour—when Mum and Dad are beyond seeking assurances against mortality. As, probably, am I.

In this place—so colorless it always escaped attention, where even time felt slovenly and dull, unable to muster much in the way of event—this future feels like the first thing to find us. I can feel its breath, hear its clatter on the rooftop. Future is a destroyer, splattering complacencies of now—all that was for decades anchored in the safe, unchanging ordinary—like ripe tomatoes at the actors on this stage.

In a house where you can spend all day just looking for a pen, it wouldn't seem that Fate could find its mark. Blank windows, weak light, misguided seagulls, nowhere near the sea. Except for the solid bastion that was the mill—with its high, omniscient clock tower set against the sky, once reflected in that stalled, spread-out turn of the river—this tattered mill town escapes the attention of the world and in this way has always felt safe.

Along that potholed road I come, clunking and bumping past square houses with peeling paint and shades drawn, through the twin puddles that I named as a teenager "the duckfeet of sunset." And there, at the end of civilization, stands the home of my formation, tufted with grasses, aged by the un-bother of application or agency. They're all sleeping inside, all content with screws loose and dots unconnected, reins dropped to the gusts of helter-skelter.

This is an honest house, I think as I turn off the ignition, built by my grandfather Stig when work made the world solid and sensible and well. Its walls and windows stand sturdy, blank and unadorned. "A ragged beggar sleeping." John Greenleaf Whittier speaks from fifth grade.

My footsteps ran out on that potholed, puddled road when I was still tender in the bone. The event never spoken about, until now, has sat forever inside like a dead gray beast—undigested, stifling dreams and motivations, keeping me careful and unreal, as if I bear disaster inside, as if something will suck me under or implode if I move too much.

I'm on a mission to come fully alive. I want to enter all the closed-off attics and cellars and closets of my life, free myself, and find new light. I'll recover that unformed self I left behind, that one who died burning her childhood diaries. Can I find her, old and heading "wiseward" now? And still young? At least, compared to Mum and Dad.

I park in back.

What the hell is that?!

An ironwork contraption, limned in moonlight, spans the length of the backyard from the back door to the driveway. That must be the ramp! They've been talking about "the ramp," a used item my father bought through the local want ads. He spent several mornings on the phone finding this item, done serving the needs of its former owner. Max—back from China, with no more girlfriend and no more word about it—has been assembling it so my father can come out in his motorized wheelchair.

Dad hasn't been outside for weeks, I know from Margo's voice mails. He's on the verge of thin air. I had pictured an incline with railings that would just cover the depth and rise of the six cement steps that lead up to the back door. But this is a major eighty-foot-long bridge that spans the whole backyard, dipped down at one end to deliver Dad, in his dotage, to the driveway. It's a shocking sight.

The graduated sweep of gleaming steel tables at the door, over the top step. I begin a slow amble up this piece of treachery, which makes clanking and groaning sounds, as if I'm dragging a ball and chain. There's a shrill overtone, a light soprano reverberation. "Indian Love Call," a song I haven't thought about since I sang it in my loudest high falsetto and my dog howled at top volume with me, starts up in my mind. Voices rise up from junior high school. Mickey and Sylvia's "Love Is Strange," in Sylvia's meowing, twanging whine—chartreuse, if it had a color—sings in my head from that time when rock and roll awakened adolescent souls. Music reached in here. Whole vignettes of my life flash past in music as I ascend toward the back door and step back into my past.

I recall motorcycle boys—in the time of "Heartbreak Hotel"—with leather jackets and DA haircuts who played "stretch," thunking their open switchblades into the mud at one another's toes, making me tremble with the beginnings of lust and love. The diner had blowzy peroxide-blonde waitresses who offered lost teenagers cuddly pet names like "huggums" and "baby-pie" as they smooched us with their painted lips. Those were the many specks of love.

The other members of this family that is mine after all had their life, too, in all this time. And I don't know most of it. So here, in this house where I grew up, lives the clan, years on and vulnerable, irrational and strangely touching. Mum and Dad agree when I call them lovable bumpkins. Mum jokes that the two of them together don't have half a brain anymore. I find myself thinking that all four who live here—and Marisol and husband can be thrown in to make six—don't amount to a whole capable person able to accomplish the necessary tasks of living. But no one minds much, or for long. They tolerate chaos well. They don't make demands of life. And yet there is a pulse here. For all its unkempt, blighted look, this house is full of something always happening—everyone excited and rallied round. The family lives an endless parade of events that could only happen to them.

The ramp begins to jitter and groan, causing me a scare. Max doesn't always finish things. Someone should have warned me. But I'm not always sure they understand I'm coming. Reliability isn't the mode here. I've reached the high point where the contraption turns and tables at the door. Alarm takes over only for an instant. Things always come out okay, even if they might look perilous: part of that escaping-attention trend. Even threat becomes feckless and distracted and lost in its intention here, like Tootle in the meadow. I call up my own Tootle heart and mind, from the time when I lived here and trusted the safety caused by neglect. I make it to and through the door, and the whole shaky thing becomes an amusement.

I pass through the sudden slam of the deep, sick odor of Max's back porch *fumerie*—the coffee cans heaped with cigarette butts, sagging cardboard boxes heaving beer and wine empties. The wooden walls bear a nicotine varnish that oozes tars. It shocks my lungs.

This was the porch on which Mum served dinner one whole summer, when it was just us, in one of her surprise bursts of elegance. We four seated ourselves around the tin-topped table with a new white "oilcloth" tablecloth. One night she added beets to her wonderful potato salad, which I believed was the best in the world—part of the secret was a few drops of vinegar—and the beets turned the potatoes and boiled egg whites pink. This was beauty in the silver bowl that had been a wedding present to my parents. The beets were disappointing to my child taste, but I recognized an expansive moment, and that screened-in porch exists as a splendid pavilion in my memory, though it measures not more than ten by twelve. One learned to relish small pleasures here.

I flip the switch. No light comes on, but I can see by starlight that Mum's plants—including the twenty-five-year-old jade plant—still throng the wide porch railings, insisting on life amidst broken lamps and doorknobs, bug sprays, and assorted hardware. A basket of laundry is so coated in dust it looks cast in plaster. It stands in the way: the laundry sculpture.

Feelings are never without their opposites. And each one has its range. All of it has music. The earliest music of my life is still here; "Goodnight Irene" sings through me in Dad's voice as I creep quietly across the kitchen where darkness hides the debris underfoot and the cabinets with all their doors off—another of Max's unfinished projects. He took the doors off the cabinets intending to sand and finish them and lost the hinges, and they prove to be too costly to replace. Dad spends all day on the phone, calling all over the country.

The dark dances with molecules of past. I used to treasure my childhood notion that invisible specks of ourselves live on in all the places we've been. So here would be the last indestructible particles of my long-gone grandparents, who lived upstairs until I was thirteen; the younger flesh and bones of my parents; Steve and me as children; the three tender babies; and my old lost friends. I'm back to the little room, as if I never moved upstairs when Nana Dagmar died and Grandpa Stig disappeared with his fishing poles, leaving his liquor bottles in the trash at the end of the driveway. We had not even a note until he phoned a week later to say he'd found a nursing home near the river where he could fish. That upstairs is Margo's apartment now. She slumbers overhead, her golden Rapunzel hair arrayed on her pillow. Max sleeps below. In their same bedroom off the kitchen, Mum and Dad stretch out their last moments in peace—or maybe I should say push the envelope of duration—in their shared bed of nearly sixty years.

I fall into bed in the little room—face up—and acknowledge that, in spite of the ache of it all, there was once a twinkle here. Not that I can't hear my lost wails and whimpers still careening around this room, but there is also that old air of fairy tales. I carry scenes of enchantment, tableaux made up in my head when I was four or five. I call up one imaginary collage of impressions created in this very place. A giraffe is munching and a camel parades, proud and splendid along the hypotenuse of sprouting palm trees, all against some black velvet background, suggesting they come out in the dark, prevailed over by a plush, midnight-blue sky and moon. A tiger steals from behind a castle, and happy monkeys on a honeymoon face each other, sharing bananas. The camel glows. The giraffe gleams. The tiger is fed and friendly. A young man and woman face each other, centered in the setting. *The blue of her hair meets the gold of the day* (I used to sing it that way), and the man is smiling because he loves the woman—and some future promise is held out to me in the voice of Bing Crosby. The whole picture assures me of a one-day-someday, and a feeling that I can't wait. That vision remains in my unconscious as one of my personal "desktop" displays.

The ramp speaks in the night breeze outside the open window. A metallic squeal softens to a whine and a sigh. The sound repeats and lulls me to sleep.

After more than forty years, I'm feeling that I never left. When I took off at eighteen, I thought I was punishing them, though they'd in turn made certain I was gone. My sisters took over my upstairs bedroom. My cut-off longing for my mother never ended. It has taken many shapes and forms over the years in all the various substitutes I've sought. I turned off my wishes, took my bitter freedom, and went off and joined my own generation. I made a new family of friends and all these first notions of life were eclipsed. Six of us found each other. The Grapes, we called ourselves, and turned our "sour grapes" attitude to "bravado wine." We needed no one but ourselves and our dire loyalty. But I never stopped blaming my parents when I was stupid, blaming them when I was lost, reckless, blaming them for my failures, blind spots, and missing pieces, blaming them every time I "died." I abandoned others. I showed them what it felt like to be me. But in the end, I suffered it all myself. The ones I hurt live on inside me. I wish someone could have told me.

I visit now to reconnect in a real way with the only people who will ever be my parents.

Max is out there early this morning, working on the ramp, building my father's way to his last freedom. There's urgency as he works his way with a power screwdriver down the gradient to finally anchor the bottom so the ramp can deposit Dad on land and he can head out.

Everybody's here. Margo is taking ice cubes from the freezer and crashing them into her tall glass, leaving the tray on the counter to melt and drip. Dad is carrying on about his orange juice and banana. Dad has the high forehead, fine cheekbones, and chiseled features of his own father. Steve and I have both told him his demanding ways are obnoxious, but he's thoroughly unashamed. Mum brings his breakfast, pronto. His peeled banana indeed has no strings, the result of a negotiation process that could be wished for the world table: hearing and honoring the "other's" desire. I believe they both feel the momentousness of this ritual: the world in a grain of sand.

Something about this dance—his calling "Lorraine, Lorraine, L'raine," like Brando's primal wail for Stella—is endearing and annoying. He doesn't want Mum out of his sight. And he enjoys this squealing. It's a performance and it's outrageous. Doctors and social workers warn it's too much for my mother, with her beginning Alzheimer's, but Mum doesn't show suffering. She just comes bobbing over. His fair Dulcinea just materializes in the trappings of dreams come true. My parents are real. No pretense. An easy acceptance of life's flaws. They laugh together in simple moments. I like joining them in this timeless now-puddle or muddle of mindless contentment. Rural happy, country happy, lard happy. All thought out of mind.

I sit with them, but soon feel antsy and go outside to watch Max working. Margo sits in the pen with her present cat to protect it from the foxes and coyotes. She's made this pen with mismatched pieces of fence and scraps of chicken wire. It attaches to the house, and makes a picture of the word "bizarre." I join her. Inside the pen are patches of tall weeds and bushes with ticks, and one cat sitting in the middle of the hydrangea, maybe one of the plants Max stole from the local nursery. There are a few hard-wire chairs in there, distorted and bent so that only some of their legs touch the ground. Some are over on their ears. Margo repeats her fear that foxes and coyotes will leap the fence and "eat Daisy." She claims these creatures have come right up and seethed at her. The grass in the pen is high, but so is the entire lawn. No one mows the lawn! Someone did start just long enough to mow some of it. But you can see how tired they got, how quickly the lines of intention petered out, leaving the lawnmower slunk right in the moment of arrest.

"Your being here gives life to Mum and Dad," says Margo. Nice thing to say. Probably speaking for herself, too. She can be endearing. She always asks about Jason—where he's living, about his work, though I don't know what she understands. I try to imagine ordinary days here.

Margo's dress resembles a lampshade—wide, with fringe at the bottom. Her hair looks thoroughly deranged as it frames her delicately featured face. This distresses me. Her "crowning glory" bespeaks her mental state. She stands and pulls on a fluffy pastel top over the lampshade and an embroidered light green bolero over that. It all sticks out like a tutu and jiggles as cloth shouldn't. I think of our two grandmothers, with their peasant women's bodies like loaves of rising dough, surmounted by breasts and arms of cumulus flesh. Margo could cut a graceful figure.

I wear black jeans and a black tank top with a tan, gray, and turquoise plaid shirt, unbuttoned, over it. My hair is shoulder length, loose, colored a golden caramel to cover the gray. I lean back to relax in the sun, to bask in the air of spring. I'm centered in a moment of pure letting go, in an unstable chair that I'm balancing by holding the frame of another unstable chair with my toes, not taking anything seriously, when Max calls in a firm voice, "I need your help."

I don't think Max has ever asked anyone for anything. His stating he needs me is downright out of character. I've never seen him be assertive.

"Right there. Hold this here." He shows me where to clamp my hand, and within two minutes, he's bolted the pieces together.

We do several more, working our way down. "That's it." And he's on to another stretch. I haven't experienced people being focused and effective here for a long time. My parents were once hardworking and handy around the house—in another long ago. But Max seems truly to be coming into his own.

Dad tells me Max is looking good. I've retreated inside to sit with him in the living room again. He says that Max earns money now, that his home-repair enterprise has taken off. The website design work is what it is.

Dad's new caretaker, Doug, is a Kenyan man, not so young himself, who's come to bathe my father. I comment on the beautiful weather and Doug says he's enjoying it himself. He's friendly and interesting, with a spiritual demeanor and a gentle voice. It's good to see my father in Doug's long, shapely hands.

I walk to town to get my parents' prescriptions. When I return, they are in the living room and Doug is out getting groceries. They tell me Doug sits with them in the afternoon and tells stories about growing up in Kenya, which they love. Doug has brought a spark. And he will become their permanent friend. A deep friendship for Dad.

I decide to walk back into town, retracing my old school route where I shuffled through leaves, pressed through wind, floated on spring birdsong, or slogged through dreary slush. I return up the finished ramp, through the back porch inferno, into silence. There they all are in the living room: my father in his recliner, Mum on her end of the couch, and Doug on the other, asleep like innocents, all with their heads thrown back and their mouths wide open—in one concerted snore.

Life Be Loved

I puzzle as I reflect on it all. Dad, a hale and healthy person, one day became an invalid, just days following Steve and I being with him and Mum at the lake in 1997. I remain grateful to David for his help in handling Dad's stroke with the local hospital that day, just following our separation. And I realize David and I have now been apart a long time. We've moved into a readjusted (redefined) category with one another that doesn't have our youth in it anymore, or the "us" of us. When we exchange our shared parking permit for the local train station—when it happens to be in person—we're reserved and curious, and a little shocked to see one another aging. What doesn't change is our deepest familiarity, having shared our most significant years. I know we both care more than we allow ourselves to know. But our voices emerge from behind doors we needed to close—at least for a while—and it makes us careful.

Our breakup had a violence and then a frozen grudge, and so far in all this time not a thawed bit of thought or feeling. Neither of us can forgive abandonment, if anyone can. Now we've done it to each other. I start having these thoughts and soon I'm torn apart, and here's my life passing. Fact is, I miss him. I enjoyed those years until I got confused, trying to be the whole person that I wish had been firmly in place before I met him. He actually has another

Janice in his life now, who possibly lives with him, and I try to act sanguine about it. I don't know much about her except what comes from Jason. But that reality inevitably causes further estrangement.

Mortality's leaden wings hang hard.

On Saturday, Margo and I walk around the pond in a local nature preserve: a ritual. When we are deep in the forest, Margo whispers and I keep asking her to speak up. Well, she's afraid someone will hear. She, who's so shrill within the family, will only whisper outside. "But the only someone here in the middle of this forest is me, and you're talking so I CAN'T hear you."

Right as I say these words, as if created by the force of Margo's suspicions, a park ranger appears. Margo's saying she wants to wring somebody's neck—I can't hear whose—and then she's worried she's been heard. And this is somehow a disaster. Is she going to be arrested or shot?

I sigh and hug her. "How hard it is to be you!"

Margo's hair, which reaches halfway down her back, is an identification with me back in about 1969. I haven't worn this style since then. And though her hair is still naturally thick, this hair that once looked like candied sunlight now personifies things out of control.

This evening—all of us sitting in the living room—Dad recalls a time, long ago, when I was home alone while they were all off on vacation (at the lake?), and I "killed the rabbits."

I didn't actually kill the rabbits, I forgot about them. They starved and thirsted and probably baked to death—to everyone's heartbreak, especially mine. I was eighteen at the time, and had been called home to take care of the house for two weeks and go from there to my job every day. I was working those sixteen-hour shifts at McLean Hospital, and I remember saving the one dollar a night it cost to live in the nurses' dorm, but I hardly recall coming home, and there must have been a car. I didn't own one. And whatever did I think about there being no money for me in college and yet they were building a summer home? I remember saying "what rabbits?" when they returned. I'd taken care of the cats, the goldfish, and the canary. The dog had gone with them.

Dad is asking if I was twelve then, and had they really left me alone at such a young age, so I remind him that I was eighteen. I say no more. I've gone back to thinking it's just too late, and they're too old.

It's later now, and it's just us three. Mum is pouring wine. Dad is saying something about feeling they had been good parents to all their kids. I perk up, thinking Dad is leading to me again. *Don't let this one go.* Dad is making emotional contact; he has me on his mind and it's coming out in quasi-ways. He goes on repeating himself. He's begging some reply. So I buzz up out of my torpor and say in a slow, soothing voice, "I think you were good parents when I was young. You both related well to young children."

"Well, what a' you saying?" my father asks.

"Dad, you did leave me alone when I was twelve. You dropped me. You stopped being a good parent to me then." I hold to my own integrity and hope that truth sets people free.

Next thing, Dad is shouting, "What should we have done? What did you want us to do?"

I pull up to a full-sitting position and search my mind. "See me!" I finally answer. "Hear me! Know something about me! Notice when my bedroom window is open and I'm gone! Every once in a while, stop to wonder . . . where's Janis?!"

"You're crying, Mummy."

Before I can say anything more she gets up with a handful of tissues, as she's done before, and starts to exit the room. Then she stops and turns back and says, "Yes. Three babies? Then, yes. I can understand. Yes. Yes. Yes." And she's gone, off to the land of forgetting, trailing yeses in her wake. How many women wouldn't understand what she's saying? Three babies all at once. Unplanned. But no further discussion will occur with Mum. She's slammed her bedroom door. We won't pursue our feelings about it all.

Mum's Molly Bloom speech is not exactly a life-affirming run of yeses. But some validation has occurred.

Has my past reclaimed me? If I could locate my old self, I could let it go.

I help my father to bed. He counts his steps across the kitchen with merriment. I sing James Brown's "I Feel Good." Mum is a ball under the bedclothes. A perverse giddiness comes over me and I tease in a churlish, wine-soaked singsong, "Cowabunga! Mummy. It's Princess Summer-Fall-Flowing-Water and Big Indian Snowball-Head here."

This is the woman who once frightened me and held the key to my heart. But she's not coming out. Poor thing. My mother simply doesn't have it to give.

"I have Alzheimer's today," she says this morning.

"I'm sure you do," I reply.

"But I don't mind," she adds.

I'm sure you don't, I think. And so she remembers nothing and just becomes cute and sweet, as before.

I will never talk to them about any of this again.

After another night passed at Mum and Dad's, I leave early this morning to visit Steve.

There's the lake house, perched just above the liquid blue—lake and sky one large spread of blue. Steve is sitting on the deck.

"Where's your gun?" I ask right away.

"The red squirrels and chipmunks are gone," he says. "It's hard to believe, I might have knocked them all out last fall."

"You and what's his name over there. What power! Guess they won't be perforating anymore."

"Nope. I miss the chipmunks."

We don't ask about each other: his mandate. It begs the question why I go on hoping for a relationship. In general, with this family, my own life stays outside. I'm only a witness.

Typically, Steve turns on the TV and rants. But after that, we have a long talk about Max's friend, Bart. Steve says Bart visits Max in the cellar every night at dinner time. So when Max goes upstairs to take his own plate of food to the cellar, he takes two. My father is angry about this. Money is tight there. And Bart is not invited to dinner. Steve has discovered that Bart has also managed to charge his own groceries on Mum's credit card. And he's having Max do his laundry in the basement, using the family laundry supplies. So Bart is a member of this cast of characters now; his name is spoken many times a day. He appeared on the scene recently to rescue my father from a fall when no one else was around. But it was unclear why he was there.

There are many calls between Dad and Steve, focused on Max putting the final touches on the ramp and his web designing for the escort service.

"Hey," Steve greets my father on the phone this morning, "you still there?!" It seems my father shares his grim laughter. Then I overhear details about the completion of the ramp, parts Max has to pick up in South Boston, and determining the ramp's safety.

"Yeah, well, have Max test the ramp himself before you try it," Steve says. "And if you think that's too dangerous, have Bart do it." He looks pleasingly vengeful.

We sit out on the deck with coffee. Dancing veils of mist gradually reveal Sunden Island, like it's a secret.

"You know . . ." I say. "I want you to know, I want someone to know, that I tried to bring up my rift with Mum and Dad before. This was not the first time. I tried very feebly to talk to them when I turned forty, then decided to let it go. Dad and Mum were visiting us then. That ended up being the screwiest conversation about how I might have ended up like the triplets if I hadn't left. Dad thought I might have fallen into the same trap as Marisol, marrying a drunk and becoming a battered woman. I bit Dad's head off: 'You think I would have been like Marisol?' I said. 'Don't you know me at all?'"

"Maybe he had a point."

"I've thought of that. Who knows what I escaped in leaving. But the real conversation didn't take place then. I let it go. They'd become so fun and easy, I wanted to keep it that way. I enjoyed their visits twice a year, going to and from the west in their Airstream. Once they were free of their children—or freed themselves for a spell, I should say; they've never been free—they had more to give."

"That's true. I had some wonderful times with them in LA."

A loud tremolo sounds over the water, a loon announcing it is here.

I laugh. "I tried to speak to Mum and Dad again up here, just after I turned fifty. Fifty was a momentous rite of passage and I thought it would be my last chance. That too went absolutely nowhere. That was the time when Mum turned on the music, got Dad up from the dinner table in the middle of what I was saying, and started line dancing, leaving David and me sitting there. We'd all been watching Jason outside, swinging like Tarzan on the rope out over the lake. Then Jason walked in to see his grandparents dancing, as if they were at a ball. He found it hilarious and started laughing so hard, he had to sit down. David and I, moved to an altered perspective, laughed too. What else could we do? It was rare for the three of us to be here. This was just following their fiftieth-anniversary cruise and I guess we were drawn to return. I'd made an ambivalent, uncertain attempt to speak about this serious thing. And suddenly they were line dancing. I decided then to give it up. That next decade flew past before I had a second thought."

It's afternoon now, and the phone rings. Steve picks up and soon says, "Yeah, she's right here," and hands me the phone like a present. It's Dad, for me.

"Janis, I went out in my wheelchair today," he says, his voice like a violin, so soft and rasping it seems to reach from beyond. His sentences are very slow. "I went down that ramp that Max made. Margo came with me and I went up Eden Avenue and across Beebe."

"You got back to the world, Dad."

"Yes, I did. I went down Winter Hill, and out on Doucette; then over to Watrous, up Scarbeau, and back up Beebe to Eden again. After that, I went back up Eden to Beebe and back. I hadn't been on Scarbeau for so long, I forgot the Finnish Social Club burned down. It's been boarded up for years now, but I remember when my mother used to sing there."

I didn't know my grandmother Dagmar in her days as a Swedish chanteuse. Dad's words have the soft innocence of a snowfall—a little sighing chant of his own. These are the roads of his life, the terrain of his childhood, and mine.

"And everywhere I looked," he continues, "everything was in flower. All the yards had color; azaleas were everywhere, all in bloom. I didn't see any of my neighbors, but I did see all the spring-flowering things in their yards."

"You probably forgot how beautiful everything is."

"That's right. It was beautiful."

"This is the neighborhood you've lived in all of your life. Where you've always been. You haven't seen it in a long time."

"That's right. I remember my mother and my father when they lived here."

"And I remember them too. I grew up some twenty-five years later in the same place, and I once knew all those same things. And you and Mum are part of what I remember. Even though I went away for a long time."

"I know that," he says with deep feeling.

Dad's words make me happy. Now. And happy from a time long ago.

"Remember, Dad, when you used to take me to the river to visit Mr. Frog on summer nights along the old dirt road that was once the old railroad tracks, running through the marshes?"

"I do! I remember!"

"We'd approach, asking if Mr. Frog was home. And most times, Mr. Frog was indeed home. I used to think you and Mr. Frog had a secret arrangement."

Dad laughs with quiet, reflective pleasure.

I picture Dad facing me in his wheelchair, like an origami moth, arms folded in semaphore across his chest, presiding over his long, loved life.

Mr. Frog and I once shared the joy of the unconditional love bequeathed by my strong, easy, very young and handsome "Daddy" when he was tall and the sky was tall behind him. It was nothing but everything, as seems to be how it is. I loved those times when precious little went so far.

Fifty-Cent Time

Life became stupid following those idyllic early days with Dad. What came after my turning twelve were the fifty-cents-an-hour babysitting days. Hours' and years' worth, and too much of it. I took all the babysitting jobs I could get, in addition to my after-school jobs in the diner, the Five-and-Ten, and, later, the factory, but those never afforded more than two skirts, two sweaters, my underwear, a pair of loafers, and one coat that would last me through high school and college. It was a brown, wide-whale corduroy "car-coat" from the Montgomery Ward catalogue that took on the shape of my rear. Even hanging on a hook—there was my rear.

One day at the lake, I said to Steve, "Talking to Mum and Dad, I've just been trying to get an emotional perspective on why they had nothing more to give . . . And from everything you've said, they withheld from you, too, in many ways—"

"My parents gave me everything they could," Steve interjected, placing his feet emphatically on the deck railing, as if he'd never maintained otherwise. "I never wanted for anything. They were wonderful parents to me."

Steve phones more often, and more than ever cuts me off when I speak. I hardly know what to do. What happened to surviving together in our complicated family? A vague quotation occurs to me—attributed to one Robert Owen, an early socialist and Quaker. He used the word "queer"—meaning mad, I believe.

All the world is queer save thee and me,
and sometimes I'm not so sure about thee.

If Steve weren't my brother, I'd have little to do with him. I have to stop clinging to the few people allotted me. I've been alone before. I'm starting to find new friends. It just takes time.

What drives Steve? In general. And now. Is it the sad fact of our parents reaching their horizon? "Something is making you very strange, Steve," I tell him. "It's hard to be with this."

He has now visited my parents at Eden and he and I have been in the family house together twice. Now we are here for Thanksgiving. His treatment of me is horrid. If I begin to speak, he either interrupts or treats what I'm saying with contempt. More than once he gets up and walks out of the room. Of course, no one else is perspicacious enough to see—all of them are sitting in a row facing the TV. The Muzak channel is on.

Steve baits anyone who will bite (not me) into an argument. Political, of course. It gives him some unfathomable gratification to explode his conservative/libertarian views at people who don't comprehend the world as he does. I'm alone in perceiving the monster in the room. This captures my predicament. Without Steve, I have no more family of my own generation. And when Mum and Dad are gone, we'll be joined in looking out for the three.

One of these days—before I become fully aware—he and I and Max walk downtown. Steve walks just enough ahead to have his back to me, talks over me, or cuts me off. He has to keep erasing me. I'm livid, walking between these two tall men.

"What the hell?" I'm truly puzzled. "Steve, you're not letting me speak. Cut it out!"

In town, he heads for the dry-goods store. Inside, he essentially instructs Max and me to entertain ourselves while he talks with an old high school classmate who's working there. He isn't going to bother introducing us. Max and I are basically being told to get lost. I leave to pick up Mum and Dad's prescriptions.

They catch up with me and Steve does the same thing again—interrupting, blotting me out, not letting me get ahead. I'm utterly nonplussed, I try to fall behind, but they fall back with me. We cross the bridge where the river sluices beside the mill. The round metal plaque of Abraham Lincoln is still there on the bridge abutment. I once thought the man on the plaque was my grandfather, Stig, who held my hand as we walked here. But I'm not in good company now, not moved to share this memory.

"I wanna stop at this fish store," Steve announces. "I gotta see whether they carry rock shrimp, that we only know in California. You can't get these things out here."

I too would like to take a quick look; the town had never had a fish store when I lived here. Well, same thing. Steve walks in there bigger than life. The guys behind the counter are eager to share his enthusiasm. Steve praises them to high heaven for carrying rock shrimp. He makes an elaborate show of purchasing three Kumamoto oysters. He's sure that Dad has never had these prize West Coast oysters.

I step outside to forego watching him show off. Max is standing there, blank and staring.

"Come on, Max," I say, and we're starting to walk home when Steve emerges with that satisfied smile on his face and catches up. His presence is now oppressive. I vow to stop acting out of desperation in relationships that will never satisfy. When Mum and Dad go, I'll rethink my relationships with my siblings. Empathy be damned. I have no empathy for Steve.

All the way home, he raves in his surly way about these Kumamoto oysters. He can't wait to see Dad's face. He raves past all the old terrains of our youth: past the mill and what used to be the town lake that reflected the building and its clock tower, now an enormous parking lot; past St. Anne's Church, where I received first communion, had my confirmation, and endured many embarrassing confessions, rounds of Lent, and the ultimate disavowal of Catholicism in my early teens. Memories of old friends rush through my mind as we go past the defunct railroad tracks where we all played, balancing on those gleaming rails on our walks to and from school, eating the winter rock salt that spilled through a rusted tear in the side of its covered well. I tune out Steve's harangue.

When did I lose my brother—and how long ago did I know?

Maybe I knew when he was just out of college and visited me and David once in New York in the mid-'70s. Upon arrival, he announced that he was going out for the evening to explore New York's bar scene. Then he left the next day. There was hardly any visit with us. He said he wouldn't be back because he had no interest in cities other than LA, which he proclaimed superior. He lost girlfriends in those days and had no clue why.

We arrive home and Steve goes straight to my father in his bed, bearing his prize oyster. "Dad loved it," he says as he emerges triumphant from Dad's room, gleeful and self-satisfied. He pushes the second oyster on Max, who can't say no. Then, to complete this whole demonstration, he makes a grand show of consuming the third oyster himself—like the king—rounding out with an elaborate sigh of satisfaction, rubbing circles on his belly, as if he's just enjoyed one of the world's great gustatorial experiences, and it's a tragedy for anyone who has to go without. I didn't want an oyster. But I got the intended insult, and have to realize that I don't like my brother.

"All the boys get an oyster," I say. "The girls get none."

This is all of a piece with Thanksgiving day. Steve cooks the turkey with narcissistic fanfare, as if no one else has ever cooked a turkey. He's brined it and refuses to tell Margo his "secret." He had Marisol purchase the bird and I wonder if he—a multimillionaire, so strangely cheap with his money—reimbursed her, our sister who lives on SSDI.

I make several dishes and Margo makes several dishes. We eat in the living room, all lined up before the TV. Steve disparages Margo's apple bread: "I just cut a piece of that brick and grease oozed out all over the plate. I had to dump it down the garbage disposal before I threw up." He goes on to boast about being someone who never eats desserts. Margo has made all the pies. And he says nothing about my Moroccan orange, kalamata olive, and cilantro salad, my superb chestnut stuffing, or my Silver Palate pear and parsnip puree. He just goes on insufferably, praising his turkey.

"Think I outdid myself this year, Dad. You're having the best turkey you ever tasted."

My folks are looking old. Mum's hair is like a static cloud of cotton and Dad's sticks up like he's had a permanent fright. Yet they smile, happy for family Thanksgiving, too far gone to get what's going on.

"Steve. Shut up already," I finally say. "Why is Steve being so obnoxious?" I appeal to everyone around me. "Steve, has all your substance abuse turned your brain to shit? Is anybody home?"

I get no answer. They are a thoroughly unconscious lot here.

"What a fucked up time we're having with Steve."

No one reacts to my comments. The Muzak is on and they're all lined up before the still picture with that hit-over-the-head-with-a-frying-pan look: Max and Margo, Marisol and Fred, and their little Joshua. Steve has stepped out of the room to call Joanne. I can hear him bragging about his successful turkey.

Last Thanksgiving I spend with you, I think, and start wondering if my brother is "coming down with" his own version of Mum's condition. I miss the brother I was trying to have. And I'm sorely missing the many Thanksgivings with my own, so-recent family.

All around the house, I recognize old, familiar spots. Stains on the walls remain like ghosts of our past family era and mark times when Mum turned termagant and came flying out of somewhere, sending jars and dishes flying and crashing. One glass catsup bottle flew through the open door from the kitchen one day when I was about ten and smashed against my parents' bedroom wall, resulting in a catsup formation that I named "Dribble Man," a splattered figure hunkering forward through wallpaper roses with wide, hollow eyes and gaping mouth askew. His head was almost 3D; his arms and legs ran long and liquid down the wall. He looked enviably contented, a squiggle of a dancer—leaning naturally into some jazz or boogie-woogie tune—hanging there.

Dribble Man was ignored by my parents; they pretended he didn't exist. But I loved that accidental creation of unpretentious dignity. Dribble Man is a love ghost. At the time, Dad just said his stock "Mummy's all nerved up again." Dribble Man is still vaguely present. But only for someone who knows.

Time is ganging up. I'm back home again and my two cats are sitting adoringly at my feet, eyes fixed on mine. I feel a timeless tenderness. But losing them is on the horizon. They're almost twenty.

Does love always mean loss? Yes, in fact, it does. For most everyone, the lover or the loved will die first or go away. The adage about old age could be said of love—that it is not for sissies.

David's diagnosis was frightening, at first. And now he's made a new life for himself, with his new Janice. My loss of him is finalized by losing him to another. And then, in keeping with the theme, I lost my whole social constellation from that stage of life. How many times can a person change context? In first moving on—leaving my fifty-cent days behind—I lost not only my parents and the only environment I'd known but also my high school friends—each a wound, especially my darling

Darlene. They wouldn't hear of college, those deepest friends; even the word hurt them. Their smallness felt abandoning. My college friends, when I met David, accused me of feeling like I was too good for them—and I did, as I stepped through the magic portal into that new milieu.

One new pair of friends taught us technical rock climbing and canoeing. Anthropologists shared films of their work in New Guinea. Nobel Prizes would happen among them. "These are the best people a society produces," I remarked to David, thinking that disciplined humility and a sense of owing society leadership in return for privilege was pure grace. Where was there a place anymore for Dad and the lumpy couch with its haywire springs to which he'd feared I'd lose my loyalty? How stunning to recall that suburban open-house visit that Sunday afternoon, our notion that the split-level ranch home suggested anything was possible. We had all felt so close in that experience.

I didn't give it up—that closeness. Nothing could ever change that. But it was interrupted.

While I was initially awed by my new society, in time I saw that all of us were humanly flawed. But of course, I don't have those friends anymore. And David is over there—two miles away—living with his new Janice. She has all those friends now. She has my husband, my country house, even my name. She stepped right into my life and became replacement me.

I can bear these losses. I had solid preparation with Mum. She was my big loss. It was gradual and intermittent, but it started early. Apparently, she left me with my grandparents when Dad was in the navy and she worked in a munitions factory and stayed during the week with her friend Mary. The eventual loss of Nana Dagmar and Grandpa Stig felt more part of the natural course of things. They were gone not long after the babies arrived, giving us the upstairs at Eden Avenue. Then Steve and I moved up and each had our own room.

Much as I loved and missed my nana, when she died, I took over her kitchen. Kids often adapt easily to losses, not understanding the finality and the mortal diminishment of themselves. My father went up and removed the sink, refrigerator, and stove. Then I painted the walls pink (I paid for the paint with my fifty-cents-an-hour earnings). It was the biggest job I'd ever done. It took all day, and I remember relishing the smell of my sweat, the new smell of woman and hard work. I was thirteen. Here on our little part of the earth, knowing nothing about South America or Europe or Africa or hardly even the next town over, I felt secure in my little pink dot.

The last thing I wanted to bring up there was my Virgin Mary. I didn't want her anymore. Her serenity was cool, but her virgin-purity had grown insipid. I set her up at her station on my headboard, then every night I launched myself from the threshold of the bedroom door—with the dog nipping at my heels—to land so hard on the bed that the statue rocked wildly. At last one night, she toppled and broke in three. I placed her inside an old nylon stocking: her head, her heart, and her womb. Then I laid her out on top of the barrel at the end of the driveway. She had completed her place in my life.

My mother must have felt my gradual removal then. We developed an ongoing argument about the quality of *things*. Following the connection we'd once had over our mutual love of certain *things*, she refused to admit differences in quality. Every day we returned to the battle over Filene's versus Zayres. She insisted Zayres's clothes were just as good as Filene's. Mind you, both stores were at least twenty miles away. I stuck to my conviction—even from my fifty-cents perspective—that Filene's goods were obviously better. "There are dressing rooms," I said. "You don't try on clothes in the middle of the aisles. And prices are higher because the quality of the clothes is better. Why can't you admit there are better things than we can have?"

What survived all the wars between Mummy and me was the cobalt teapot. Though it was out of sight inside a cabinet during the "babies" years, I always knew it was there. It was a souvenir of Mum and me awash in our silly love of *things* when

I was an only child. Singing about the teapot brought on our joy of harmonizing together, and there were all the other *things* we laughed about: word-things, like "puffer-bellies" in the song, and "pinking shears"—that word sparked pure, tickled giggling together. We sang "Mockingbird Hill," while Mum "pinked" away with those zigzagged blades at some pattern pinned to fabric laid out on the kitchen table, common pins clasped between her lips, her presence shaped the air around us.

Then the era rolled in when we began to heatedly disagree. *Things* now stood between us.

One morning as I left for high school—pulling the corners of my mouth into an exaggerated smile across my dismal face in the front hall mirror so I could proceed out the door—Mum piped up behind me, "While you're gone, I'm going upstairs to use your Chanel Number 5"—meaning that I was a snob who indulged in expensive cologne.

"Go ahead," I said. My mother had never been in my room when I was there. "You won't find any Chanel Number 5. Just because I know it's a good thing doesn't mean I can afford it."

That argument never finished, it just ran itself out. Time took it, as it took the Virgin Mary.

I did not know this experience between Mum and me was a loss never to be recovered. We'd be completely cut off from each other in just a couple years, never to recoup what could have been. I'll never know if my mother wondered what I was doing in my years away. Or even missed me. That cut-off period won't be revisited.

Here in this phase of life, there's little sign of the mother who once condemned me so adamantly to the fifty-cent life, the way Mimay had condemned her. Somewhere she's dropped her rage; she's had the ability and the will to change.

David loved my folks for their basic honesty and lack of pretense, competitiveness, rigidity, or agenda. He found them enjoyable.

He was refreshed by their acceptance of their children for what they were. They were satisfied with each of us in the package in which we came. You got plunked down in the world and you were what you were. He thought that, for all their blind spots and limitations, my parents' children were free from unwholesome pressure. Certainly he saw the downside of no expectations, discipline, or demands, no strings, no suggestion that we strive. He could also see the arrests among us, and the reasons I came through most whole.

Then there is the loss of "us," the us that was David and me, the painful break of moving out of the fused state that had sustained us for so long. We'd been good together for twenty-five-plus years. But the gnawing feeling grew inside that there was no me. That feeling built until it exploded, as if we were one egg that broke and the yolk ran one way, the white the other.

Be With Me When I . . .

David has died.
    It was the cancer.
        There is no consolation.

We're walking on a street in Paris together in a moment I love, in a morning-colored memory that will now be only mine. When we stopped there in the Quartier Latin that day, we didn't say let's remember this storefront, your beat-up cotton sun hat with the flopping brim, the once-over-lightly sun of our twenties, our feet on the uphill sidewalk, living a never-ending moment together. But I know these same frames stayed with you too. There was that old woman passing with a fresh baguette who made us smile, and the fat man with the little pug on a leash, carrying his baguette too. Those indelible moments were keepsakes. No words. We just locked together into experiences that became us.

    David. I'm drowning in *shag gosht* at the Kohi Noor in Cambridge, England, drinking *guayabas* in pre-modern Manzanillo (was it?) made by that one electric blender in town after and we had hitchhiked to the sea and dove in. I'm reliving both our episodes of *turista*. Our first agonies. Cherished agonies.

Neither of us forgot Mrs. McLeod in the Outer Hebrides—so many times we told the story—the surprise of her coming through the door to fill our stove with peat moss, then tucked youngest-sweetest us into our bed. I'm sprawled on the mossy banks of our streams in the Catskills with our new squiggle-baby. Or we three are facing the looming polar bear at the Central Park Zoo with tiny Jason in my arms, gripping my neck tightly, asking, "Mommy, what he eats?" I'll always be in those moments with you.

A ton of loss, regret, estrangement lies on top of me. How will walking, speaking, ever feel the same again?

There was an ICU, a blur of days, a wraparound northeastern winter the color of a filthy rabbit, an unbearable welling in my throat. My car was driven in David's last hours on earth by someone who was me, who had to pull off the highway to go unconscious for a few minutes at a time. Inside the hospital parking garage, the piss-and-petroleum-smelling clay color of the walls of mortality ran liquid right down my ankles into my shoes and dragged my walking below sea level, so it felt I was not getting forward. I grabbed on to railings. I pushed through hefty air. Cars stood crying empty, sounding their metallic ticks and bumps and grumbles.

The bed looked like a truss of iron crutches. He was unconscious. That woman named Janice was fluttering around announcing his and her planned wedding. That held me back from claiming him as my own. But the doctor stepped forward and shook my hand. "I remember you," he said, delivering the words with so much meaning I nearly fainted. I stood beside my forever husband and breathed. Breathing seemed strange and new and like all I could do. Then, in a clearing that had meadows flowing to the sea, my husband turned toward me, his eyes reached into mine, and in an ancient voice I told him "David: I have always loved you and I always will." His brown/

green-hazel eyes—for a moment—looked at me and appeared to turn blue like the sea, the color of my own eyes, as if we were becoming one again.

He tried to speak with that tube, that thing he detested most through all those surgeries that began when Jason was only six. Yes, I repressed all this and lived in a state of denial. Now he was to have his last bit of life with this dreaded tube in his throat. "Please don't die," I screamed. But of course I didn't. This is another moment I will never leave. Jason and Susanna were there. And all the old friends Jason had called to the bedside, after he and I discussed that. Their faces hung there long and wide and wavy, distorted by a lens of distance, love, sorrow, all the not knowing, horror, and denial . . .

It was the worst kind of denial. I had lived these last years certain I never thought about him, while I thought about him all the time. We lived two miles apart and had been married for one month shy of thirty years.

What had I done? Protected myself?

"Daddy and I were fools to lose sight of our love," I said to Jason as we walked from the hospital beneath dim streetlights and black, blustering trees to get a sandwich. "You must think Daddy and I are very dark."

"No. I don't think you are," he said. "Divorce is dark. That's what it is."

I took his hand. "I didn't know the divorce would be the end. I didn't know it was irrevocable. We loved each other too long for either one to have let go for good."

I don't like the trees this night. Nature's beauty and resonance is filling out the pain. Nature was once our lover—David and me, our generation. Now beloved Nature is cashing us in.

How does the lone member of a mutual betrayal survive?

When we parted, I was reduced—as people can be at the end of an unresolved battle—to a blubbering, whimpering two-year-old:

unheard, unvalidated, and raw. I expected to turn to our friends, the people with whom we'd gone through our twenties, thirties, and forties. I wanted their comfort, their take on things, maybe even their help.

But the whole cast of characters swept right off the stage, leaving no common story or memory, no shared grief about our parting. Nothing got talked about. Nothing got defined. And lacking witnesses, mourning our breakup couldn't happen for me. My whole long marriage sank like a leaded sun behind me and a new, lone mountain loomed ahead, without a visible path.

My new life was a thin soil in need of work.

That new now was filled with the noiseless screech of panic. I woke up one day a stranger in a foreign bed, in a room I needed practice to recognize, in a new town where I was still finding roads and parking. I started a practice in town. I moved twice and then found my house. I found myself alone. What could I do but stroke my way forward? My past went into eclipse and might as well have died.

But David died.

I didn't know one could weep in sleep.

"David, we missed our last ten years together." I talk aloud. My footsteps groan against the floor. The cats crouch, watching.

The lasting ache of our breakup turns this decade to nothing. A large illusion. All this avoidance and denial renders your death the worst possible blow. The feelings that stood hard between us were barred gates in the way of any reconnection or review, except in matters involving Jason. We continued our focus there.

I grieve with Jason and Susanna.

I can never forget the sound of their snow-packed footsteps on the porch steps that day after it was over, the door opening, the crash of reality all over again, the utterings, the gibberish of disbelief. Then the three of us huddled with knees touching, like a clover, regrouped on the leather couches in the damp-feeling light of my living room. Jason—at twenty-seven—looked demolished, following the courage he'd managed throughout his father's last days and hours. I couldn't make this all right for him.

Sadness rained down us that day: three washboards steeped in the river Styx.

David was sixty-four—abruptly halted in the middle of his lifelong work. All his loves and passions cut off.

There would be yet a different meaning to sitting with friends who were there when David and I began together, friends with whom we were young: sitting on an eternal riverbank, inhaling the spirit of the day, emerald in the varying glows of youth and promise. I feel the miles we all traveled together, the memories of him we could share. The old friends were not there following the divorce, and they're not with me now, following his death. They'll come, express sympathy, and disappear again.

That parting with him—now ten years ago—was to be Forever. I didn't know that then. Death trumps any hope of repairing what is broken.

I look back on myself in that time apart, running back to the city on weekends, recounting the story of my marriage and breakup, over and over, with new people, strangers to him and to us. This did nothing for my healing or for those relationships. Waves of people came and went and I no longer remember what was said. I grabbed on to anyone who could hear me. I recall intimate restaurants, a framed stormy seascape awaiting shipwrecks on a living room wall in a New York apartment I'd no longer be able to find. I hardly remember the names of those I involved in my compulsion to share. With doctors and prescriptions, I got control of myself in time, and then tried to manage states of depression and those awful sleep attacks. David knew none of this. I didn't fully get it myself. I thought my wretched feelings were about certain new men in my life, knowing full well they didn't have that kind of meaning.

Until we all surrounded him while he lay on his death bed, I hadn't seen anyone since our separation who'd known us both, or had known us together. His friends had remained loyal to him. I suppose they thought I'd quit the club, trashed and burned my membership.

I cry with Jason. The friends cry with Jason, too. That's when I cry alone. New friends empathize but can't cry with me about David, whom they didn't know.

Grief unmirrored never stops. Cry alone and you cry forever.

It turns out he was ill for many of our years apart (one, two, five?). Our contacts with each other were too few and too guarded to let me know he struggled with a worsening condition. And I only had input from Jason, whose knowledge was incomplete. Jason was David's and my only connection. He was seventeen when we separated. With our focus on our son and not on each other, we got together for Jason's birthdays and graduations and his goings and returns from the years he spent in Nepal and Bolivia. Jason told me that Susanna once made the observation that David's and my continued love for one another always showed at those gatherings. But we knew all too little about one another.

His death is a meteor that has hit and taken out my center. This whole last ten years has been thrown into sudden eclipse. When I can, I'll limp back and recover who I became without him. It's certain that I've grown and he must have grown, too. We never got to bring our developed selves back to each other. The new Janice appeared in his life after we parted. I don't blame him. But this fact helped to seal the breakup.

Heartbreak takes a course of its own.

I'm fully back in our tender years together, over my head in memories. "Light My Fire," songs like a bow across my nerves. "Hey, Joe." "Bobby McGee." Weren't you the soul mate with whom I shared one thatched April Cottage (older than America), outside Cambridge, in the English countryside, humbled by our honored fifteenth-century-lineage dormouse who traveled in a hidden passage between the Inglenook fireplace and the pantry and ate all our crackers? And our borrowed dog, Spot, who sucked up his dinner like a vacuum cleaner every night that year? Remember that hedgehog that so gradually unfurled under our watch, in our kitchen? It was the year that Jimi, Janis, and Jim died—all at twenty-seven—the start of huge losses of our own generation. Dinner was at the Kohi-Noor every night: "our Kohwee." Indian food was new and we couldn't get enough. How are those times not a continuing present?

All those foreign places, for the first time, where no one in either of our families had ever dreamed to go. Mexico in 1968 was magic. So was England. The Isle of Skye. Paris. Provence. Les Baux. Florence. Venice. Jerusalem. Then back home, all those Augusts in the Catskills, inhaling full, starry nights in one together breath as we lay on the mountainside, glorious Perseid showers lobbing shooters that nearly took our heads off. How many light years out into the universe would I have to travel to be back in these moments still hurtling through time? Piece by piece, this world we discovered through joined senses came to belong to us. Our formative experiences together were prototypes of everything to follow. We came to feel the same in rhythm, humor, sensibility, and conviction. What a natural pair we were. And what homecomings with our friends when we returned from travels, bringing treasure-stories of days and nights that changed us. I felt loved as a couple.

That very fusion of our beings became the source of our terrible anger, that and me feeling submerged in his shadow. The explosion of self, torn from other, severed our link and shattered all the happiness of our symbiosis. I can't enter the antechamber of our undoing yet. What can I say? He was the center. I was the satellite. It was a natural order then.

Right now I can't stop picturing him all day—off to the woods outside our funky Catskill cabin with his worn *Bhagavad Gita* or *Upanishads* or some volume on mysticism waving like a metronome in the back pocket of his farmer's overalls, grouse firing out of the sun-stung silence—thunderous warning how nature can shock you, aware or not. These memories have stayed in full Technicolor for me. The two of us are there this minute, I can hear his laughter: us sitting on the mosses, or flowing in our skin down the giant boulders that in ancient times bounded downstream from the waterfall as if born of the great water, molded by the flush and gurgle of time to make cushioned perches for living things. We felt simply Always then. Time just hung suspended.

I'm back there, feeling us both alive. We're in our twenties, driving in cars in good times with Kevin and Laura on backcountry roads, finding old abandoned houses full of handwritten letters of once-renowned artists, in the wilderness, or in secret small French restaurants beside an errant river branch where some famous chef escaped into anonymity and set up a private world of his/her own vision, open only to a few. The Catskills was like that then, a place people went to drop out of the mainstream, a sublime land of drop-outs. There were some truly unique, interesting people among them. Imaginations flourished there.

Sometimes we are back rock-climbing with the tender instruction of Duane and Thalia, or canoeing, doing the outdoor things we learned from them. Or we are fine-dining all over the city with Michael and Bea, or back in the mountains, swimming in a hidden lake. Most of our New Year's Eves were saved for Paul and Felicia, in their outdoor hot tub, with strawberries and champagne, surrounded by snow.

Did he step out of all these pictures when we parted? When did he leave all these memories to me? Did they all come flooding back to him as he lay dying? As they flood me now, in highenamel colors, all glossy and idealized? He didn't have this loss that has me back in the past as magic. I've lost the present. I know better, but right now I can't see it otherwise.

A yellow road looped and rounded into the sky, with vistas of meadows and homes with chugging chimneys, the whole landscape a heaving patchwork of cozy farms that wagged like glad puppies. We traveled this road on weekends to our mountain retreat. Birds settled in rows along the barely visible power wires that spanned distances in graceful catenaries. When Jason was a tiny boy, he'd say the birds were having a "bird-day" party.

One Friday afternoon—driving on that road—we spotted, off in a sunny glade, two children sitting on a small arched wooden bridge with fishing poles and bare feet dangling. The girl had chaff-blond braids and the boy a kind of light-brown mop that stuck up at the crown. That enchanting vision dominated our weekend, a confirmation of some innocence that cynicism just couldn't deny. Returning that Sunday, we sought that bridge of our fond recollection. And there were the children, still there, still fishing in the same position two days later. Made of painted wood.

We gasped.

"I feel like someone died!" David captured exactly the full wallop.

This memory replays for me.

"David, we're sixty, and you're dead, and we never had a good conversation or a loving touch again. We blew your last ten years."

So the memory-stories go to Jason and Susanna, and to my current wave of friends, who were not there, of course, and who have their sorrows and memory-stories, too, in pasts where I was not present. All that is good. But the pain goes nowhere, like the sound of the tree's fall—unreceived. My thirty-year life with you, David, is swarming me down whitewater rapids as all the memories come screaming back inside my head. And I don't want to come up for air. It would feel like parting all over again. Some stubborn infant inside myself that lives without comfort won't hear my wiser self making sense.

After all the explosions and slamming and blaming and withdrawal, marriage counselors and mediators and lawyers, I am back to the *Us* that is David and me. But it's gone.

Gone like the mountain lion on our high wilderness road who ignited our vision and vanished all in the same pleat of time. Not before we had locked on its flashing yellow eyes. That miraculous cougar crouches atop the safe-deposit box of memories I now hold alone.

We're both owed gratitude for sharing our best years. Never-ending tears are about thwarted love—frozen like those wooden children on the bridge who were so real for a time. They were me and you, of course: our love, our marriage, our youth, our crude incompletion.

Tragedy

I wake up and it's true. I wake up and everything is true.

Poor Once More *

When I was thirty-eight, I entered a state of shock one day when I realized the "not-me" experience of turning forty was straight ahead. Forty was going to hit me hard. I spent a long, late afternoon—while my dentist kept me waiting—sorting through all the women's magazines in his waiting room to see what they said about forty. This was 1982. I had three years to go.

I found I'd immersed myself in a realm where women were only young. There was no such thing as a woman of forty. Except for advertised products that promised to ward off the unspeakable ravages to come, there was no hint that women actually aged. I sat stunned, absorbing the implications. Forty would put me in the land of the invisible. Would I still be whole? Would I still be considered a woman? Would men still like me? Why would a well-married woman, a mother, a reserved person be having this thought? I burrowed farther into the magazines. Finally, in an advice column, a woman asked about her aunt, a woman of forty whose husband had died. Her aunt was ready to start dating, she said, and didn't know how to go about it. The advice columnist (a woman) answered: "Men like younger women. So older women should take up fulfilling hobbies and concentrate on their interests, their families, and their friendships." No mention of women finding love again, or even taking their own careers seriously. This was the era I grew up in—my life is forever yoked to this spoke on the wheel of time.

There was no music that fading afternoon, walking to the beat of traffic that moved like time up Madison Avenue. The avenue was the sound and color of dread as I headed home, bereft as one could be. What would happen to me without my husband? That was the loaded question. He had a diagnosis then. And I was not facing that harder truth. A couple months before, David had located a node on the left side of his neck one evening, as we sat drinking black Russians. "It's tender, Jan," he'd said, palpating his own thyroid. He explained that it's a bad sign when a node becomes tender upon drinking alcohol. Within days, he was diagnosed with a rare form of medullary carcinoma of the thyroid. An unsettled life ensued—one of surgeries and monitoring levels of calcitonin, a protein the thyroid produced. And here I was weeks later, wondering what would happen to me. The money would run out. My earnings would never sustain my son and me. We'd become poor. But the more pressing question was, could I be without him? He was my only friend. What would be left of me?

A brilliantly colored painting in the window of a Madison Avenue art gallery leaped out as I passed by. It was oil on glass in reds and turquoises. The peasant European scene depicted was vibrant. I spent until full-dark deciding, and then paid more than I'd ever paid for anything in my life and brought this work home as a gift to David. The artist was an Eastern European who'd set out in magnificent colors a metaphoric place both our ancestors would have known. "It's our two peasant grandmothers in the backwoods of the old country," I said, "laundering their clothes in tubs. I had to get it."

The gift was puzzling to both of us. We paced up and down our Park Avenue living room, wringing our hands about the amount I'd just spent. We were not big spenders—except for on where we lived, which was already foreign enough—and not at all used to having money. It seemed I was beginning a midlife crisis of the worst order. I thought I'd just bought a fucked-up gift and that I must be crazy.

Before that—during the acute crisis, just following the diagnosis—David and I walked many times in silence to our spot in the American Wing of the Metropolitan Museum, hearts pounding like kettle drums. We sat holding hands in that nearly private, out-of-the-way spot (that now has a restaurant) on our same bench set inside the glass wall, facing onto the grassy knoll outside. I scoured my being for every creative speck of hope, every consolation, every ray of light. His life was threatened. I had never been so hard-pressed to find words of comfort—for both of us. Every test result showing elevated calcitonin levels meant the possibility of another surgery.

Before the first surgery, we went to the Caravaggio exhibit, attempting to immerse our recently normal, non-afflicted selves in the world of art we loved, a world greater than us. Jason was with a neighbor. Doing this kind of thing always worked to take us out of ourselves. But that day we came across the painting of Judith with her long knife, beheading Holofernes, and David nearly fainted. We flew to our sitting spot, where I held him tight, we looked up our grassy knoll, and we (I?) talked ourselves out of that panic until we had turned it to humor. I remember clutching one another as we made some grim joke and allowed ourselves a downpour of crying laughter.

But I couldn't think beyond our six-year-old son losing his father. Both of us were unable to go there. I took Valium on the surgery days and walked nonstop around the city at an almost running pace, like someone on fire trying to escape her body. David's secretary came with me, at his request. I've always hoped she felt okay about it. He and I had been one being. Now we were cleaved in two by an illness.

David found a new doctor, expert in his condition, more concerned about his quality of life. The tests became less frequent, the results somehow less catastrophic, the whole process less upsetting. And somewhere in that time-frame arose the words "slow-growing," "chronic," and "indolent." Words of hope. And, I suppose, denial. We returned to our normal life. But that was already a land of disagreement, which was about me wanting to emerge and him feeling threatened by my changing—all of it handled in the most clumsy, most misunderstood way possible. Frustration turned to anger, which turned to rage and our ultimate break.

    David. I so regret that we were not what we could have been then. Both unformed and incomplete, I think. I wish we could have found another way. The amazing part is we first loved each other just as we were—raw and imperfect.

How to bear the unbearable? I drink a bottle of wine every night and watch our past on home videos, which begin with Jason as a newborn. Then I play all our sixties music and feel David's breath, his voice, his laugh in the air. All our best moments run through me. When tears join music, sadness becomes sublime. I dance because I need to keep moving, until I fall exhausted after midnight in my living room. I have to do this.

    I start with Janis and Jimi, Beatles, Stones, Doors, Chambers Brothers, Leon Russell, Bob Dylan, Paul Simon, Jefferson Airplane, Fleetwood Mac—every song we ever knew. I arrive at Procul Harum, popular in '67, when we met. "Whiter Shade of Pale" is so deep with me. But "Too Much Between Us" rends my heart: *"Be with me when I need a drink. be with me when I die."*

    How could I have known this would be the song to strike the deepest nerve of my grief? That song: I feel held in the palm of its hand and I move to the purity of sadness, because this is all there is—for hours—until I'm a puddle on the floor.

    Someone who is me carries on like a toy of Time.

A memorial service will be held at the medical school, three weeks following his death. In the meantime, Janice II holds an immediate service in a local art museum, once an elegant home on a hill. Some of the old friends I've never seen since the divorce attend. We say hello. I'm in such a state that I can't fully register what's going on. Many people I don't know speak in tribute to David. Janice takes the stage to announce that she and David had wedding plans. I can't imagine this is true. And I'm shocked that she'd use this forum. Her friends step onto the stage one by one; each laments her fate and pronounces her "the widow."

From what bits I knew, I thought that David was trying a new self with Janice, being someone he'd never been. I could empathize. Jason told me that Janice had many friends and she and David were socially busy all the time. They gave Halloween costume parties—something that had never been our thing. David and I were a reserved couple that thrived on our few friendships. I know David drew his new Janice into our old friendships. Must I picture her spending weekends with Kevin and Laura? Canoeing and hiking with Duane and Thalia? Fine-dining with Michael and Bea? She moved into our Catskills cabin, took over my dishes, my decor, my landscaping. My bed. She praised that precious mountain retreat in her speech. It seemed this stranger just moved into every aspect of the life I left.

I'm too stunned by the whole nightmare to get up and say anything. I haven't prepared a eulogy. Sitting in the audience, a few of my new colleague-friends are incensed by the performance, and they tell me later they were puzzled at my seeming paralysis. But this seems to be Janice's show, and I feel how much I had lost touch with David; that long alienation stands in my way. Though I don't believe what I'm hearing, I can't know the truth for sure.

Afterward, in the main room—where hors d'oeuvres and wine are set out—I circulate among the people I know. Three of the old friends come forward to say hello. Their grief-sentiments are genuine, but our greetings quickly run their course. I do feel touched by Duane, who gives me a long, cherishing hug. Then Paul and Felicia of the New Year's Eves and Passovers come forward to sympathize about David's dying too young. I know Felicia doesn't mean it when she talks about getting together again. An uncontrollable drowsiness is pressing like rising barometric pressure, and I feel like I'm being called home. I need escape. I need the protection of sleep.

When I park before my backyard entrance, something makes me look up into the trees at the skyline. A bald eagle sits majestically on one limb, looking down as if it's been waiting for me. I stop, stunned.

"Oh, David," I say. "Pity me that I should have known how ill you were. I could have asked. When we had Jason's last birthday dinner together—you and Janice, me and Jason and Susanna—we went out close to home because Jason told me you 'couldn't walk.' I took that to mean you couldn't travel comfortably. You certainly didn't look well in that, your last month on earth. Jason had warned me about this, but told me a scheduled adrenalectomy was going to restore you."

"What a loss!" Steve exclaimed loudly when I called to tell him David died.

I told him about the memorial service to be held at the medical school three weeks hence.

He said, "So—I probably don't need to come to that."

"Why would you think that?" I said, furious. "You'd better come. This is your duty and obligation, to me, to Jason, and to David. To our family."

A sensible person would have cautioned me to know better. Steve didn't argue.

Now, with three weeks to fill, a couple of my new friends invite me to join them on a tour of California wine country near Santa Barbara—to get away. Death so strangely holds no reason not to go. Since we fly into LA, we first visit Steve, who picks us up at the airport and gives us a grand tour of the city. He wins the affection and gratitude of my friends. He is great at showing a good time in his own territory.

I spend the first night alone with Steve, thinking we have a lot to talk about, while my friends stay at a hotel. But he makes no mention of David. I arrive at his splendid top-floor apartment with the all-new kitchen he's put in himself and the deck he's built out over his beautiful garden. He owns the building and rents out the two apartments below, all of which he gutted and refurbished himself. I plan to sleep that night in the living room with his 200-gallon fish tank, then continue my travels with my friends the next day.

Steve opens a bottle of Cabernet as soon as I arrive, then produces some pot, which I haven't done for more than a decade. I attempt to take it slow and settle in for an evening of gathering memories together. I think we're going to talk about David. Neither of us has lost anyone close before. David used to visit Steve when he had meetings in LA. I fail to consider that we're starting early on a combination of substances I'm no longer used to. And that I've had three hours added to my day, coming west. I'm vulnerable altogether.

I end up overdoing it. I'm in quite an altered state when Steve begins showing slides of the Guanajuato mummies he took on his last trip to Mexico. He claims that the mummies were victims of a cholera outbreak in the mid-1800s, buried locally in dry climate and soil conditions that preserved the bodies, including the nails and hair. Much later I will learn that these bodies were exhumed when their families could no longer pay the annual tax on their grave plots, and then put on exhibit in the Mummy Museum, which has become a major tourist attraction. Kids in uniforms make school trips there. I'm thinking the whole thing is horrific. Many mummies are lined up standing against a wall, and they appear terror-stricken, cast forever in mid-scream.

"This is all very creepy," I say. "To put them out there on display like that seems like a humiliation."

Steve just treats it as an interesting phenomenon. I'm too altered and far gone to think showing these slides is a strange thing to do right now. I pass out.

When I come to, Steve is on the phone with Joanne, speaking in a calm, unaffected tone. "Yeah," I hear him say, "I think I just killed my sister."

I become fully conscious and pull myself upright on his leather lounge. "What the hell . . . ?" I sputter.

"You should'a seen yourself," he says, as if I've been entertaining, "your eyes rolled up into your head and your mouth was hanging open. You were drooling."

"I don't think that's funny."

He looks like he enjoyed the whole spectacle.

"Were you going to call an ambulance if I didn't come to?"

I don't get an answer. I vomit heavily in the bathroom, then find my way to the couch in front of his fish tank and fall unconscious until I leave early the next morning. I don't tell my friends what happened. I don't know them well yet. I hide the fact that I'm hung over. I'm wondering about my judgment.

David's death has changed me. Steve is moving into focus more than ever. Even though I'm seeing him differently, I'm still clinging. And why? If we weren't siblings I wouldn't be hanging out with him. I've regressed with this latest blow. I had resolved to keep my distance for a while. Now here I am again, hoping I have someone in the family to turn to, when I don't. Where am I beyond David? But I'm not beyond David. And no one is with me now.

Shortly after I arrive home, Steve phones and we have a disturbing talk that begins vaguely on the subject of death and completes my growing reservations about my brother.

"I don't want to be the first to die," he opens this strange conversation, and I don't know why I hang in. "I want to be the last."

I reach and pick up the lid of my mother's cobalt teapot on the shelf. I've ignored the fact that the lid is not just chipped, it's broken in half, though the halves fit perfectly together, like puzzle pieces. My brother and I are broken apart. Why is Steve the way he is? Did our family do this to him? Or is this just the mold he came in?

"I want everyone else to die before me."

I assume he's talking, specifically, about his siblings—including me. Joanne has some kind of protected status; he never talks about her unless it is to quote her take on a movie, or her politically liberal point of view, which he finds delightful.

"That's quite a horrible thing to say. Do you mean to say this? You sound like you wouldn't have any feelings about the demise of any of us." To say this now, when David has just died, has me feeling that the bottom has dropped out. A feeling I know well with Steve.

"We get over things."

"Did you have feelings about David dying?"

"Only for a minute. One day when I was walking across the Golden Gate Bridge, it hit me that he died. I actually burst out crying for a minute, then I started throwing up over the bridge railing. But I pulled myself together and that was it." He vomited away his feelings. One way to avoid feeling them. *What was he doing on the Golden Gate Bridge?* I wonder.

"Won't you feel alone with everyone gone before you?"

"Nah. Are you kidding? When I used to visit assisted-living places, I'd see people in their seventies and eighties who'd just met each other. They'd all love each other and have a great time. I won't miss anything."

Bob Dylan's Mr. Jones (Ballad of a Thin Man, 1965) runs through my mind: *"something is happening here, but you don't know what it is."*

"Don't you have relationships that you're invested in?"

"Relationships don't work. Relationships all come down to there's finally a deal-breaker. Basically, people suck. Strangers are the best. Some are fascinating people."

Steve goes on to tell me about the old man on his block. "Remember Melvin?"

"Your old neighbor you're so fond of?"

"Shot himself."

"Jesus. I don't want to hear this now."

"Guy was in his eighties, learned he had lung cancer, did exactly the right thing."

"Hope he said good-bye to the people in his life who'll miss him."

"Guy's one of the coolest heads I've ever known."

"Because he took the pragmatic way out of a nasty illness?"

"That was just his last act. Guy was cool in everything he did."

"One of your gun buddies."

"Yup."

Happiness is a warm gun, I think.

Qwerty yowls when I hang up, as if welcoming me back from another planet.

*from Emily Dickinson's poem: *I Never Lost as Much But Twice.*

Empathy

The medical school memorial will be on February 2, a Thursday. I'm going to tell the audience that I love my husband. I'll wear my full-length hippie skirt, the fabric so thinned by time I'll be walking in a mist. Beautiful thing that David loved, it's a fitted, full-length, A-line skirt with patches of different material arranged in a pattern of horizontal pointed flags wrapped around me in colors of burnt sienna, purple, black, and tan. David knew me as someone— at my best—unable to speak in a group of more than a handful. I'll overcome my inhibitions, I'll do it for him before a few thousand people; the auditorium will overflow into live-streamed areas. Jason will compose a piece of music for his Dad.

Steve takes the train from the airport today and I pick him up at the station. He'll stay in Jason's room. Jason and Susanna will sleep out in my office, opening up the queen-size convertible sofa.

Margo calls to say she'd like to attend. That's possibly problematic. I worry that she'll be disruptive. I don't have room for her to stay in the house. And she and Steve can't be under the same roof. But if she wants to share this memorial for her brother-in-law, then she belongs. She knew David for decades. She was part of my wedding party. Since I'd lost all my college friends by the time I got married, she and Marisol were my bridesmaids. They were fourteen. They wore deep-plum, velvet, floor-length gowns my mother made. Otherwise, I paid for the wedding, having saved from my part-time jobs: $1,000 total in 1969. Max and Steve and David's younger brother (who disappeared forever after into a cult) were ushers.

Our beautiful wedding took place in an old New England mansion, with chamber music and candle lighting and exactly one hundred guests. We were married by a cantor, not a rabbi, which comforted David's parents. My parents didn't mind, though they needed some education about being Jewish.

So Margo has a place here. I make a reservation at a local hotel. I'll pay for her stay. She too arrives by train; I get her at the station and check her into the hotel.

What an evening. The landscape is blanketed with new-fallen snow, reminding me of Joyce's story, "The Dead," of that dominating power of what's absent. Everything is cloaked in one white sweep of sameness—the garden bench, the Lenten roses that stay in flower all winter, the shrubs, the leaning tree trunks hosting deep white pillows, deck chairs, table, land and rooftops—a picture of oblivion. Even the picket fence is draped with wind-driven, fluted snow—like wedding cake buttercream.

I bring Margo home for the evening and we all enjoy pizza and conversation. It's good to be surrounded by family, with the "dark night of the soul" enclosing my lighted house. My nonstop crying is interrupted by this presence of others. I've developed mile-deep circles under my eyes. We all—except Margo (who disapproves)—drink wine, and Steve grows increasingly hostile and belittling of her. She is trying to place David's soul in heaven, to reunite him there with his parents.

"Yeah, let's think about David's social life in heaven," says Steve. "They're all sitting having tea."

Margo doesn't respond. For me, this is business as usual. The only one to react is Susanna, who retreats out to my office before midnight. I say a few things to manage Steve, but no one understands that Susanna has left what she considers an intolerably nasty scene. We in the family have gotten used to different standards.

It's late. Margo says she'd like to go to her hotel. I give her my car keys and explicit directions (she's a good driver); the hotel is three miles away. She gets hugs and warm embraces from Jason and me. "Come back for breakfast at nine," I tell her.

Then Jason says he has a prize malt whiskey to share. I'm tired and alcohol-filled enough, so I leave the two men to their strong brew, say goodnight, and head upstairs, pleased that Steve is here for Jason. Jason needs the men in his life now.

Voices, shouting, rouse me out of a sound sleep. I fly through my bedroom door and stop at the top of the stairs to hear Jason yelling at Steve.

"You don't give a flying fuck," Jason says.

"That's what you say . . ." Steve's voice blurs, so I can't understand the rest.

" . . . have your own agenda," Jason continues. "No matter what I say, you'll only hear what you make up."

I can't make out Steve's words that follow.

"You're fifty years old and you still have your father. You're the rich Park Avenue kid now," says Jason clearly.

Steve begins again. Both are loud—but I don't think out of control. They're certainly having a disagreement. I don't know if I should interfere.

"You don't care what I'm feeling," says Jason. I wonder to myself if he's talking to his father, trusting Steve to bear this anger. Jason's father has just abandoned him forever. But Steve wouldn't understand it this way. I don't know whether to go down and stop this, or to let it serve the purpose of emotional expression. Should I really hope that Steve is trustworthy with my son? Why would he alienate Jason? There are long moments of silence. Jason sounds like he's in tears. Then they start again. But though they're yelling, they're not escalating.

I sit here listening but leave it alone. Would Jason want his mother interfering in this argument between two men?

Then Jason says, "I gotta get outta here." I hear him gather his things.

Steve says something like, "Maybe you'll think about . . ."

They've been drinking that strong stuff, I reason. Jason leaves. The back door slams. I go back to my room. I don't want to talk to Steve when he's inebriated.

I think of all that Jason has lost in losing David—his guidance, his advice, their never-ending chess game. I run through their times in David's lab where he showed him current experiments and educated him in neuroscience and cell biology. They went camping together and spent days in the mountains catching snakes and salamanders.

I fall into a disturbed sleep, under the full weight of heartbreak and more, not sure what has just happened and if Jason needed me tonight or not. We are all coping with overwhelming loss. Jason is twenty-seven. Not a child. But too young to lose his father. He'll be spending the rest of the night working on his musical composition for his Dad.

I fall into a twilight sleep of jagged dreams.

The phone wakes me. It's a man's voice with an Indian accent: enraged at me. The hotel manager is ranting in the middle of the night.

"What?" I keep asking. "What's happened? Is everyone all right?"

"She call police. She call police. I cannot have police here at two o'clock in the morning."

"Is she there? Put her on the phone. Please. Margo, what has happened there?"

"There were men outside, talking under my window," she says, as if—of course—their intention was to attack her. She was right to defend herself.

"Margo, you are so wrong. You've made such trouble . . ."

The manager comes back on. "They are young men, working here, taking time to smoke out there. One is my son. There are no bad people here."

"Put her back on again. . . . Margo, this is a terrible thing you've done with your imagining—"

"I'm not imagining. You have never understood that I'm being stalked. You have never been sensitive to that issue as well as the fact that I'm a rape survivor. They were out there for longer than a break. And after midnight."

"Margo. We all need sleep tonight. He wants me to come get you and there's no place for you to sleep here. I have to promise him you'll behave yourself."

"I can't have men following me."

"Margo, shut up and stop it. Or I'll come over there now and put you on the next train home!"

This works.

How can Steve and Margo come here and behave so badly? I've just lost David and could use comfort. I won't get that with both of them caught up in their own visions. What a profound lack of empathy in this family! My empathy now is only for Jason and myself. I believe Steve is jealous of Jason on many levels, but on the most primitive, I think he feels Jason took me away from him. Of course, I can never address that. And Margo has this strange fixation. I've tried to get her to tell me the first person who ever raped her, but she reels back through many, never getting to the first. I believe this is the psychotic mind-state in which thinking something makes it true. I throw the blanket over my head and snuggle with my comforting cats.

I speak with Steve, up early next day, like me. I've made coffee, but he's "not a coffee drinker," he announces with a superior attitude.

"What happened last night?" I ask.

"Jason got pretty out of control. I didn't know what I had on my hands there. He was pretty aggressive."

"I heard two people being aggressive. It sounded like Jason was expressing a lot of emotion to you. I couldn't make out much of what was said. And you'd both been drinking. I debated coming down to intervene. But it seemed Jason was expressing feelings that were right for a young man who's just lost his father. I thought it might even be healthy. I don't know if you knew you could be serving that purpose."

"I didn't."

"I think these were things he had to get out. His father has left him and he's overwhelmed."

"I was thinking Jason and I were going to have to end our relationship."

"What? He just lost his father, and you end a relationship with your family?"

This strikes a wound. What a disturbing attitude. Is he really this callous? Who is he? Who does Jason have in his life?

Margo walks in. Her winter hat is frosted with snow and the flaps look like fallen bunny ears. I can't look at her.

"Look at this piece of roadkill the wind blew in," Steve says. He can't resist.

"Stop picking on her!" I say fiercely. Why is he so mean to her?

Margo always seems strangely unaffected by Steve's attacks. Just as she is impervious to my anger at her for calling the police and upsetting the hotel owner. She asks for a tall glass of ice and fills it with coffee.

The memorial service is at overflow in the medical school's main auditorium; ancillary spaces hold the telecast. There is a full stage-sized audio-visual display of David's life; Jason and I gave the AV department a selection of family photos. David's own baby pictures and shots of him as a child play across the stage to Glenn Gould playing Bach. He and I are together in many of the photos—both in our twenties. Then there is Jason and our family of three. And last, there is David with Janice, standing on a bridge.

I don't think there is a dry eye in the audience. Margo is quietly sobbing beside me. We learn later that David brought in more research grant money than the medical school had ever seen, and any research grant with his name on it was automatically funded by the NIH. Extraordinary in this era.

An exquisite life-sized poster of David, the scientist lecturing, is set on the stage. I didn't know how far he'd excelled in stem cell research. How have I not known? How out of touch we'd become. I feel a desperate pride. I was there at the beginning of his whole trajectory.

His many students and colleagues from the past say hello and embrace me. All our old friends are at this ceremony.

Colleagues speak. Former and present students speak. Some of the friends speak and refer to times together that included me and I'm touched. I speak. Janice speaks. Jason speaks and plays the piano piece he stayed up the rest of last night to compose. That brings even more tears.

"For those of us who know and love David . . ." I begin. My voice is delivered in quiet shreds by the microphone. I talk about when we met in 1967. How he chose neurology as his specialty and he expressed his fascination with the human brain. I fell in love with this man of passions. I tell the audience that our marriage lasted just minutes shy of thirty years. I don't say I'm guessing that a broken heart is permanent and lasting.

Emotion breaks through my voice as I tell the story of David when I first met him as a medical resident in Boston. He was then participating in a kind of reverse strike at Boston City Hospital, called a "heal-in," that involved full admission of patients to the hospital. The goal was for residents and interns to be paid more than pennies per hour and to not be so sleep-deprived that clinical judgment could be compromised. They didn't admit any patient who didn't need to be there, but normal procedure forced them to operate in triage fashion on these patients—mostly homeless alcoholics—patching most of them up and turning them out. Now they were overburdening the institution, until it screamed for help. The *Boston Globe* was on board, the bishop of that archdiocese was with them. This was my first vision of the rebel, the maverick, that David always was.

Later a woman comes up to me in the hall and says, "I have to tell you, you are a classy woman." She tells me she's an English professor at a local college. She had invited David to come and explain the human brain to her students. David was known for being able to explain things well to non-scientists, so he'd given a talk to this English class that they never forgot. This voice of a stranger is most stabilizing to me.

Following me, Janice speaks. She stands behind the podium—fingering the string of pearls around her neck, holding them out to the audience—and explains that this necklace is her "engagement ring" from David; their plan was to marry in the early spring. There is a mild stir in the crowd. She says that David was "the love of her life," and that their most frequent discussions were about whether it is "worse" to be black (like her) or Jewish (like David). I don't hear much more. I can't imagine this life; this is not the David I knew. Anti-Semitism only came up significantly once, when David and I first began together. I asked him what one does about it. He said, "First you go to Columbia, then you go to Harvard."

When it's over, Steve says, "That was atrocious. When have you ever heard David—ever—complain about being Jewish? Ever see himself as a victim? Never. That was an insult. It was outrageous." Jason tells me later that Paul, David's colleague/friend, nudged him during this speech and said, "I think you're going to have a lawsuit on your hands."

I move through the dozens of deeply familiar faces from David's past laboratories. People I knew for years and now haven't seen for years. I'm moved to a pitch of feeling. Each one of these people is meaningful. Someone tells me that every one of David's protégés is successful now in some part of the world.

Paul was right. Janice sues Jason—the sole inheritor of David's assets—for everything. Thus begins a horrendous time. Kevin is executor of the estate and helps Jason through the next years of strife.

I don't know yet that I am going to find my way back to Kevin and Laura. That we will embrace again and consider ourselves friends and family. Eventually, we'll learn that David voiced strong opinions about never marrying again. He'd said it was not his thing. Someone quoted him as saying, "Marriage is something you do once, when you're young." I will think it is a statement that he remains married to me. That your first, young marriage might have the truest hold.

But all this won't surface for a few weeks. The mystery to me is why he left her nothing, and it's possibly just because he didn't think of it. He possibly denied his approaching death on some level. A little empathy for her would have helped.

Reckonings

I've kept to myself to try to reconstitute. To tend to the need for mourning.

On May 1, less than four months after David's death, Steve calls to tell me Max has been in a serious car accident.

It's a Sunday afternoon. I've just spent a day hiking with some rewarding new friends. It seems Bart was driving Max's car and, according to Steve, "got into a pissing contest" with an aggressive driver who forced them off the highway. It sounds like a gruesome accident. The car rolled over several times and caught fire. Max was pulled unconscious from the wreck by a stranger—a Marine—who moved him to safety and left the scene. Max was taken to the hospital with numerous concussions and his left ear was partially severed. He had a broken collar bone and wrist. Apparently Bart was not injured. I don't want to be pulled into this catastrophe. I don't have the capacity right now. I'm glad he's alive. I'd like to stop at that.

A day passes, and I speak to Max on the phone. He's done the necessary things, like contacting the insurance company, and getting the medical treatment he needs. Indeed he is shaken and scared into sensible action.

At least for a while.

Bart tries to get Max to make a statement that will get him (Bart) off the hook. Bart was going over the speed limit, in fact, and provoked the monster who forced him off the road. And it was Max's car. Steve manages to talk Max into not giving Bart anything. For once, Max appears to heed common sense.

In spite of my wish to extricate myself from the family for now, I phone Max again to suggest that he never let Bart drive his car again. Max agrees. Then there is the insurance question. It looks like Max will get a not-bad settlement.

As the physical shock of the accident recedes, Max begins dreaming about being able to move out of the family basement to a place of his own. He seems to appreciate the irony that this near loss of his life will finally give him a life. He's full of plans to finally live on his own, after almost half a century under our parents' roof.

Both he and Bart are interviewed by insurance company agents. Bart manages to escape any penalties to himself, thanks to the no-fault insurance state he lives in. Max is assured that he will receive at least $50,000, some of which will have to go toward his medical treatment. He starts thinking this is not enough. He sees an accident lawyer's ad on television, and the rest is predictable.

"Max, you almost lost your life. Now you're going to let some crook take your compensation?" I can't plead enough.

And that's just what happens. Max goes straight to this person's office and signs a contract he doesn't read. The insurance company grants him $50,000 for everything. This crook, who promised him much more, just helps himself to half the $50,000—leaving Max with $25,000, the need of a new car, and some expensive medical bills.

A month later, I stop on my way back from a summer conference on Cape Cod. Dad's eighty-seventh birthday is almost here. My parents are aging away.

I encourage my father out for a walk. He'd been going out in his wheelchair every day with Margo. But she's run away to the monastery again. I walk behind him in his wheelchair down that amazing outdoor ramp. He looks as pale and ghostly as someone down from heaven, and he concentrates on motoring forward in a way that makes me feel his whole lifetime is pushing him forward: the old man at the end of the child, large straw Panama hat moving as if on coasters. He's moving faster than I can keep up, even as I run. Old-age determination seems to have made for the decision not to care, and Dad has foresworn all sense of caution.

"Dad, cars come around this corner," I call after him. "You're all over the road. You have to stay to the side."

He's not even listening. I have to wonder if he goes out every day like this. That ramp might be a curse. Who's taking care of him?

By the time we get to the schoolyard, through the baseball field, we're positively flying. We've covered more than a mile.

When I ask him later if he heard me talking to him on that junket, he says, "Yeah, I heard you."

What is the scene here now? I haven't been here, quite consumed by my own fate. I don't have energy for this situation anymore. I want to be home lamenting David and me, imagining ways we could have done things right. And then I want to heal.

I end up spending two nights. Margo returns, but takes a day off from taking care of my parents, since I'm here. I'm seeing my parents to their end. I regret that David didn't get this from me.

I order dinner for all from a local Chinese restaurant. Right after dinner—in the living room, amidst the rubble—Mum turns on *Wheel of Fortune*. Nothing could be farther from the well of tristesse I've been living in. I try to take the remote, but Margo, who's fully back, tells me this is a program Mum never misses.

"Make hay while the sun shines," Mum cries out, having named the aphorism before anyone on the program, when only the A's and the U are turned to show.

"Ma is really good at this," says Margo. "Ma, you could have won $7,000," she praises her. "Ma always gets these before anyone on the show," she informs me.

"A rich man needs nothing. A poor man has nothing," my mother calls out when only the A's, the O's and the N's are in place.

Then Mum turns on *The Godfather*. Margo says Mum watches this every night. Dad decides to go to bed. Max brings in the wheelchair and helps him.

"*No Sicilian can refuse any request on his daughter's wedding day*," Mum cries out, in lip-synch with Tom Hagan, as if she's talking to us. Following a few more of these and making someone an offer he can't refuse, she clicks off the TV and says goodnight.

My parents have entered their own worlds. So have I. Dad had such a determined independence on his wheelchair romp. And Mum—who "can't remember a thing anymore," as she's stopped even saying—knows all these aphorisms by heart. Adages have always been her specialty; these bits of truth and meaning seem to provide her hold on the world, her guideposts, her survival.

Will I be here again soon? Yes, because they're dissolving into thin air before my eyes, but also because, right now, I'm not doing well alone.

Way After Sunset

It's August and I'm here again. Dad makes his way in his wheelchair across the kitchen. Entering the living room, he waves his good right arm, offering an absurd salute to his Barcalounger. Max walks behind and waits while Dad transfers to his recliner. Dad's feet come last—like two dead, plucked chickens, one especially limp and wagging—his "dropped foot." Max places Dad's feet on the recliner's footrest, gently puts socks on him, turns on the fish tank light, and takes the wheelchair back to the kitchen.

That leaves the three of us in the living room. Mum and I are on the couch. Healthy fish swim forward behind glass, uttering O's. Max set up this two-hundred-gallon tank to the left of Dad's recliner. It's a pristine, well-kept, beautiful thing.

Dad's voice is a constant stream. He mutters continuously about news and sports; he reads the want ads out loud and carries on about used gadgets and tools for sale. His nonstop sound is like his proof he's still here. Today he goes on about teams playing baseball when we're at war (we're in Afghanistan and Iraq), how no one remembers that they didn't play during World War II. He harps on this. (It was actually in World War I that baseball games were suspended. In World War II, many professional players joined the services and weren't available to their teams.)

"*Mike, I'm innocent. I swear on the kids.*"

"Will you turn that off, Lorraine?" Dad pleads. "And put on the Red Sox. You watched *The Godfather* last night and the night before."

My mother cheerfully complies. Both ignore his contradiction about watching baseball in a time of war. I go out and take a drive into town to buy food for dinner.

Upon my return, I find Dad still in his recliner—with his newspaper—whistling through his teeth while reading. His whistle is a single, perseverating note, like a bird call.

"Dad, you're whistling again."

"Yes. That means I'm thinking."

"Thinking?!"

"Yes. When you hear me whistling, it means I'm thinking."

My parents' elderliness is shocking, as if they've donned disguises. Or some hand flew down and cast a spell. When did this happen?

"Janis," Dad says, "you must be getting this heat wave. I bet it's worse down by you."

"Yeah. It's pretty hot. But I'm not noticing very much."

"You don't notice the weather. What the heck is that?"

"I'm still feeling so sad about David. I don't notice much else."

"About what? Oh, about David. I know you're sad about David. Jeez that was sad when he went. What a sad thing that was."

"It's eight months and I'm still crying. All the time."

"I wish I had told you back then not to get a divorce. I wish I'd just said, 'No, you can't do that,' and put my foot down."

"You couldn't tell me what to do. I was fifty years old." I wonder how much our parting was about loss of youth, albeit youth already long gone.

"*I need a million dollars cash.*"

"Mum, turn the TV off, please. That constant sound is annoying."

She joins our conversation. "Horace, nothing you said would have mattered then. She'd made up her mind. Yes. Where is that damn thing?"

"Well," Dad considers, "David tried to tell us you shouldn't leave. He didn't think you could get along in the world. He thought you didn't know what you were doing and you were making a big mistake."

"What a vote of confidence from David! But you know, David was pretty rigid by then. Our horns were locked. He pushed me out too. He should have recognized that."

"Who is it we're talking about?" Mum asks.

"About David, Mum. We're talking about David."

"Oh, that's right. David. He died so young. If that didn't just take the—what is it I want to say—if that didn't just pin the tail to the monkey."

"On the what? Lorraine," says Dad. "That's wrong. It's not a monkey."

"That's true. I meant on the—"

"The donkey," Dad jumps in. "You mean pin the tail on the donkey."

"Pin the tail right on the big fat rump of Fate, if you ask me," Mum says. "That's where that tail landed."

Do I know why I'm talking to these two now sweet people, whom I left so long ago for a wider world? Talking about my larger life, which they wouldn't understand?

"If he treated you badly, he didn't love you," Dad says. "That's all there is to it."

"The point is, Dad, the divorce happened for a reason. Things had become bad between us. And we were both angry. We had to get distance. We ignored our love."

"You shouldn't have left if you still loved him," Dad says. "Look at you now. Why did you do that? If you left him, you couldn't still love him. That's what I say."

My mother sighs. "Horace, things are never that simple. She was mad at him. You can be mad at someone and still love them."

"Yeah, but you don't divorce someone just because you're mad at them. Now look how she's suffering. She's feeling like the divorce was wrong."

"No, Dad. The divorce wasn't wrong. We had a terrible fall-out. Could you please turn that off, Mum?"

"Yes, I'm trying to find the thing."

"He thought you'd gone out of your mind," says Dad.

I think about us in the early '90s, new to that university town, a move we thought would provide new growth. We separated when our fighting was too hard and nothing helped. Except for our connection to Jason, mine and David's world vanished. My parents are the only adults left to me who knew David, who knew us. That's why I'm talking to them now.

"Who is it we're talking about again?" asks Mum.

"We're talking about David, Mummy."

"Oh, yes, that's right. I know that. Did he die? I think he died, didn't he?"

"Yes. He died."

"Of course, I know that. Listen to me. Talk about someone losing their bananas."

Most cultures and religions mourn their dead in communal rituals. I so long to be surrounded by our old friends, to share our grief. Only they can know or imagine mine. Without those gatherings, I think mourning can never be complete; true mourning can't be accomplished without those witnesses.

"Mum, that's the telephone."

"Oh, for heaven's sake. They all look the same; feels like you're gonna launch something."

These are my witnesses.

I explain, as if I'm lecturing, about the profundity of betrayal. How once David had the girlfriend, there was no getting back. And I didn't fully know my own feelings. Ultimately, I think we had to show our worst faces to each other, show our dark sides as we never had. Now I feel like I'm living in one of the hell realms.

"Would he have wanted me back?" I wonder out loud. "I'd have been hurt by his rejection."

"After you rejected him? What sense does that make?" says Dad.

"It went both ways, but I'm left holding all the blame. Because he died. That is the saddest thing he could do. I can't even remember the anger. It all dissolved because he died. It's as if I died."

"Well, it wasn't your fault that he died." Dad's voice has lowered to a plea.

"I bought a house two miles from him. I was always looking over my shoulder to know he was still there. Yet I failed to see."

"You couldn't know everything if he was with someone else," Dad sympathizes.

"That is true. It was thirty years and then a shoddy, bull-in-a-china-shop ending."

"You can't be eating your heart out now," Dad says. "It's too late. What happened happened. That's all. It happened. No one can go back."

I don't go on about having lacked an identity in my marriage. What does it mean to have grown up in times that denied most women whole-personhood, but then having been of the generation that made the difference for the next? I spent years dependent, submissive, and agreeable. Then I became aware. Then he went berserk. Someone should have helped us.

Mum chimes in: "Did he ever take up with a girlfriend or anything?"

"Yes, Mum. It's that Janice Bonnick, who's suing us. We've been talking about it all these months."

"Oh, yes, that's right. I'm getting forgetful in my old age."

"If he had a girlfriend then he didn't love you."

"Horace, for Christ's sake."

Two hanging plexiglass birdfeeders outside the window host nuthatches, chickadees, and the warning blue jays. Max put them there for my father to see from his seat. All this bird life has been going on as we speak. David and I had birdfeeders outside our cabin in the Catskills. We were avid birdwatchers.

"I'm the one who should have been with him in his demise. Not some new person he'd put in place, possibly out of desperation."

"You know what I think?" Dad grows ponderous. "I think you think you killed David. That's what I think."

"She could think that, Horace," says my mother. "When she thinks how he was ill, maybe the breakup upset him and the stress made his cancer worse."

"I'm amazed you understand, Mum and Dad. You are quite the mystery package. You always have been."

"I say that's a hell of a way to feel. How can someone live like that?"

"I think he never got it," says Mum. "Did he have a girlfriend?"

"When did he start seeing that girl?" Dad asks.

"Some time after he'd given up on me."

"If he was seeing that other girl even when he was still with you, then he couldn't love you at all. And then you shouldn't have loved him."

"The point is, people don't know what to do when they're insecure in the relationship they've trusted. And they don't want to find themselves alone. I believe he never stopped loving me and I never stopped loving him."

"That's what I think. I think that's true," says my mother emphatically.

"He would be glad to hear you say that, Mum. He loved both of you."

"And we loved him," my mother says.

"Yeah, we were fond of David," Dad says. "He was a good guy. He was honest. And I don't believe he would've lied and gone with some other girl. I don't believe that for a minute."

"He wasn't being dishonest. He was being desperate, and frankly, fucked up. His answer to his relationship going sour was to run away. He had the last word, for sure. Death is one big last word!"

There are downy woodpeckers at the bird feeder. I go off into a lone reverie. When I come to, I have no idea how much time has elapsed. I feel as if I've been deep-sea diving. The TV is off. Dad is whistling and turning pages.

I feel shocked into waking.

"Mum? What are you and Dad up to?"

"Oh, I think you fell asleep. Daddy's reading me the want ads." Dad is whistling through his teeth again. "He's still trying to get the right hinges for the kitchen cabinet doors that Max removed. Now Max can't put those doors back on."

Their whole day has actually been about these hinges. Life's true desperation easily falls by the wayside in the face of some concrete necessity. Every day's platform is a progress of details—sometimes a cluster, but usually taken on one at a time.

"You're spending a lot of time on this."

"The dishes get dusty and splattered with cooking oil; the cereals are getting moths." Dad shakes his head. "We don't know why he took the doors off. He doesn't know why he did it. I've called the store. I've called the company. I've tried the want ads. He lost the hinges and it would cost $3,000 to replace them." Newspapers and leaflets are strewn beside him on the floor. He throws down a last page, as if that's the end of that. "You know, Janis," he says, "we know how much David's dying has hurt you."

"It's too bad he died so young," Mum says. "You might even have found a way to be together again."

"We got cut off mid-storm. I remember how you and Dad used to fight and argue when I was growing up. You'd have broken up if that had been an option. But people didn't divorce in these parts then. You had a stormy relationship."

"What?" Dad says. "We didn't fight!"

"Yes, we did, Horace," Mum says. "We fought all the time."

"When you retired and bought your trailer, you were the same age I am now. You thought of it as a new beginning. You traveled the whole continent and became best friends. Now you're dear to one another. At my age, you didn't know that was coming."

"No," Dad agrees. "We didn't know what those next years would bring. I wish you could've had the same with David. I wish you hadn't gone off track like that!"

Mum echoes, "What a mess that all was!"

My parents tried to help us, and they witnessed our sad ending. Of course, they couldn't understand our problems. But they had love and compassion.

"If only we could turn back the claws of time," Mum says.

Suddenly the back door slams and there is a loud clattering of metal in the kitchen, a sound of something on wheels. We all sit looking toward the kitchen door, expectant.

Max rolls into the living room, sitting in Dad's wheelchair. He has a six-pack of beer in his lap and a peculiar smile on his face.

We all sit looking at him in one surprised, speechless question mark.

"What are you doing in Dad's wheelchair?" I ask.

"I just went downtown."

"In Dad's wheelchair?"

"I went to the package store. It rides good. They wait on you first. Everyone feels sorry and they let you go ahead of the line."

When Music is Your Only Way

In October, Dad began deteriorating and was going down fast. I thought we were looking at his last weeks on earth. Steve was at the lake house with Max, doing repairs. I called him.

"Steve, I think Dad's going under. He's weak. His blood pressure has fallen. An ambulance is on the way."

"We've gotta get this insulation in under the first floor today. I can't stop now."

Many of these cross-conversations followed.

But Dad will hang on for almost another year. He returns home restored to his now normal. Max fills their home with the sound of Charlie Parker's "Harlem Nocturne." Dad heard Charlie Parker play at the Apollo in his navy days—"the most beautiful song I ever heard."

Steve's voice resounds over my kitchen speaker. He's called to tell me our parents are broke until their next installment from Social Security. No mention of health issues.

I pick up the phone. "Where's all the money going?" I venture. My parents bought a small condominium apartment a decade back that they rent out for an additional small income. They have that and the summer rent from the lake house.

"I'm looking at their credit card bills," Steve says. "Margo's been buying their food at top gourmet markets."

"Don't forget she's the family cook. She's buying and cooking for all of them."

"Well, she's spending like a queen. Dad told me she bought stuffed pork chops for all of them the other night. She paid $12 a chop. Dad can't eat that stuff anymore. Neither can Ma. Max doesn't care what he eats. Last week she bought five pounds of wild salmon for the four of them, then leaves the leftovers on the counter to rot. She buys fresh arugula, leaves that out too. No one eats it. Dad doesn't like it. He's never eaten that stuff. She buys truffle butter, pink sea salt, and fresh flowers to put in that pigpen."

"Who can deny anyone the pleasure of flowers? You cross a line when you start controlling every detail about how someone lives."

I put on Pink Floyd's "Money," and puzzle again about Steve's involvement with this family. Most people go on to their own adult lives and leave their past behind. It looks like Steve has never done that. I know nothing much of his relationship with Joanne, except that, though they remain together, their one attempt to live together failed. They now live four doors apart on the same street.

Margo told me that Steve surprised my parents one Christmas, over twenty years ago, by arriving in a gigantic box with a big bow. He'd had Max package him in the cellar. My parents opened the box, hardly expecting Steve to burst out.

What explains Steve? I imagine he—like me—was quite displaced and thrown off when the three took center stage. But he was only five.

My own return to this family is different. I've lost all my meaningful people: my husband and our friend-family. My son is launched. My life has dried up. My parents are ancient and there's the mess of our unresolved past, now spilled all over us. I'm seriously but only temporarily regressed. I'm only touching down for a while. I'm not here to stay.

Those years when I was not alone, all that time with David, were music-filled; that whole, world-changing rush of '60s music has never stopped playing in my head. We marched against the war and for civil rights in those days and saw success in those efforts. Those decades when my husband was always home by six and my son needed me were the best. David was my "primary" adult relationship. There's been no other. Throughout my marriage, I sought friends of my own to bring home, knowing that having no one but David wasn't healthy, but each time I met with only limited or temporary success. Alone with the music now, I'm our "Sad-Eyed Lady of the Lowlands." I haven't lost our music. The music is still here.

"Why is the divorce still a wound and not a scar?" The man in the soft brown room speaks. This psychoanalyst's golden Ganesha sits on a shelf, watching over. I've sought good help.

"He died! I'm crying because he died!"

"You are not crying about his death yet. You are crying about the divorce."

This is true.

"You were running away." This man in the soft brown room shocks me.

"You could not bear to be left again. You could not have that done to you again—what your parents did—to be in the passive position. To be abandoned. Again."

I'm speechless. And back for a next appointment.

"You were running probably from the first moment of diagnosis."

"What you're saying is unbearable for me to hear."

"There were other reasons. You are not psychotic. There were problems in this marriage."

I couldn't realize all that was driving my panic when I was facing forty. I now understand how many ways David's illness—about which I flew into a near-psychotic state of denial after his diagnosis—was affecting me. I was upset all the time. I thought it was about losing myself. Me at forty just wouldn't be me. But I was ignoring what was really looming: the threat of losing my husband. Panic trumped love?

  Our poor, imperfect love. Our music will remain. But no consolation exists.

  It seems to me this is why the divorce remains a wound and not a scar.

  Does this explain my altered behavior during that time? We were not only coping together with the diagnosis, I was also coping alone. The illness made us different. I did not have cancer. One night I arrived almost an hour late to meet him in a restaurant. I'd kept stopping to do errands on the way and I simply lost time while he sat waiting and worried. We'd never been late for one another. It's something we wouldn't do. I couldn't stop apologizing, but had no explanation. I wish I could say this was the only instance of my strangeness. By then I was acting in some ways like a stranger to both of us. Besides that, arguments about our unresolved conflicts escalated. Then our life collapsed. We left New York for a new opportunity in this university town and bought a house. But even in the new setting, we could not negotiate our disagreement. Then I moved out because he wouldn't. Our marriage ended and I was alone and fighting for air.

  I now understand the mind-state I was in that night I came late to the restaurant. Losing track of time identifies the dissociative experience. All these years I've only been mystified by my behavior. I had no explanation. I worried about my ability to love. It's monstrous that we might not grasp the motivation of our regrettable actions, fail to get the whole picture when it matters. David must have wondered about me for the rest of his life. I wish he and I could rehash those times now. Now I could explain.

On "David's side" of the bed sprawl the clothes I threw off when I crashed tonight; they rustle and sigh as I move in dreams and semi-waking. Not my husband but my vacated self sleeps beside me. In those dreams, David and I are back, climbing the Flatiron, outside Boulder, our "peak experience"—the same day (July 21st) Neil Armstrong and Buzz Aldrin walked on the moon—having learned rock-climbing from Duane and Thalia in 1969. Jim Morrison sings about turning out the lights. I'm ahead until we get to the top, and then we have some dream mission that I can't recall and he takes the lead. I happily follow.

This is how we were. I didn't realize then that his bravado, which everyone bought into, hid his own need for care and nurture. He was good at taking charge. It was easy to just trust and follow. It was a blind insensitivity, I think now. Where was my love and caring?

"Mummy, I get so sad . . ."

Mum and I are nestled together on the lumpy couch in the Eden living room, holding our drinks. I'm on my second glass of wine.

If I can't find comfort at home alone, why do I find it here? Because here I'm not alone. And though I want us all to come to terms that allow me to move on, I'm seeking solace, too. But it doesn't stick. What if I had our old friends? Or one close friend to talk to? What if I still had Darlene? But I'd have to be fourteen again. The sister I begged my mother to adopt when I was an only child, we'd have each other now. I need to gather myself up and invest in my new friends.

"What's that?" says Mum. Strains of Nino Rota's symphonic score are playing softly on TV. We are alone in the living room. It's late. I've been moved to express my nagging self-doubt to Mum.

"What did you say?"

"I keep thinking . . . It's so sad when I think . . ."

"Think what?"

"Mummy, I question my capacity to love," I say in a strained, teary voice.

"Oh?"

"I may lack the ability to love."

Mum looks baffled, looks like she's searching her mind. "Well . . ."

"What?"

"Well. Just do the best you can."

When everyone went off the deep end here, my parents became the entrapped keepers of an asylum. When that matrix of bewilderment became too snarled, I think they just learned to speak the language of madness and finally joined the inmates.

"It's us against the mentally ill." Steve's refrain echoes. How he and I are bonded.

When I was fourteen, I often sat on the sill of the open window in my pink bedroom upstairs, smoking Lucky Strikes, listening to music on my pink clock-radio and looking down on Mr. Balamin's two apple trees, the same apple trees I got lost in when I washed dishes at seven in the pantry below. In full blossom, those trees looked like pink cumulus clouds. No matter the season, I forever saw those trees in full dress, as if they were paper dolls with tabbed-on gowns. I began leaning daringly out, a little more each day. I wanted to fall into their pillowy arms and be magically cradled. I knew branches couldn't hold someone falling, that I'd go straight through—like a for-real rock-a-bye baby—and, presumably, die. Then Mummy would rush to my crushed body and finally understand how much she loved me. Too late. She'd wail and moan and feel bereft, sorry for the way she'd treated me. But I'd have gone off in the hold of an angel, never to look back. And Mummy would stay, punished by her love, and sorrow would stab her heart cyanotic blue.

I smoked hard. I wobbled. I dared myself to lean out farther every day. The dog, sleeping on my bed, would wake and watch, alerted. Then—almost too late—I'd hook my bare left foot under the windowsill ledge and catch myself.

When hunger demanded that I descend the stairs, I found I couldn't eat. I moped in the kitchen, sorry I wasn't dead. There were the waiting piles of diapers and the sink full of dishes. I was no longer cuddling cute babies. I was getting out as soon as I could.

What saved me from falling into the apple trees when I sat there smoking one day, regretting my inability to inhale, was a song that came crashing over the radio like a message from the land of hope and promise. Just as I teetered on my perch, one Jerry Lee Lewis (1957) squawked "*Goodness, gracious, great balls of fire* with an outrageous verve I will forever treasure. I was suddenly shot through with that brash humor and thrill of being alive. I belly laughed and changed my course—never to lean out over the apple trees again, never to smoke again. I embraced Rina-Tina with all my heart. She licked my happy face. There was life out there, and the cloud I saw now held a future. I was thoroughly restored to my senses that day.

And—the golden realization of that future is that I created a family of my own that wasn't crazy. David was the father I wanted for my child: a strong guiding presence, sure of the world and how to be in it. David found his coordinates to some extent by chance and luck, but also due to his overall strong talent and intention. His career came together. He followed a very near set of interests in becoming a neurologist, and that opened into a vista one day. Then he felt he'd stumbled on his own gold mine in neuroscience, and every move he made going forward built upon the last. We often toasted Ramón y Cajal, the father of neuroscience, with our evening glasses of wine. David's surprise and humility, his pure gratitude, was infinitely endearing.

The Reluctant Supplicant

Marisol calls to tell me Mum has had another fall; she's been ambulanced to the hospital and has internal bleeding in her right arm. Margo is camped out there, spending the night at my mother's side. That leaves my father home with Max.

I wait until morning to call my father. "How you doing, Dad?"

"Well, Max, he doesn't answer when I call him. He won't come upstairs. He's really angry these days. He doesn't like me at all."

"How are you getting what you need?"

"Well, Margo calls from Mummy's hospital room. But she does things that aren't right. Last night I told her I got from my wheelchair to bed by myself, and got my left leg up with the strap. But I couldn't reach to get the window closed and Max didn't answer. I told Margo it was okay. I got a pillow against the screen to keep the cool air out. Ten minutes later, sirens are coming up the road, police cars and fire trucks. All these men come walking in and I said, 'She shouldn't have called you. All that's happening is I can't get the window closed.'

"'You don't have anyone here with you, sir?' the policeman asked me. I said, 'Well, my son is down in the basement. But he's not answering right now.' Well, they went right downstairs. Suddenly Max comes up in his pajamas, goes over, and slams the window shut. I've never seen him so angry. The police tried to talk to him, but he just walked right through them as if they weren't there and went back downstairs.

"Next thing I know two firemen are fixing my blankets and putting my pillows under me and behind my head and pulling up the blankets under my chin. They were tucking me in, for crying out loud. And one of the firemen got me a glass of water and gave me my medicine. I said, 'I don't want you guys having to come over here just because I have to go to bed.' And one guy said, 'Why not? You pay your taxes and you don't have kids in school. Might as well use us, we got nuthin' to do most of the time anyway.'"

Dad goes on, "At night we only need help if we fall down. I can pretty much get myself to bed now with this motorized wheel chair. I just have a little challenge getting my left leg up onto the bed. But I worry about Mummy. She usually stays up after me to watch *The Godfather*—because she forgets it from the night before."

"*The Godfather* is never done."

"That's right. Each time is the first. Then, if she's had too much wine—that's probably what happened the other night—she's apt to fall down. She doesn't remember, so nobody knows. That's our only problem. But I hate having people coming all the time. Every day, an army of people shows up at the door first thing in the morning: first comes the Coumadin lady"—Dad's been on Coumadin since his stroke—"then the nurse, then the social workers, Meals on Wheels comes when Margo's away. I like when Doug comes. He's the only one. But most of all I just like to be here with Mum, watching the news and having a good time, just the two of us. I'm happy this way. Even though I'm paralyzed on my left, I still like my life. I'd be happy to live another hundred years. I like baseball. I like being with Mummy and I miss her tonight."

"I know. But you certainly don't want the police and fire departments there to get you to bed."

"Well, the night before last, Fred and Marisol came over. They take good care of me. They do bother me with their prayers, and that's why they come. But they got me to bed. Then I had to have them praying over me and giving me lectures about God."

"Trying to convert you."

"That's right. That's what they're up to."

"That must be annoying."

"Yes, it is. It's very annoying. I don't like it that they think I have to have their God and believe like them."

"Do you tell them you don't like it?"

"No. I don't. I don't want to say negative things to them when they're helping me out. I just let them do what they have to."

This is Dad's passivity—a passivity that always frustrated me and especially frustrated Steve.

One bright green day as I cross my backyard, cradling an abundance of fresh spring lettuce bestowed on me by my neighbor, I hear the phone ring. Inside, Dad's voice talks out on the speaker.

"Hi Janis. I want to talk to you about something."

I pick up the phone. "Hi, Dad, what's up?"

"I have something on my mind, something that's bothering me, and I'd like to talk to a therapist."

"Really?! You, Dad? A therapist?"

"I don't want you to tell anyone."

"No, of course. I didn't know you were bothered by something. Can I help?"

"Yes. I need to speak to someone right away."

"Do you want to talk to me? You know I'm coming there soon."

"Yes. I want to talk to you."

That next weekend, I close the living room door and tell everyone to stay out for a while, so I can be alone with Dad. I can feel breathing through the keyhole, ears steaming through the door. But in the room, we're safe.

"Oh, those look nice there," I comment, sitting down on the couch next to Dad in his recliner. We're facing two sepia portrait photos of my parents in their early twenties, set side by side atop the TV. These are a new addition, a present from me. When last here, I took many of the old family photos—smoldering away in the greasy brown paper shopping bag in the attic—to try to save them. Among a mess stuck together, I found these portraits of young Mum and Dad. I had them restored and framed and I sent them as a gift. Mum has a full-lipstick smile with sparkling teeth and looks like a movie star. Dad's wearing a suit and tie, his hair is slicked to one side, and his eyes are bright and happy. He'd probably not gone into the navy yet. It was before they were married, maybe even before I was conceived. Probably no one has seen these pictures for decades. I had the cracks and scratches touched up. So, on this rare occasion, with the TV off for once, we sit talking before these two beautiful ghosts.

Thus begins a shaggy tale that grows more bizarre as it goes along.

He's back in World War II in the Philippines, in the submarine that underwent serious bombing—in which all aboard survived. We have forever known and repeated that Dad prayed to God then, for the only time in his life. Everyone knows about the foxhole believer.

"Is this what you want to talk about? The submarine?"

No. It isn't. What's on his mind is that during the time he was away, he thinks my mother was carrying on with a man here in the neighborhood.

I choke and swallow the wrong way and almost have to open the door and plow through the busybodies for some water. He doesn't notice and goes right on.

"Well," he begins, as we both fix our eyes on the photo of my mother—glamorous then, as I've never seen her, somewhere in the early 1940s—but innocent-looking too, because she was so young, in her satin blouse with a looping, sequined scrawl across the top. "When I was in the war . . . first I was down in Mexico and then I got to the Philippines and, you know, some of the men went to prostitutes. I didn't want to do that. I had Mummy at home and I had you. You were a new baby. There are some things I just can't think about."

"I can't either, Dad. Really."

"But Mummy, I found out, used to visit some single guys in the neighborhood. She and her friend Shirley would go to their house and play cards with them all night long. One was a guy named Arsenault. She was spending all her time with him."

I so don't want to hear any of this. No matter how old you are, you don't want to think of your parents as other than your parents.

Dad's speech, softened by age, is like a voice wearing slippers. He gestures as he speaks with his one good hand, long and elegant. It flies and brushes and motion-shapes his words as his left hand lies still, like a dead animal, done in by the stroke. At certain points his live hand goes to his lap, as if he's patting his last statement in place and smoothing the page. He's wearing many little Band-Aids all over his arms and hands where his pale, thinning skin is tearing and ripping.

"When I came back, she still went over there and stayed late. Once I went over and they weren't there. They'd gone to a bar called the Firefly. They were sitting at the bar together and they pretended not to see me."

"Dad, where was I? I must have been less than a year old."

"My mother was taking care of you. We were living over there with my mother and father then," he nods through the window toward that tiny saltbox I remember so well. "Then they started dancing and I went over and spun that guy around so fast, he didn't know what was happening. I threw him against the bar."

"Dad, this isn't true."

"Yes, this is true. This is true."

"I can't imagine you like this. You're mild-mannered, understated—"

"The police came and talked to me and in the meantime, Arsenault took off in his car, and then Mummy got in her car"—she had her brother's car then—"and took off too. I tried to follow. That night, I stayed out driving around and finally, a few hours later, I found that guy parked down by the river, where he looked passed out. I got a huge rock and I—"

"No. You didn't. Don't tell me this." I want to cover my ears.

"He jumped out of his car and I chased him. When I got close, I threw the rock, and .... and ... I just don't know how men are supposed to resist a girl like that." He's riveted on my mother's picture again.

"Did he get away?" I'm thinking my father could be having a first episode of dementia, which can manifest as sexual jealousy that is probably delusional. He's always been a quiet man.

"That time he did."

"Was there another time?" I'm asking in spite of myself. If this actually was therapy, the therapist might join with him and explore his feelings and fantasies completely. I feel such empathy for his suffering, but my instinct is to try to close this off. He'll just whip himself up and spin his wheels.

"Well, not really. Not the way I wanted."

"Dad, this is so in the past. This memory is distorted by time. Think of all you've been through together since then. Can you just let go?"

"I can't. I can't stop thinking about it."

"What do you want now?"

"I can't trust her. It's eating me up."

"That was more than half a century ago. Didn't you ever talk about it?"

"No. She said it didn't happen, but I never believed that."

"Poor Dad. You've been thinking about this all this time?"

"No. I'm thinking about it now. I can't stop thinking about it now. Once my mind starts going, I can't stop. I lie awake in the night and the early morning and think. There's no way a man wouldn't go for a girl like that."

"You need medication. Medication would help your mind calm down."

Could this story be true? And he's held it in all these years because he valued the marriage more? I try to imagine my naive, unworldly, Catholic mother as a foxy lady prior to her bellicose housewife years. She does look sexy in the photograph. I wish I hadn't sent these pictures.

"She betrayed me and I can't get over that."

"But now. She's just a cute old lady, your best friend for decades. Why now? Why would you be thinking about this now?"

"I just do. That's all."

"Have you spoken to Mum about it now?"

"No. She doesn't remember anything anymore. There I was, away fighting for my country, and she was going behind my back and . . ."

"You've been inseparable since you retired and traveled the country and grew old together. She's been caring for you all day every day."

Dad sits silently concentrating on my mother in the photo.

"Look at the handsome young god beside her," I continue. "You were her lifelong love." I nod at his photo. My father was chosen to model for a magazine when he briefly passed through New York in his sailor uniform, this small-town guy, who'd never seen the big city. That magazine is still somewhere in this house; I fear to think where and in what condition.

Well, he isn't going that way.

"Medication," I offer again. "There's medication for this."

"I don't want any more medication." His good hand airplanes around and lands.

Mum's lace curtains separate over the open window behind my father's head and dance in on a summer breeze to stroke my father's cheeks and shoulders. "They were all running around, drinking, going out in cars. And my mother kept trying to get her to come and take you home with her."

"Did she succeed?"

"She was trying. But they were just interested in their good times. Dancing through the war. They'd go to Boston to the night clubs. The war wasn't happening here. And she was being a good-time girl while she could."

"Jesus, Dad. How did you know about all this?"

"Boyzee told me." Boyzee, his high school buddy—long gone.

And I'm still trying to picture my then churchgoing, small-town mother callously dishonoring her marriage. It's a new vision of Mum.

"Medication could help you stop this thinking about it all the time."

"I don't want to stop thinking about it."

I recall finding a delicate white handkerchief out on Dad's workbench in the garage when I must have been about five. It was edged with rainbow-pastel lace and looked like an angelic love message fallen there among the gruff, greasy tools. It had a blot of lipstick perfectly outlining Mum's lips. And it stayed there. No one ever removed it. I assumed it was a kiss to Dad.

This story doesn't touch him.

"What if I put these pictures up here on the bookshelf, so you don't have to see them all the time." I take the pictures and set them up beside him, but not where he's facing them. I accidentally touch a plastic fish glued to a plaque there, which is stirred to rise up and sing "Fly Me to the Moon."

"One night we were all dancing outdoors at Norumbega Park," Dad says. "Then there was a thunderstorm. The band kept playing, but next thing I know, she's gone. She just danced off and away."

"What about the way she's danced off and away now? Your lives are ending. And your wife is losing her mind."

Dad becomes suddenly lucid. "I'm afraid that when I die, she'll be looking for me."

"I guess that's a sad thought."

"She'll be going around the house looking for me after I'm gone. She'll forget I'm not here. She'll just look for me all day."

"Maybe that won't be an unhappy quest. Mum doesn't demand a product of her efforts anymore. She lives in an eternal present. The journey—the anticipation of finding you—will be her happiness. All the while, as she searches, she'll be holding you in her mind and in her heart. The looking—not the finding—will be the point of it all."

The door bursts open. Swirls of cotton-candy hair rush in like a stampede of summer ghosts, and a plate of food is plunked down in front of my father.

It Has to Be Love

How many ways can love go wrong?
"I've gone crazy with grief." I'm talking in the soft brown room.

"You cannot face that you hated him."

"No. Because he died. I can't feel the hate of the divorce anymore. All my anger has evaporated into thin air. How can I be whole?"

All love contains its opposite. Hate is a reality. But ours led to a breakup. My sadness wears helpless jowls and puts bloated blue hammocks beneath my eyes. Every time I try to let go, even for a minute, the reality comes slamming in anew. It doesn't stop. Winter, spring, summer, and yet another winter have shot past. My life bumps and jerks along. I walk along the waterway every chance I get. I attend Sierra Club meetings and I join those good people I've found to hike and kayak. But I'm still up late nights, moving to the dream music of Procol Harum and drinking wine. There is a Cape Cod conference on bereavement and mourning. I'll go

And I'm feeling the condemnation of Time. Dad is moving on. The world will be without him, too. Will I lose my bearings? The loss of Dad will repeat the loss of David. Qwerty and Elemeno will only be mine a little longer. And Mum. Mum soon won't be Mum anymore. This is how it goes. I don't want to lose myself. Not yet.

Love doesn't always hold betrayal, but it always entails loss. What love do I have now? My son and Susanna. That's a lot. I feel some attachment for my siblings. I'm even looking forward to seeing them all. Yes. I'm going there again. Where else can I go?

Steve won't be there. He either stayed at the lake or went back to LA. No one seems to know.

Getting there will be like arriving on the moon. But I'll tuck in all my inner darkness, which has no place there. I'll be a kind of stick figure, a person without insides.

Steve calls before I leave home. He's just had a phone conversation with Dad.

"Wait'll ya hear this. We were just talking and Dad said something about going to meet his maker soon. I said, 'I thought you didn't believe in that stuff.' Dad said, 'Well, I'm not so sure about anything anymore. And you know the girls, they just don't stop.'"

"Yeah. Dad's been baptized. I'm outraged. Marisol told me. They brought in some maniac pastor. I said, 'Marisol, you can't just let the guy have his own point of view?! His own integrity?!' But she just insisted, 'He's better off in God's hands.'"

"This'z what I can't stand about Dad," Steve says. "He can't stick to his guns. The guy gives in to pressure. I never thought I'd see the day he'd go for this stuff. After all the times he threw those priests out of the house. Who was that redheaded guy? That Father Conroy, or something like that. I remember Dad chasing him right down the back steps." (I too was there that day.) "The guy flew headlong into the bushes. His briefcase went flying. I was so proud of Dad. And Dad shouted after that jerk that what someone believes is their own goddamn business and no one else's. That's the one thing he stood for all his life. Now those little shits have baptized him."

"Wonder if they brought in a bathtub of water and plunked his bony old body into it?" I say. "They're 'total immersion' believers, you know."

"I just get madder every time I think of it. There was a whole stupid ceremony."

"Me too. But, remember, he's eighty-eight. And you know? Really, I mean—actually—think about it. What's the harm?"

Steve is silent for the moment. He seems to relate to this. Then he goes on. "I said to him, 'Dad, how are you feeling about the state of the world now that you've found God? Is the world looking better?' Then Dad said, 'No, the world hasn't changed. You've still got the selfish people running things and the poor people who've got nuthin' to say.' I said, 'So, are you just one of the poor people with nuthin' to say? You just let the selfish people baptize you and have their way?' He said, 'Well, I guess so. That's what they did. They baptized me. So I've got a soul where there wasn't any before. And it's a wet one!'"

These are Dad's last moments. He was in the hospital again last week, and I felt on the phone that he was asking me to come. He's growing profoundly feeble. Qwerty, dear-best-friend cat, who's twenty-one years old, has been in the same stage of dwindling existence as Dad—they're fading away together.

It's June. Everything feels gone again to Jell-O. Except for work, my world feels so small that it pinches, while my sadness over David remains a swamp without borders. I'm feeling Jason's loss of his father, too. Jason thrived on his father's certainty about the order in the universe and humanity's progress. They created a splendid saltwater fish tank together, and worked on its upkeep every weekend. They had their own shared humor and their continuous chess game. Jason, my son, I wanted you to have your father, as I've had mine, well into your waning years.

Time requires one to keep pressing ahead. Jason and Susanna are my new family. And I'm finding some really satisfying friends. I'm filling this new niche. But right now Dad, at his end, is calling me.

Following an early morning in my office, I take my forest-mushroom of a life and put it on the road. The inches that run beneath my tires all the way from here to there are like the minutes between then and now. As always, my music plays. It's Janis Joplin all the way, wailing about trading her tomorrows. Traffic slows to a standstill on I-95, due to road work; I sit glued to one spot on the road, glued to my present life's metaphor—one spot. It's so hard to want to be moving, with energy and ambition, efficiency and planning, to be pinned in place, as if fixed with chloroform. Fatigue claims my consciousness. I feel my nose ground into wondering what is to become of me after all—like a child, who has no control of events, might wonder.

I drive up Eden Ave into a sunset-drenched sky, the same sun that once flooded one Caribbean horizon, as if baptizing young David and me in a "total immersion" sunset; we were sitting on a rocky prominence that faced west, experiencing our joint wonder during those years of discovering the world together. All sunsets forever after have been me and David.

I turn into the driveway, which is ablaze with this sunset magic, to find an abandoned, misshapen brown bag of groceries sitting pathetically on the ground behind Margo's parked car. She bought groceries, got them out of the car, then gave up the task and left them sitting there under the broiling sun. She probably ordered Max to bring in the groceries and he dug in his heels, as he does, because she's so bossy and he's not able to say no. The sight of this lone brown bag is disheartening: costly groceries have perished. I'm going to tell her she's inviting the foxes and coyotes she fears.

"Here I am again," I mutter, and pick up the greasy bag to haul up the ramp with my suitcase. The bag is dripping melted butter.

Dad looks paler and thinner than ever. But he has his appetite. Cooking here, though, is a challenge. The oven doesn't close all the way and only one burner on the stove works. Margo tells me that Dad says he liked the food in the hospital better than what she makes at home. She gets no praise for her cooking. Max goes out and buys his own submarine sandwich every day. Dad doesn't outright reject her cooking, though he complains it's not good (it's not); he eats like a horse and weighs like a feather. He's always been that way. But it's exaggerated now.

And my Qwerty is doing the same—dying in old age, but eating all the time. Strange to have my cat ailing in the same way as my father. Appetite must increase when, though your body is wasting, your will is to live—which both Dad and Qwerty are demonstrating in tandem.

Max shows me his website advertising himself as a web designer. We're down in the old coal-bin basement. The homepage on his website has a Quentin Tarrantino-worthy bloodbath with some torn flesh object in the middle. On closer look, a nearly three-dimensional picture of Max himself emerges, lying on the gurney in the ER immediately following his accident, complete with head wounds, dripping blood, and the ear hanging off like a small ripped animal. "Welcome to my website," the narrative begins, and then tells the story of the accident in gruesome detail.

I suggest that this is not the most enticing invitation to his website, that many people would be put off. But oddly enough, he's gotten a number of new clients. Maybe Steve and I have been on the wrong track all this time, trying to fit him to the mainstream world.

Why do we keep applying reason where it doesn't fit? When are we going to get it that the joke is on us?

I spend the weekend going through their finances. Handling the finances was always Mum's role, keeping up with their two rental properties. She still pays the bills and maintains the checkbook. Margo oversees. But now the rental checks to be deposited stand on the kitchen windowsill over the sink, where the report cards used to go to be forgotten, between the dusty candelabra and the jungle of stained, dirtied, and superbly thriving African violets. The checks get bleached by the sun and spattered by the garbage disposal. They eventually get deposited because my father reminds Mum and Margo. But the credit card bill is never paid on time. Numerous other services and insurance policies have been canceled because of nonpayment. Until now, Dad would always get on the phone to get them reinstated. But no more.

What a mess my mother's desk is, where she sits during most of her waking hours—if she's not before the TV—holding papers, reading them over and over, looking for her lost checkbook. Her desk is in what used to be the pantry with the window where I once stood on the stool and washed dishes forever, looking out into the neighbor's apple blossoms. Now I find dozens of pieces of paper cascading off her desk and a few hundred unused, empty envelopes from all their service companies, some with my parents' return address written on them in Mum's handwriting. Many have postage stamps. Most everything appears to have been paid eventually—but not on time. Some bills have been paid twice.

I sort through current bills in the living room with the TV on its Muzak station, everyone numb, lined up, sitting, and staring. Marisol came early to find out what time to arrive for dinner and misplaced her car keys, so she's here indefinitely. Margo and Max are in their pajamas. Margo rocks in the rocking chair, chewing hard and loud on ice cubes, a trail of spilled iced coffee leading to her from the refrigerator—good for finding her, if she were lost.

"Is there a stapler?" I'm desperate for an organizing principle. Max and Margo have a brief discussion about whether there ever was a stapler. Max comes back twenty minutes later with an ancient stapler, its corroded metal flaking. He pries until its rusted jaws cough open. I see that two staples are left inside.

"There are no more than two staples in this house?" My voice quavers and actually sounds threatening.

"Y-e-a-e-a-h."

"Then we will go into town and get staples, first thing in the morning." I sound like a Marine sergeant. "We'll get staples. We'll get a stapler. We'll get a pen. We'll get scissors, a pencil sharpener, Scotch tape, and paper clips. And we will not lose them."

No one seems moved. I know that the mess of their finances needs more than a stapler. I put the pile of papers I'm holding on the floor beside the couch. That's when I note that the floor is littered, among all other manner of debris, with hole punches. (Do they actually own a hole punch?) I also notice the rug has a huge stain, as if something large bled to death in the middle of the room and its gore soaked into the rug.

I sputter over the mess. Max tells me he vacuumed on Tuesday, but the hole punches appeared on Wednesday.

"What year was that?" I say, sipping wine from a plastic coffee cup.

Dad is so weakened that he's beyond use of his wheelchair. They've managed to get something called a Hoyer lift, which looks like a gigantic prehistoric crane and occupies half the kitchen. Max and Margo expertly load my father, like a giant baby, onto this Hoyer lift, haul him from his living room chair to his bedroom, and put him to bed. They've been instructed and have clearly practiced and do it like a dance. They even take slight bows when I praise them. I relinquish my irritated state of mind.

"Look," I tell them because they're actually very sweet, "I'm not here to feel superior. I'm here to fix the finances and find the checkbook."

I go in and talk to Dad. He tells me he thinks about dying and how it will happen. "You don't know if it's sky above or sky below where you'll go, if it's a hurricane sweeps in and takes you. I don't mean like what the religions say. But I don't know whether to think a big wave comes in with an undertow or a north wind or you get sucked into a maelstrom. Then either you're part of everything—the sea, the sky, the universe—or you're nothing. I hope you don't suffer. Best if you just nod out and disappear from this world. But what becomes of everything you were? Is that all real anymore once it's gone? Does it all just evaporate into thin air? Like you were never here? Even after you fought for your country in the biggest war? On a submarine bombed off the Philippines for all the world to know? What happens to that? Does everything turn to nothing?"

"I hope it will be a good experience, Dad, that it will feel right and natural. You will be deeply missed. You'll live on in all our hearts for as long as we all live. You're dear to all of us. You're dear to me."

"Sometimes I just have my mind on baseball," he says, pointing to his own little TV on the bureau, which Max set up for him. Max also stuck a clear plexiglass bird feeder with nyjer seed on Dad's bedroom window, and goldfinches are busy there.

This morning, as I'm sipping coffee in the living room and reading, I hear Dad wake up.

"Mumma—are you still alive under there?"

I hear her muffled reply.

"Hallelujah! Still here. You and me. Another day." *Dad's back with Mum*, I think.

Soon he's being flown across the kitchen by Margo and Max, as if in the beak of the stork. The skin of his scrawny arms and legs hangs like limp tatters, flapping in the transit breeze.

"Here I am," he jokes. "The flying wonder." Dad bears indignity well. "I said good morning to my darling and my darling said it back and we're here again, looking at another sunrise. Another day with my bride, my bluebird of happiness." Dad's unhappy obsession about Mum in her playgirl era must have lifted—at least for now.

His darling happiness bird comes padding out of the bedroom in her slippers, laughing at the whole production, which is all any of us can do, including Dad. She brings his orange juice and banana these days. How could what he said about her be true?

Max and I walk into town.

We walk along the railroad tracks. Did I ever not know these tracks? Again I remember how my friends and I balanced all the way to school on these polished rails of precision steel, glinting in the sun, leading to a somewhere out of here I would have given anything to know.

"Why did you break into that woman's apartment that time?" I ask him. It happened over thirty years ago, but I've never asked before.

"Uh-uh-uh-uh . . ." His voice goes flat, and I understand he's fudging an answer. "I liked her computer."

"What an answer."

"Y-e-e-a-h!" The monotone, drawn-out word can be heard as slightly sorry and empathizing that he can't give you more. It agrees with you and evades any truth.

"What was it like being in jail?"

"Uh-h-n . . . the food was good."

I have to wonder if I'm talking to a person or an illness.

The old mill that gobbled up my teenage years stands ahead. The whole complex has been revitalized into a new-age office building. That five-story brick bastion of old has glorious, sparkling windows. We walk inside to see that the original floors have been redone—the long undulating planks are polished and polyurethaned—but nevertheless warped with age. The pipes, vertical against the walls, must still clang and bang. There is a lovely café and offices behind wide, glass-paneled French doors.

"These are stunning!" I say, touching the wood.

"Yeah, these are nice." Max reaches his hand to touch the wood where I did.

"How many of these people working inside know what stark lives these old buildings harbored before the architects came?" I wonder aloud.

"Yeah. They'd be surprised." Max is studying his hand that touched the wood.

I worked in this mill for three summers in high school and for stretches after school. I spent one whole summer winding gift ribbon onto cardboard spools and sealing their cellophane wrap (and occasionally a finger) with a hot burner connected to a lever. I spent the next summer typing bills of lading with a creepy boss who rubbed my back and bra fastener every time he offered an instruction, and a Mrs. Landhawes—second in command—who offered her Librium (precursor to Valium) all around whenever her alarm clock went off.

The money I earned that summer was what afforded me my wardrobe for the last two years of high school and into college: the two skirts, two sweaters, and pair of loafers. Both skirts were good-quality (from Filene's)—"straight skirts," one gray, one a tan, gray, and light-blue plaid. One sweater was gray, the other tan. I went through life in those clothes until I met David.

Max and I go to the drugstore, the only big-box store in town. Last time I was here, stubborn semblances of snow—storing the winter's dog urine for timed release—clung to the edges of this parking lot.

Max stands up front near the registers, spacing out, while I shop. Walking home, he tells me—because I ask—that he doesn't hear voices anymore and the radio in his head he once thought David had put there is long gone.

We come back later by car to pick up pizza. I drive home an unusual way to soothe my nerves. How many haywire tree rings do I bear—just from this little lifetime—in so many contexts as to make me unrecognizable, even to myself? I imagine the thousands of generations there have been on this planet. Think how many unrecorded moments have been lived, never to be known. The route up over the hill that runs beside the mill, passes along that well-made brick building and all the shining windows that were clouded with dust for more than a century. Max knows the history of this mill. He's telling me there are over a million square feet in more than a dozen buildings and how mechanization brought about power looms. Max knows a lot of things.

All the way up the hill beside the aqueduct along the mill wall that sluices one long beard of whitewater, a titillating memory arises that takes getting around the corner to fully materialize. This part of town—up over the millpond—has meaning. Across from the mill there is a side entrance to an old wooden church hidden behind a crumpled pocket of mossy earth that looks like a forgotten place. I recall a sunny summer day when I dared a much older boy to chase me up the hill by sticking out my tongue at him in a sassy, provocative manner. He lit after me. No matter how fast I ran, he was faster. He was probably eleven. Every look back revealed his warrior thunder, his determination, and I could not stop looking back. How I loved and feared his strength of purpose. I dove into this crumpled, mossy opening. Inside was a tiny glade with light veiling down. Pastel anemones clung to the rise like delicate ballerinas. Then, Boy—I didn't know his name, even then—flew into this little pocket-glade or earth-womb, if you will, like he was coming over the goal post.

I was so noodle-kneed I probably couldn't have spoken English. I could no longer feel my ankles when he caught me. Then he didn't know what to do. We were suddenly steeped in some summer liquid fantasy, in that town of ours that was smothered under long, heavy winters every year. We were clammy and we moved like fish. We were all of a sudden everything to each other in a world where that can never be true. He had caught me. He was just a boy. And I was eight.

In what was almost a dance step—me like a rag doll in his clutches, actually standing on his toes—we suddenly dared to look into each other's eyes, and that unnerved us so that we both collapsed.

The rest is wonderfully awful! He fell back against the banking and we had a scuffle that smudged us with loamy dirt. I writhed and punched. There were hands on me, and there was child-eros. Then what did he do? He threw me over his lap—as he must have seen in some movie or advertisement of the day—and spanked me.

Beyond humiliation, I finally freed myself and we faced each other, flushed, sweating, and overcome. I felt both so outraged and embarrassed that when a surprise tenderness welled up, I grew steamy again. A cloud of vapors from our mouths caught and stalled in each other, making a bog of child-breath. And that was what swarmed my mind for the rest of the day; our locked humidities left the lasting impression.

"They made navy blankets in there during World War II." Max is talking beside me. He's been talking for a while now, he who never talks. He's become positively loquacious.

I return my full attention to my driving and face the road. Sitting in the passenger seat, Max begins ruminating out of the blue. I wait to receive some peculiar notion from his original mind.

"I guess, since you're the oldest, you'll be the first to die," he pronounces. I flinch as reflections of thin, upright trees parade from right to left like Hebrew corduroy across the windshield.

"Then comes Steve. Then comes Margo. Then Marisol." He nods, to emphasize his new realization. "I'll be the last."

"I'm glad I'm the youngest," he finishes.

Time

At home, I live with what's left of my family here: our two elderly cats. Originally Jason's pets, they came with me in the divorce. They're Tonkinese—magnificent Egyptian figures with friendly temperaments like puppies. It's uncanny that Qwerty, the dark cat—named for my endless typing career—required an emergency stay at the cat clinic (suffering from renal failure) in the same square of time that Dad was ambulanced to the hospital. The day after David died, the cat was out licking the floor of the back porch and the metal threshold at the door. While his behavior expressed the bizarre feeling of that day, we recognized something was wrong.

"Please hold on, Qwerty," pleaded Jason. "Not now. Please. Not now." That was well over a year ago.

But the time, as the Chambers Brothers (1967) once proclaimed, has come. David was always on this side of that song with me. I always thought those boring, repetitive workdays of my youth could not amount to time passing, that I'd get time off and for my slowness to mature. Aging would be delayed. But David's death has made me know that I too will be swept into the whitewater of senescence right around the next bend.

Dad's in the hospital and I'm back. He's in hospital white and he looks waxen, the "disappearing into thin air" color of his personal dread. I sit with him. He's in and out of sleep, but eventually awakens and we talk a bit. He's glad I'm here.

In this lucid moment, I say in a hushed tone, "Dad. Do you think . . . if we had everything to do over again? Do you think . . . what happened with me . . . would happen the same way? You know. If we could rework? Replay?" I sound like I'm speaking with my high school voice.

I can see the memory salts sifting through his mind: maybe he's picturing me at three, in my rocking chair in the road, singing to the sunrise. Or he's recalling us four Mohawk scouts in the woods on Saturday mornings. Could be he's making breakfast in the kitchen: hash with sunny-side-up eggs on top for us and cereal for the three hungry babies to be fed with the single bowl and spoon. Maybe he's running through the unexpected family prosperity that came later: the cottage, the lake, end-of-the-week Fridays heading up there from work with the second family; maybe the sunken boat at the bottom of the lake tumbles through his mind.

He strains a little as he speaks but finally says, with honesty: "I don't know."

I became one person out of all this and not another. But where did this one begin? What limitations of mine have played out in the whole story? What can I do now?

The hospital staff tell me they'll discharge Dad tomorrow. He's improved. I decide to stay for another two nights, rather than remain in my home among complicit silences that pronounce me dead along with David. Here, at least, I'm not alone. Here—seeing my parents on their way—this is one place I belong.

Margo and I take a long walk in the nearby nature preserve. When we return Marisol is already there, with her little Joshua, and they've started on the pizzas Max and I brought from town.

She has no idea about making the length of their visit reasonable. If it's four o'clock now, they will certainly stay until eight.

Joshua proves to be one hyper, out-of-control kid, very hard to contain—reflecting the environment he lives in. He's already overweight, because Marisol overfeeds him, as she does herself. They are both fat.

"Marisol, why can't you tell him he has to wait for us all to eat together? He screams for food and you shove it down his throat."

"I can't let him go hungry."

"Teaching him to wait is not letting him go hungry. A person can sit with his hunger until it's time to eat." I try not to feel thoroughly annoyed the minute I see them. Marisol is already shouting—about food—ordering her husband, when he arrives, to find her Diet Coke, as if it's an emergency. Joshua, who appears excited to see me, projects himself across the room like a missile, lands on me full force, then slobbers and rubs the food dripped on his shirt all over me. I throw him off and grab his arm. I'm firm, but I know he's reflecting Marisol when he acts so out of control. He blocks his ears with his fingers when I speak. Marisol yells at Fred and at Margo. Margo shouts back. We're all blown about by this storm of screaming.

"*I need a man who has powerful friends. I need a million dollars cash.*"

"Mum, please turn that off," I plead.

I make Joshua understand that his drooling and messing with his food makes me cross. "No one wants to be near you when you do that," I tell him. One wants to love a kid. But managing him is hard. Soothing doesn't work. Being commanding doesn't work. He's soon banging a pot with a large metal spoon. I take both objects away.

Marisol's continued yelling feeds the chaos. She shrieks about Joshua needing the salad she brought right away and about his not liking her pasta spirals, which are strewn on the living room floor. This urgency is full of psychotic anxiety and it is Joshua's model of behavior. How could I not feel hopeless and wish to escape? Marisol and Fred love their child, but they can never provide the kind of structured environment he needs. I bring out the child-puzzle he brought and try to settle us in the corner. But he can't be engaged. He's overstimulated. He won't come out for a walk around the yard with me.

Within an hour of their arrival, my nerves are frayed. When I find myself yelling over everyone to try to quiet them down, I go out and walk around the block to pull myself together.

Fred tries to engage me in conversation, but the chaos is too much. His wooden, Frisbee-size cross hangs from his neck. His tall body can handle large adornments. Apparently he's been getting in some trouble at work; I wonder if he goes there wearing this thing. Jason has often voiced the opinion that "this cross keeps Fred from murdering Marisol, which he probably wants to do several times a day. Let's just hope he never takes it off." I've never seen him without it. It seems he's now employed in the food-service part of a nursing-home enterprise and he's paid about ten dollars an hour. Yet Marisol, who doesn't work and spends much of her day sleeping (possibly due to her medication), hires sitters to care for Joshua.

Fred continues trying to talk with me, as he always does, about music from the '60s—his passion from childhood and a love of mine—while failing to see his son dump a new bowl of pasta spirals into the potted ficus tree beside him.

Later, after everyone is gone, Margo turns on *A Raisin in the Sun*, which she has preselected, after my father is hoisted and flown like a football pass across the kitchen to bed. "Touchdown," I yell after them. Max has long since exited the living room. Mum and Margo and I begin the movie. The relative silence is like warm, honeyed milk.

Then Mum says with utter shock, "This isn't *The Godfather!*" She begins thumbing anxiously through the *TV Guide*. "What happened to *The Godfather?*" She is quite agitated. "I thought we were watching *The Godfather*."

"No, Ma, you watched *The Godfather* last night and already once today," responds Margo. "This is *Raisin in the Sun*."

My mother gets riveted to the drama, and whenever Sidney Poitier or Ruby Dee expresses strong feeling, she's physically and verbally moved. "Oh, poor thing. Imagine . . ." She sits forward and calls out her empathy to Sidney Poitier as he pours his heart out. When the wave of emotion is over, Mum is back to the *TV Guide*, asking where *The Godfather* is listed and isn't that what we're watching, and why not.

Margo repeats, "We're watching this movie tonight."

"What I did last night is under the bridge." Mum laughs and makes a mock-frown, as if some part of her accepts her worsening condition without complaint.

My mother hasn't lost her personality. Will the same be true of me? Will I be so accepting in my old age? I wonder what my fate will be. Will I have the means to survive? I don't want to burden Jason and Susanna. Maybe I'll have Margo and Marisol as my caretakers. My money will support us all, but I picture us living here in this sordid dump, probably because they wouldn't go elsewhere. They'll read to me from the Bible all day and engage pastors to counsel me.

"Mum, a change is good for you," I offer. "You don't just want to watch the same movie every night."

"Well, I don't see why not," she says, setting her *TV Guide* down. She pauses, then looks at me and at Margo. "An old fool is the best fool," she pronounces.

Page One. Page One. Page One.

Steve and I will manage the estate—this special-needs trust. Our saga will remain stalled at the beginning, and will end only with the demise of some or all of us. But I hold to my notion that the three are getting better—mellowing. Setting them up should be straightforward, though we'll always need to manage their money. We might have no idea what we're getting into.

Steve believes that taxpayer support of people who want to get everything for nothing, who don't go out and work, causes their ruination and ours. Big government, he believes, coddles these people. He feels there are too many of them and that they'd be better served by having to stand on their own two feet and earn their own way. Ironically, we will be caught up in maintaining SSDI and HUD benefits for the three ad infinitum, while trying to see that they have a small financial cushion that's managed by the trust. Steve will become an expert in food stamps, housing, and disability allowances, and will counsel them on all of these benefits—with their limited capability, the three prove unable to act much on their own behalf.

Steve had Max advertise the lake house for summer rental on Craigslist. When weeks passed with no response, Steve was not able to find the ad on the web. Finally, he found it listed under Rhode Island. Max's logic was that a lot of people from Rhode Island like to rent in Vermont. He didn't seem to get that they would then look under Vermont.

"If I wanted to vacation in Jamaica," Steve explained, "I wouldn't look under California, where I live, because lots of Californians want to vacation in Jamaica. I'd look under Jamaica. Other Californians might want to vacation in Alaska."

Max changed the ad.

In the meantime, Steve asked Margo to go to an office supply store to photocopy Dad's life insurance policy and mail it to him. He received several copies of pages four and seven, none of pages two, eight, and ten. In total he has nineteen pages of the ten-page document, but not all of the ten pages.

"This is why they can't hold jobs," Steve surmises.

I'm here again to see my ailing father, and Margo is at her most assertive, shouting at the Bagnewskis across the street as well as at all of us. She says we don't see how these neighbors torment her with their noisy dirt bikes and their chain saws. We don't understand that they know she's fragile and just want to upset her. There's truth in this and I'm about to say so, but she continues that we also don't get that one of these neighbors' relatives fondled her breasts at a party when she was in high school.

This escalates. Mum is shouting back, having the rage reaction that Margo induces.

"Please everyone, I'm trying to find someone to love around here." I yell myself until my throat hurts and have to wonder what I'm doing in someone else's act. Dad, home and in his recliner, bursts into tears and blubbers and sobs.

"Will you stop that, Dad?" I say. "Please. Someone act like a grownup. Stop this crying and sniveling. Be an adult among the babies and I will too."

"You harass these people more than they harass you." Mum is aroused and focused, referring to Margo and the neighbors, and knows what she's about. And Margo is like someone clawing at her own cage.

"I'm having nothing more to do with you," Margo throws at me. "Nothing more to do with you," she throws at Dad. "And nothing more to do with you." She hurls her keys at Mum.

My mother, seated on the couch, looks around herself, as if Margo might be talking to someone nearby, and, seeing no one, says, "Well, I'll just take that sitting down."

Margo runs out and takes off in her car. I have the thought that she could have an accident, driving in that state of mind. She can be irrational and have her fits. But she would never intentionally hurt anyone, including herself.

I have to leave. I have a long drive ahead of me, and I could have an accident too.

Margo's freedom plan includes some idea that she'll move out; hard to imagine where, but I can identify with feeling trapped. This is the dull and limited environment that Steve and I made our way out of. The three are not able to do the same, mellowing or not.

"Sometimes she just thinks she's the cat's mittens," says my mother.

According to Steve, who learned it from Dad, Margo is thriving more than ever on the gourmet circuit these days. She studies recipe books all day, then sets off on her daily jaunts. I'm glad for her in one way. Why shouldn't she feel alive?

Except that Max told me no one eats the foods she buys. Then everything is left out to rot on the counters. The French triple-cream cheese (Brillat-Savarin) melts off the counters and "hangs like snot," reaching for the floor.

Steve speaks to Margo. I try to talk with her on the phone from my home too, when she's returned from her angry flight.

"I'm not trying to make you angry, Margo," I say. "Maybe buy just one treat per week. Buy something just for you, nothing out of the ordinary for them. And forget about those neighbors."

But that's not why she was angry. She was angry because someone let her cat out.

End of the End

Dad is dying.
Another stroke has left him unable to speak. Margo puts the phone to his ear when I call and he manages to utter my name. I try to fathom what he's feeling, trapped inside his failing body. Is he freaking out, or at peace? Margo thinks he's in a state of horror and Max thinks he's "just riding it out." I tell Dad I'll be there on Friday. It's Tuesday. I'm telling him to wait for me. He taps the phone with his fingernail to let me know he understands.

Qwerty is dying too. The course of their death plights is as if synchronized. Both have been dying for months: crisis and rally, crisis and rally. Emergency treatments happen on the same day. There's been more than one good-bye with each of them. Dad's strong appetite is gone. Qwerty has stopped eating altogether.

Jason called his two cats from the same litter "twins." Lemmy's full name was Elemenopee, which Jason once thought was all one interesting word when he learned the alphabet. He has numerous short-version nicknames. The cats attained personhood because of their duration and their engaging personalities; these two loving friends fill my rooms. My father knew these cats on all their visits and I recall how he played with them as they sat on his lap. Now, both Dad and Qwerty hang in through repeated hospitalizations. Eerily, I'll be driving Qwerty to the vet exactly as the ambulance gets Dad to the hospital. Both live in wasted bodies, holding on with strong wills.

Qwerty lies ailing here with me. My father lies ailing four states away. Both show the same keen spirit, even as their bones melt like icicles and their bodies turn to straw. Similar sounds whimper and whisper in their throats. Three weeks ago, Dad still maintained that he loved his life, even with his disabled left side. But Steve tells me my father wants to end his life. Probably both points of view are true. I fear Dad and Qwerty might finally die in the same moment. I want to be with both of them at their end.

I remind Dad of my early life with him, all the frogs, toads, fish, balloons, and bedtime stories—tiny fingers of memory are still cradled in his big kindling hand. Dad taps the phone.

"Those are precious moments, Dad."

He responds in sounds not unlike the purrs and ghost-meows of the cat, and also manages to whisper my name, "Ja Ja-nis," in syllables, whenever he can—if not in his full voice, at least in his sweetness. It's a tender experience.

"I'll be there Friday," I promise. "By late afternoon."

The cat stations his frail body under my desk and computer, where I sit. At night, I carry him downstairs, put him on the couch beside me, and watch rented episodes of *The Sopranos*. He crawls into my lap, bearing his body like a limp old sail borne on a brittle mast, and sleeps contentedly. Lemmy sometimes hovers or sleeps nearby.

Qwerty and I have a number of long good-bye sessions. I recount memories of all our twenty years—our life as a family, that once-happy constellation of husband, wife, child, and pets.

Tonkinese are extremely social. They both used to run with me when I covered a couple miles on our cul-de-sac. Not long ago, Qwerty, this dark, seal-pointed beauty, was the star of a dinner party I gave for a new group of colleagues and environmentalist friends. I've developed a circle of people with shared interests, though I wish I saw them more. Qwerty seated himself on one welcoming guest's lap—a respectful distance from the dinner plate—yapping and animatedly participating in the conversation. Always lively and present, he and the last TV repairman had an instant friendship. The man didn't want to leave. Whenever I ordered from catalogues on the phone, because he was so vocal, he became the subject until, finally, the person completing my order would say, "Tell Qwerty the package will arrive in two days." My writer's group made him an honorary member. Then Robert, who "hated cats," would arrive saying, "Where are they?" He'd then lie on the floor and let them surround and conquer him, causing me a spot of affection for him. I've found a veterinarian who comes to the home. The first time she came, Lemmy circled, supervising her handling of his brother.

It's Monday night. I interrupt my TV watching, take this skeletal being off my lap, and set him on the couch while I go upstairs to phone my father. Dad's whispers bear the sound of pure innocence. When I come back, the cat is gone. How can this be? He can barely move. I finally find him in the litter box, nestled in the beige clay grit like a killdeer, the bird that nests in beach sand and can hardly be seen. The sight is shocking, sad, and—strangely—almost funny. His symbolism is profound. Dying is a turning to waste.

"No, Qwerts, I'm not going to let you turn yourself to crap right now."

I bring him back upstairs to his spot on the soft towel on top of the wall-to-wall carpet under the computer. He lasts the night.

It's Tuesday morning and I'm sitting at my desk. My feet are on either side of Qwerty, propping his poor body up on the floor. I phone the vet. When Qwerty is comatose and still, he looks comfortable, and I really don't want to put him down.

I discuss this frankly with the vet, but using euphemisms, knowing it's possible that animals understand language when they've lived with people for twenty years. But I have to be with my father on Friday. Every few hours, the cat wakes up, cries out, and struggles. His meows are such gaunt, effortful rasps that I'm moved to tell the vet to come. Then I call back to say he's comfortable again and we should wait.

Sitting with my feet holding the cat, I phone Dad, say loving things, and end with, "Until Friday." His fingernail taps the phone three times. "Friday" has become my mantra with him.

I imagine Qwerty knows the dilemma I face. All day—Tuesday, July 10, 2007—this dear friend sleeps peacefully between my feet, looking comatose for hours, while I type. Then he wakes and struggles like a fledgling bird, trying to make his body work. I see patients as scheduled. I tell Qwerty I'll be in by eight. I hold him close, stroke him, and make him comfortable.

When I come in through the back-porch door, I hear a whimper-meow. He's found strength to call down and let me know he's waited. I know he hears my footsteps coming up the stairs. I find him lying on his side in the middle of the floor, having pushed out from under the desk; he lifts his head and seems to beckon me down to him. On the floor, with my face close to his, I extend my open palms. His meows are now a flight of repeated gasps and labored breaths. Then—the most incredible thing—looking into my eyes, he extends his two front legs, picks them up, and emphatically places them as one unit in my right hand. I close my hand lightly but firmly around those legs and he starts moving them back and forth—large, straight, forward, swim-like strokes, deep from the shoulders—having gathered up all of his last. All the while, he's holding my gaze. His back feet find my left hand and he pushes firmly against my palm so that he moves forward, using my hand as a launchpad for what seems to be a pushing off, taking flight. He appears to be going somewhere. And Qwerty dies, his eyes deeply locked with mine.

I will never forget those long, plushy-furred but emaciated legs moving so purposefully in my hand. The vet softly enters the room where I sit holding my old friend. She affirms that he's dead and swaddles him in something soft. He's still beautiful, his turquoise eyes wide open. "Oh, I'll never forget this little face," I say as I kiss those cheeks and let her take him away.

Lemmy sleeps by my left ear all night.

This morning, I sadly go through the motions of yoga before work, now with only one cat, not two, circling my postures and settling on my back when I parallel the floor.

Friday has finally come. I leave very early in the morning. A cat sitter will come to be with Lemmy. She knows him well and will spend time with him.

My tires roll again, inch by inch, from here to there—all those inches of the road, I reflect, are the product of human labor, the original workers probably all dead by now. Generations flourish and work and die. I relive a conversation I had with Dad when I was nine and we were driving together along one Sunrise Hill Road, a tarred road that turned soft in the heat. Sitting beside him in the front seat—taking in what was then an idyllic, houseless, forested landscape that ran alongside a wide, plunging stream—I asked if he felt terrible knowing he would die some day.

"I only feel bad thinking it will hurt you," he answered.

This drive is hard, like the highways ahead. It's early and it's hot. The sun has just barely extended its rays and already the steering wheel, even with the AC, is moist and glistening from my grip. That insistent sleep demand that began after David and I parted keeps coming over me. Twice I pull off the road for a twenty-minute crash-nap. I wake up thinking David is beside me. How I wish he were.

When I finally arrive in my old hometown, I see Erisman's Ice Cream Stand still there. I feel the most powerful urge to eat that ice cream. Dad and I—sometimes Dad and Mum and I, or Dad and Mum and Steve and Nana and I—used to pile into the car to go for this ice cream together. We'd park with the car doors thrown open and leave the motor running while we got our cones and ate in the car. Then the ice cream family grew too large for one car. I feel a pang of pity for the triplets that, through no intention of their own, their arrival created two families—families that could not all go for ice cream, or anywhere, together. But when I drove at sixteen, I took the three, and sometimes Steve, too, to Erisman's. Another family constellation. It was fun making those children happy.

I surrender to my ice-cream desire. I sit behind the steering wheel with a scoop of butter-crunch on a cone (Mum's and my favorite flavor) and recall when I worked here in high school. Scooping ice cream was the hardest physical labor I've ever done. Mr. Erisman, the boss, was a mean and exploitive guy who made his teenage employees put a nickel in a cup for every taste of ice cream they took, so they felt justified in stealing. Every now and then, I made skinny Dad an elaborate banana split and snuck it home under a jacket or a sweater.

Finally, I arrive at my parents' home and ascend the wheelchair ramp onto the back porch with all my dread in tow. One warped and rusted lawn chair sits among the boxes and bags of beer cans and wine bottles. I go straight to Dad's bed, a hospital bed supplied by hospice. Mum is there in their separate bed beside him, herself overwhelmed by sleep these last months, maybe years.

Dad looks wan and tired as never before. He manages again, with struggle, to whisper my name and I take his hand. He slowly whispers the names of all five of his children and within hours begins slipping into the convulsive movements we come to know as death throes, with a very dramatic "death breathing." When Greta, the attending hospice nurse, arrives, she explains the phenomenon of Cheyne-Stokes respiration: it is rapid, deep, and loud, with stops. It sounds very uncomfortable. But she assures us that people who've returned from this experience have reported no discomfort. Wish we really knew.

Margo is permanently stationed at Dad's side. Now Marisol arrives, and they stand like sentries. I don't want to be annoyed. They have every right to be here. Margo's been Dad's devoted caretaker. But they're all over him. They crawl into his bed, they merge with him, they read their Bibles aloud. To me they feel like suffocating monsters. Mum and Max and I find ourselves retreating to the living room. When I brave my way back in to hold Dad's hand and talk to him, it means dislodging the two fatsos. (It's a sad fact that Marisol is obese, partly due to her taking Stelazine. Margo is not fat at the moment—she works it off, when it happens—but her presence always feels large.) I have to stop these hard feelings; imagine the lives they've had, these two once-adorable tots. They are losing their father too.

"Let me have some time with Dad," I say calmly. They leave, and immediately start a ruckus in the kitchen—squabbling or praying, I can't tell. I manage to steal a little time alone with Dad, but it's not open-ended. I feel them waiting to come back in.

Dad seems largely in another world. Part of me wants to hold my breath and just get it over with—one of the worst feelings in all our existential predicament—waiting for someone you love to die. I talk to Dad, give him a little bouquet of words to take with him. I vote for the existence of an interminable soul, continuing greater realization beyond life. But of course, death could be immediately final, with nothing beyond. As far as Margo and Marisol are concerned, you rise up to sit in the sky and watch over your loved ones forevermore. It's a lovely idea.

Greta returns after midnight. She moves my father's position. He's been lying on his left cheek too long and there's a bruise spreading that remains for several hours. I lament feeling helpless. Dad looks like a foreign body. Greta asks us to leave while she changes his sheets. She has an expert touch and I feel assured that she's making my father comfortable in this strange journey. I don't take an active role in death. I'm frightened by it and don't know how I can improve. What would I do if I had more courage? In some cultures, families bathe and groom the body. And how much have my folks and I broken through our old estrangement? How much hold does that still have?

I haven't found a process here, much as I can't have a process with Dad now. It's like living under an occupation. But why didn't I take a strong leader position in helping us talk frankly about what happened when I was twelve? Mum and Dad and I could have realized how simply human we all are. One late afternoon several months ago, when Dad and I were alone in the living room, he began to say how he and my mother felt that I'd gone above them—that I felt superior and, I suppose, left them in the dust. They could have gone on to voice those feelings. I had started to tell him I felt they'd preempted my leaving by jettisoning me first. But at that moment, Marisol and Fred and the little screamer busted in. And there was no return to Dad's and my conversation. The fact is, a class difference did develop between us. A profound separation. Dad once said outright—when I was about fourteen and our family was upset all the time—that I was a snob who thought I was too good for everyone. We should have revisited the pain of all that.

"It's true," I answered at the time, casting my eyes over the chaos of baby detritus. It was not the fact of our limited means or our modest home that made me disdain the situation. It was our being overwhelmed—all day every day, without recourse. The helplessness and stupidity of our predicament distressed me, as did the feeling that this could only happen to us.

David and I shared the amazing plight of upward mobility. It was a thrill-ride to experience the good life we'd never imagined. But refining our vision of wealth and privilege took years, and we came to understand that living well is an art, a development of values and a refinement of taste. He and I finally took that route on separate roads. Our post-divorce houses were better reflections of who we were: his a post-and-beam construction perched above a river in the wilderness, mine a New England–looking Civil War–era gem, both modest and understated. As Mum would say, a fork occurred in our once-together road.

Greta tells us there are only hours left. Max and I try to get Mum to sign papers authorizing cremation. Mum sits on the living room couch, holds the papers, and reads them over and over again. Margo and Marisol finally agreed to cremation. They believe that burial is necessary to allow the body its final resurrection, but since they had their way about getting Dad baptized, they compromise.

Mum finishes reading both sides of the paper, then says, "What's this I'm signing? This is a cremation authorization."

"Yes, Mum," I say, "you have to authorize cremation because you're his wife."

"Well, is this what he wants?"

"We believe so. Steve and Max and I think he would prefer this to burial."

"Is he dying?"

"Yes, Mum. He is dying now."

"I know that. I do know that. I do." She looks down. "This says cremation authorization."

"Yes. Please sign. It has to be you." Max steps over and hands her the pen.

Several times, she poses the pen over the line and stops short.

Then she disappears and I find her in bed in the little room. Greta clears a place for herself to sit in the front sunporch. I hold

Dad's hand one last time, then retreat out of resignation and fatigue. Margo and Marisol are waiting at the door. I don't hate them. This is our reality. I've never tried to get to know them better. I should do that, get to know them beyond their nonsense. Find out who they really are. I will do that.

At 2:00 a.m., I open up the living room couch. A monitor beside me is tuned to Dad. I listen to his breathing, and it's as if he's right next to me all night long. But only as if... Maybe it's not just about those two standing in my way; maybe in going to bed I'm opting out and not admitting my lack of courage. Maybe I'm running from death. But no. If my sisters weren't there, I wouldn't be in here, leaving Dad alone. Mum would be there, too. Max would be there, a quiet presence in the background. There's no question, my sisters take over and crowd others out.

Dad moves into that phase called the death rattle. Before dawn, I go to him. My sisters have been there all night. I remind myself that there was a time when I actually did have Dad all to myself, those seven years when I was his only child. Five of us are losing him now. My sisters have rushed in and staked their claim. They won so long ago.

Max appears and right away screaming voices order him to close the window and move the dresser back from the bed. I yell at them to stop yelling. Max has never been able to defend himself.

This goes on all day Saturday. At one point, I find Margo in bed with Dad.

"Get out of there," I yell.

It's Saturday afternoon, and Dad is slipping further. Max comes into the living room where I'm sitting with Mum. We're repeating our round about the cremation authorization, but for the moment Mum and I are silent, solemnly reckoning with the moment. Dad is about to die any minute.

"Do you want to go for a walk around the nature preserve?" Max suddenly asks me, as if this is an ordinary day.

"No way!" I exclaim, irritated by this jarring intrusion.

An hour passes, he and I again try to get my mother to sign the document. Same ritual: she studies the page as if she's never seen it, gets to the end, turns it back over and says, "This is about cremation."

"Yes, Mum. You need to sign it," I repeat wearily.

"Well, I need to read it over first."

"You just did, Mum. He's going to die soon."

"Well, I need to read it again."

I want to give the papers to the men who come to take Dad to the funeral home. No one here can be trusted to do it tomorrow, and I won't have the time.

In one go-round, Max and I both sit to the right of Mum on the couch—me next to her, Max next to me—when suddenly his hand falls onto my thigh. I quickly remove it and jump up. "Max, what the hell?" Then, not knowing what else to say, "Let's talk."

We step out onto the smoke-infested back porch.

"Max, you're having some kind of thoughts and fantasies about me..."

"Y-e-e-e-a-a-h," he answers. "I think about you a lot."

"Well, I don't know what you think is going on?"

"I just think about us holding each other," he says.

"What do you mean?" I ask, already wishing I hadn't.

"Well, it's not so much about having sex," he launches in, as if he's received my permission, "it's mostly just holding each other. I want to hold you and touch you. A lot."

I'm dumbfounded.

"I want to wear your clothes," he adds.

All this is stated as if we're talking about the ordinary.

I'm creeped out and feeling for my brother at the same time. He's losing his father, and longs for comfort. I understand.

"Max, you have to know. I'm your sister."

"Y-e-e-a-a-h-h," he says flatly.

We return to the living room. Mum is studying the cremation authorization. We both stand in front of her. She looks up, then places the paper carefully and significantly on the table. "For heaven's sake. Can't I at least wait until he goes?" she says.

"Of course you can, Mum. I didn't understand," I say. "I'm sorry."

Dad dies at 10:00 p.m. His skin turns a dun mushroom color and his mouth opens wide, as if to let his soul escape. He is one month short of his eighty-ninth birthday. As my eyes flood, looking at my father, Max enters the room behind me, holds up his camera, and snaps a flash photo of him—eliciting shrieks from Margo and Marisol, who are still at their places on each side of Dad.

"Stop that screaming! Both of you," I holler back. Their loudness is more shocking than Max's action. And Dad's moment of death is lost.

"He can't come in here and take Dad's picture," Margo shouts. "It's disrespectful."

"You don't tell anybody else how to experience their father's death. If this is what Max needs, weird or not, you respect that. It isn't harming anyone."

My sisters jump up and take clippings of Dad's hair. I drop any aggravation that distracts from the truth of this white-hot moment. Dad has gone into thin air. Greta has us leave the room again and she dresses Dad in a wine-colored, satin-looking sweatsuit—something he would have liked, and certainly chosen for him by Margo. Then we're all invited to see him in his final resting state.

There are families who would do what the hospice worker just did. But I never bathed or dressed my father when he was alive. I couldn't be close to his nakedness in death. This seems a sad limitation. I had the same limitation with David. I wish I'd been all possible things to him in his last days. David, you're the site of so many personal failures. Mine, and yours, too. I wish we'd been better, but we were young and both "unfinished."

With Dad, I know that my imperfections are all right. I don't feel remorse and heartbreak as I do with David. With Dad, you never had to get things right.

The large toenail of Dad's right foot has turned iridescent, a nacreous purple-gray, like mother-of-pearl. This seems to have happened just as he died. The toenail turned to shell—as if Dad might be returning to the sea...

Two young men in suits arrive and place him into a body bag and lift him onto a stretcher. My sisters walk with them. Max and I walk behind. My mother is standing in the kitchen, but she runs now into the living room—"I don't want to see this. No. I don't want to see."

I go to her and hug her and tell her that whatever she wants to do is fine. I tell her we'll be right back. Then I walk behind the little crowd making its way through the debris on the sunporch, lit only by the streetlight (our front house lights don't work), and down those front steps of Dad's own making with his father, on that day I remember so well.

"Take a good look," Max says to me, as they pass our father through the double-doors on the back of the hearse. "You're seeing him for the last time." He and I follow out to stand in the road and watch the car drive out of sight.

Dad's last moment on Earth occurred on Saturday, July 14, 2007, at 10:00 p.m. He waited for me to come and he uttered all his children's names.

We all return—fatherless—to the living room. My sisters wail and hold one another. Mum is sitting on the couch. I sit beside her and put my arm around her. Her face is wet with calm tears. Then she reaches for the cremation authorization, picks it up, picks up the pen, and signs it, just like that. Max promises to take it to the funeral parlor in the morning.

This morning, Max comes upstairs early, while I'm pouring a cup of coffee.

"I have to apologize for how I behaved last night," he says.

I'm shocked on top of the full roll of other feelings I'm experiencing. "Yes?!"

"I behaved very badly."

"Yes?" There is a silence while I pour milk into my coffee and stir. "Did you stay awake last night over this?" I look at him.

"Yeah. I couldn't sleep at all. I behaved . . . abominably. I hope you will forgive me."

Abominably.

This is the most expression I've ever known from Max. I appreciate his sincere attempt to make it better.

"I hope you will forgive me."

"I do understand, Max. You were feeling the loss of Dad."

"Y-e-e-e-a-a-h."

"We all went through Dad's death last night. None of us is in our normal state of mind."

It's Sunday, midmorning, the day after my father died. I take leave of everyone, having offered what comfort I can. Months ago, I signed up for a conference in Provincetown on the Cape—and once again, death provides no reason not to go. Had he not died, I'd have canceled.

Since Dad is to be cremated, there's no reason to rush the memorial. We've set the service date for Saturday, a week away—to give people notice and a better chance to get there. So strange to have no reason not to attend my conference as planned, when something so momentous has happened. When someone has died, all urgency is over! I bring Mum her morning coffee and she sits quietly on the couch. I stay another few hours in silent solace. I'll be back on Friday.

This day—the first day in eighty-nine years that my father has no more existence, the first day in my life that no man on Earth calls me "daughter"—is strangely still and saturated with mystery. Out on the Cape, I stand in the sandy parking lot of a restaurant where I was first taken by my parents and Nana when I was about five and we all ate fried clams. The air feels portentous. The sun looks stunned and ghastly pale. Milky light spills over everything, as if the sun is melting down over the trees.

"Dad, what would you think if I told you that you died last night?"

Incredibly, the trees begin to rustle and stir, as if in answer. Their nodding speeds up until they're casting their branches around: giant headdresses on giant dancers who start with some slow, ponderous agreement. It's a fabulous frenzy, a unified chorus.

Suddenly, they all go curiously still and wait. Then the motion slowly resumes, until trees are again hurling their branches around like strong arms of old-world laundry women slapping wet, dripping garments upon rocks on the riverbank. Then they slow again to something like a sacred hush. They seem to huddle their leafy heads together and come up with some universal dance, choreographed before my eyes.

I don't doubt what's happening. It doesn't even feel extraordinary. It's God in the face, this day, this week, this gathering of energy, this rush and stop, this dull knowing that my father is gone. Grown old and gone. Qwerty gone. Grown old and gone. David gone, cheated of the rest of his life. Me, closer every day to my own demise. The sun has poured its warm liquid glow down on the world in a new way today. I've never seen light like this.

No Song to Write About It

After that sunny day with the mystery of trees astir on the Cape and a summer wind I've never known, Steve comes from California to be with my mother. I phone him, but in keeping with his taboo, we say nothing about how he is or how I am. I wonder how much more I'll visit without Dad there.

Friday has come, and I'm back. The house looks stark, pinned in place by a cloudless blue sky. The ramp is gone, as if it vanished into thin air with Dad.

Steve comes out to greet me. We actually hug. He tells me about plans for Dad, says my mother sleeps all the time and that it's strange without Dad.

We walk up the crumbling back steps.

"It must have been a tough week for you here," I say.

He agrees but assures me he's spent time up on the lake, continuing his assault on the red squirrels. He's shot eleven just this week.

"Perforating the foundation again, are they?" I say, uncomfortable with the subject of killing right now. I should have known he didn't just stay here with Mum. I can't blame him. I say something limply sympathetic about the murdered squirrels.

The Cape Cod conference on trauma gave me a deeper understanding of the defensive function of dissociation, that altered mind-state people can enter to escape a heavy reality. I've arrived here full of thought.

Everyone is in the living room, in their usual places: strung along the wall like birds on a power wire, facing the TV.

I speak into the sluggish silence: "Greetings from Provincetown."

It feels too difficult to launch right in about Dad. I could ask how everyone is, what's been happening, although those questions don't always receive normal treatment. But I see myself entering our family tragedy from a comfortable, protective distance. I'm making my way back from the seashore. It seems a neutral subject, not likely to elicit tangents, bizarre flights, or dull silence.

Attention is turned toward me.

"I haven't been to Provincetown for a long time," I offer. I'm sure it's a place they must know well. "The place has changed quite a bit." I don't intend to go on long, because I'm braced for Steve to interrupt.

He doesn't. No one especially responds. But no one brings up anything else. That leaves me hanging, feeling the need to fill the silence, though I know this is one silence that shouldn't be filled. I should linger and let the real subject surface.

But I need steps up to talk of Dad. I'm trying to transition from where I've been to where I am. So a nervous state takes over. I avoid our new reality, and continue running unchecked through impressions of Provincetown. *Stop talking about Provincetown*, I say to myself. Yet I run on about ocean breezes, sailboats, and lobsters. I tell myself I'm just taking the long way around.

Steve doesn't stop me. Max is in Dad's recliner, staring. Mum is on the couch. Margo is rocking vehemently in the antique chair Max acquired from the furniture refinishing place, once his daily workplace. Steve sits with his back to the fish tank. I sit on the couch with Mum and continue talking.

Finally, I shut up.

The TV is on, the Muzak playing. No one else speaks.

I start again. "Dad must have loved Provincetown. He must have gone there when he spent all his childhood summers in Gloucester with his cousins. I felt he was with me this week."

But I'm filling a very difficult blank. Our father has died. Steve's lack of cutting and abusive interruption throws me off completely and makes me uncomfortable.

Suddenly Margo jumps up, pointing toward the window behind me and Mum. "Look. Look at that!" she says. "There's a rabbit. Right out there in the yard." She says this as if it's a holy revelation.

"Oh, look," says Steve sarcastically. "It's Dad. Everyone say hello to Dad."

Margo sits back down and resumes rocking. "I've been talking to Dad," she says.

"Oh?" I'm the one who responds. "And is Dad talking to you too?"

"Yes."

"How is that?"

"He enters my prayers."

"How very nice. How is he?" I'm picturing him in saintly robes.

"He's doing fine. He's up on the lake."

I refrain from asking if he's walking on the water, or if he's been disturbed by Steve shooting all the squirrels. All I say is, "Nice you have a special line to Dad."

Then Jason walks in, just back from a recording session in LA. A flurry of hugs and embraces dissolves back into stasis. Then he takes a seat on the couch with me and Mum. "How was Provincetown?" he asks.

I'm sorry to say a further run of impressions ensues, how much Provincetown and gay culture itself has changed. People there are friendly now, I say, not exclusive the way they were in the past. "They meet eyes; they say hello; they hold doors open and chat." I stop talking, feel the weight of lethargy all around—then nervously continue, starting and stopping. I probably could use some help here with reentry. Wouldn't that be nice!

I stop myself. "Where's that rabbit?"

Margo doesn't argue or press on about the rabbit. Jason signals me not to ask about his trip. I know he had a dicey negotiation with his producer; we'll talk about it later.

But now Steve has seized on the subject of homosexuality, which is not the subject I was talking about. He's been triggered into bringing up The Folsom Street Fair, a distasteful-sounding annual street performance by a subset of the gay men's community in San Francisco that Steve has attended and photographed to feed his negative vision of humanity and God knows what else. "Men fornicating in the streets, walking around buck naked. You've never seen anything so disgusting in your life," he chooses to explicate. He must be talking about elsewhere-and-not-here for the same reason I am.

"Steve," I offer, "I'm talking about nice people making a place beautiful with front-yard gardens, inviting to outsiders. This other thing sounds gross."

I have to assume everyone is in the same state of mind: a tiny bit dissociated. I press my feet hard against the floor, my back against the lumpy couch, and remind myself again to be quiet, breathe, and be here now. I should just say how hard it is that we've all lost Dad. But Margo gets up and storms out of the room, saying that God disapproves of homosexuality.

I ask Jason about LA. anyway. He needs help with reentry too.

But it's not going to go that way.

Margo returns, carrying a tall glass with clinking ice cubes, chewing on ice and announcing between crunches that there will be no more talk of homosexuality. I miss Dad. He's always been my reason to be here. Mum is largely out of commission. Her sweep of hair glows. But she's gone. I'll visit her again, but it won't be the same.

For unimaginable reasons, Steve now brings up my Uncle Armand's suicide some fifty years ago. Mum looks shocked.

"Armand was Mum's baby brother," I explain to Jason, as if he didn't know, while turning off the TV in a way my mother won't notice.

She turns it on again. She's not fighting with me. She just has no memory.

Suddenly, she sits forward and lucidly says, "I don't know if I should say what I'm thinking right now. But I will. My mother was a fat, lazy slob who left us all on our own. She never got out of bed and I had to take care of her and protect her and find food for my younger brothers and sisters."

Jason and I openly cheer the triumph of her moment, thinking this might be her first admission ever of the burden of her growing-up years.

But Steve is back on suicide, saying he often wanted to leave a gun next to my father in his bed. That's where he's going.

"Maybe that wasn't Dad's thing," I retort.

"*I had heard you were a serious man*," Mum calls out.

I grab the control.

From here, the conversation is a melee. There's my voice still bringing in the sun, the tides, the shifting dunes. Steve is back on Folsom Street. His tone is angry. No one responds, and the room grows silent. Jason asks Max about his awesome fish tank and gets an answer that quickly runs its course. A remark floats through about bears around the lake, a question that, oddly, leads to talk about the music industry and the lack of sidewalks in Los Angeles. Jason and I each say a little about our travels to fill the tense silence. My mother appears to have left the room.

Suddenly, Steve jumps up, grabs his straight-backed chair, whirls it around, places it in front of the fish tank, and sits down with his back turned to us, staring at the fish. Steve is sulking.

Leadership is needed in the Ahlenberg living room. And if it's up to anyone, it's up to me. I'll bring it up. "How is everyone?" I'll ask. "Do we want to check in with each other? All of us together and each of us alone has had a major loss. Sometimes it's easier to talk about other things." What's been the drag on me? I don't want Dad to be dead.

Margo leaves again and Mum is nowhere to be seen and definitely not coming back. She's probably snuck back to bed.

Steve whirls around, body and chair. He, who never allows conversation in his presence but has been letting us go on and on, has been building up a head of steam. Now he explodes. "Well, congratulations, you two have taken over the room, talking about your own business, completely excluding Max and me. You'll notice everyone else has left. I'm going to sleep. Hope you're satisfied with yourselves. Good night."

It's eight o'clock.

"Max shares my opinion that the two of you are selfish, talking about your own thing and ignoring the rest of us." He turns back.

I'm aghast. I'm alarmed.

"Wait a minute, Steve," says Jason. "We weren't stopping anyone else from talking. Come back and let's talk now."

Steve, who is exiting the room in a huff, whips right back in again.

"Let's all talk like civilized adults," Jason says.

Steve hears this as a suggestion that he's acting like a child, and it's too much provocation. He storms toward us, looking violent, and looms intimidatingly over us, jabbing his finger as he yells. Jason and I quickly rise to standing. I think he's going to hit Jason, who is both shocked and provoked himself. Just as it looks like Steve is about to throw a blow and Jason just might respond in kind, I step between the two tall men and push them apart.

Steve keeps saying to Jason, "We have to go outside and talk."

"Oh, no," I say. "Not with that rage in your eyes. Back off!"

Suddenly dishes crash in the kitchen, my mother calls out, and there is a thump that sounds like she's fallen. We three run to her, Max trailing behind. She has come from her bed into the kitchen and stepped on Max's cat's dishes, which I and the visiting social workers have repeatedly pointed out as a danger;

Max has been asked a hundred times not to put those dishes there, right in the path from the bedroom. There are four dinner plates on the floor, each one strewn with the last crumbs of cat food eaten over the last week.

Steve goes rushing to my fallen mother, shouting "Oh, my God! Oh, my God! Look what the two of you have done." He helps her up. She says she's upset by the yelling and asks us all to promise we won't fight anymore. We promise. Jason and I hug her and reassure her. Then Steve gets her back to bed.

Max tugs at my elbow and tells me he does not agree with anything Steve said.

Then we four go outside, at Steve's insistence, and stand in the yard. This somehow moves Steve into a better spot.

"Once long ago," he says, "Dad and I were looking up at the stars, and he said to me, you see how small we are in comparison with all the universe . . ."

"Yes," Jason says. "We should all appreciate how small we are. Grandpa was so wise."

Steve visibly calms down. He starts repeating, "Yeah he was such a great guy. There were a lot of things he understood. He loved his family." Then he finally says, "*This* was the night I wanted to have tonight. This is just what I wanted us to be doing."

Jason and I talk on our way back to the motel later. Jason remembers that Steve was good with him as a toddler.

"He was great with me until I entered my teens," he says. "Then something happened and he couldn't deal with me anymore."

"That must have hurt, Jason."

"Yeah. But I got used to it. I've got Daddy's family. I don't really need Steve. It doesn't hurt me the way it hurts you."

"You and I were probably not at our best tonight, either."

"Yeah. We weren't. There's no song to write about it."

After All

Deaths often cause violence and rifts in families. My brother and I only continue our connection as active co-executors. I agree to drive the many hours back to my mother's house one weekend in the fall to start the financial ball rolling.

Except for issues concerning the estate, it will be four years before Steve and I will see or talk to one another again. Jason's relationship with him will cool indefinitely.

It's a cold Saturday morning in our rude New England mill town, a week before Thanksgiving. I decided not to stay in my mother's house during this visit. Margo said she would not be able to clean because she's busy taking a course and she'd have a nervous breakdown if she cleaned, which I suspect is true. Not only is the house a mess, she tells me, but Mummy has taken all of Daddy's clothes out of his drawers and closets and put them in all the chairs and in his recliner, maybe imagining she's put him sitting there. I asked if Mum is entitled to a cleaning service on the home health care policy, but Margo said she has no time to call agencies while she's taking her course. She's reading Noam Chomsky and Jonathan Kozol and is having to write papers. She is finally going to have a career, so late in life—in special-needs education. She tells me most days she doesn't even brush her teeth. But I see improvement, and no one is more her champion than I. She couldn't have read these authors in the past. Her brain was too twisted, her days too fractured. Her mellowing has been a lifetime in coming.

I phone my mother several times before leaving the motel this morning, but Mum doesn't answer her phone anymore. I call Margo, headquartered upstairs, right above Mum, and she says she doesn't want to get up yet.

"I told you I have to get Mummy to the bank today." I'm walking toward the car, talking on my cell phone. The words I utter into the cold go up in plumes before my face. "Our appointment is at ten, and they close at noon. Could you please get her up and remind her? I've told her, but she can't remember."

"Well, I don't like what you're trying to do."

This sounds ominous. "Margo, please cooperate. I've explained what I'm here to do. I'm carrying out Mum and Dad's wishes, according to their trust. I'm co-executor, and I've come a long way to get things going."

"You're not. Ma is executor. I've read over the trust and she's executor and you're not."

"Mum has signed over certain duties to me and Steve. Things she can't do herself. Mum and Dad put these protections in place for this day." Steve set up today's plan with the bank.

"You're trying to take advantage."

"Of what? We're getting Mum's signature verified and put on the Trustee Certification form, because she's lost all her identification. She has to sign her money market account over to the trust now or there'll be a tax penalty. What else can I do to help you to understand? I'm coming over there to get Mum now."

Clouds gather like burly polar bears. All is still; not even slight, ragged wafts ruffle the brush of the meadows I drive past.

I arrive, hold my breath through the solid block of cigarette smoke on the back porch, and notice that instead of coffee cans filled to overflowing with butts, Max has lined a large, perfect bird's nest with those cigarette ends; they're all arrayed in a neat spiral to the rim. The design has the perfection of the nautilus seashell.

I don't know what to make of this piece of pollution. Or

is it art? It certainly has wit, humor, imagination. A kind of integration? Max loves both cigarettes and birds. Bluebird boxes or bird feeders are stationed outside all the windows now and smoking is his way of life. He's given up drinking. I'm hopeful that he's mellowing, too. I'm not expecting miracles, but I am thinking that brain disorders might become less disordered in midlife. Margo and Max are embarking on careers. Marisol is establishing that family of her own.

I find Max in the living room in his pajamas, staring with glazed eyes at the TV, which has a fixed picture and is playing Muzak. As usual.

"Hi, Max." I note that the house is as much a slum as ever, all presided over by one huge HDTV, which is probably the only thing anyone here sees.

"Is Mum awake?"

"I don't know."

"Well, I guess I've driven all these hours to find out."

Mum's amazing plants are now lined up along the counters and windowsills in the kitchen: more African violets, the prayer plant, the Tibouchina. Mysteriously, each plant has a single piece of paper inserted among its leaves. They look like supplicants bearing messages. I look closely. One piece of paper is the electric bill, one is the phone bill, one the property tax bill—all hailing On High. So, this is how Mum remembers to pay the bills. She doesn't forget her plants. Her Christmas cactus is as old as my youngest siblings. It's in full blossom but with many of the flowers fallen to the floor and trampled, a scattering of petals to prepare my procession across the kitchen.

I knock loudly and call outside my mother's room. I hear her voice and push hard on the stuck door, which squeaks and squawks until it blasts open and I go flying in.

"Hi, Mummy. It's me. Can you get up now?"

"Am I dead?"

"No. You have a day to face."

"Well . . . if I'm not dead." Her fingers are grabbing at her bedspread.

"You're not dead. What are you doing, Mum?"

"I'm trying to get home." She's pulling out of sleep.

"Where is that?"

"Well, it's right on the tip of my tongue."

"You must have been dreaming. Remember I was coming today?"

"Oh, yes," she lies and sits up. "Oh. It's you. I'll be a monkey's whatsis."

I hug her, noticing that her bedside clock says two fourteen. It's actually nine thirty. "This is where I left you three months ago. Have you been in bed all this time?"

She laughs.

"Would you like to get up now?"

"Well, is there a day happening?"

"Oh, Mummy, you don't have your mind anymore."

"Well, I don't miss it."

"Can you please get dressed? Do you remember we have an appointment at the bank?"

"No. I don't."

"Remember I told you?"

"No. I don't."

"You have to sign your money market account over to the trust. Then Steve can pay your bills online. You've lost your wallet, and no one here is capable of finding it. You have no picture ID, no social security card, no identification at all."

"I'll be damned."

I get a pair of slacks out of her closet and place them on the bottom of the bed. "I've got your Frederick's of Hollywood fashions here. A woman named Linda has your signature on file at the bank. She'll verify it and we'll be all set. Let's go. Linda's waiting. Please get dressed."

"Where's the daylight?"

"Look. Here." I pull up the blinds. The gray light that enters through the window lays like lead. The naked trees outside, when lit copper and bronze in a sunset, resemble muscular, young warriors. Today they look stalwart and stark.

"There it is," she says, happily. "Where's God today?" She turns her face up to bask in the limp daylight.

"God's waiting for you at the bank."

Standing in the kitchen—in a cloud of fruit flies—I ignore the white dust spread all over the floor, as if something made of flour has splattered down from above. Margo must have been baking. I've promised myself to ignore these details. I'm not here armed with rubber gloves and scrubbers and chisels to attack the refrigerator, which I know contains revolting, fermenting messes. Pure chaos trails in Margo's wake, especially where she's been cooking. She takes the role of family cook seriously. An acne of jam and spilled soup dots the counter. No one cleans up. The next meal gets prepared on top of the last.

"Hurry up, Mummy," I call out, resisting these distractions. The big clock beside the refrigerator says four thirty-eight.

I began cleaning this house right after the babies were born. It's as if I never stopped. I'm stopping myself today. Later we can all relax and visit, maybe even take care of something else. But for now, Steve has convinced me that no living person, not even our mother, should be running around without identification and no verifiable signature. This simple single thing will get done.

I knock again and offer Mum coffee. She pops out in her charcoal slacks and a smart burgundy sweater, as if she goes out on the town every day. Margo knitted this sweater, gave it skilled cables and complex swoops around the collar. Margo is superb at knitting. If she chose to knit for a living, she could earn top dollar. But she's unable to do anything in a sustained way. Her special education course is an unprecedented achievement. (Actually, Margo has told me recently that she completed two additional years of college over the years. She took pre-med courses: organic and inorganic chemistry. But she couldn't go further in her education until now). Margo also buys all my mother's clothes with a nose for bargains; she keeps my mother well dressed and well groomed, but can't do the same for herself.

Mum steps along with pride and a smile. She looks vibrant. Her white hair gleams, swept in one long, smooth wave around her pretty face. Her eyes remain their vivid blue. She still has her beautiful smile. Her teeth have turned brown, but her skin is pearlescent. She takes the cup of coffee I offer her, brings it into the living room, and sits down on the lumpy couch.

"Drink up quickly, Mum. We have to get to the bank." The fruit flies are swarming and making me itch.

"Why are we going to the bank?"

"I'm not going to tell you again."

"Oh, yes. They say I'm coming down with Alzheimer's."

"That's right. But it's okay. We're taking care of everything."

Margo appears—tall and overweight right now—wearing what look like flannel pajama bottoms, decorated with little white men that flutter down the floppy pant legs as if poured from a shaker; her top is an old sweatshirt and her thick, waist-length hair looks like a hayfield gone to seed. But she's still beautiful, with Dad's chiseled features and high cheekbones.

She goes straight to my mother's freezer, takes out the ice tray, and presses cubes into her oversized plastic tumbler. I refrain from saying anything when she leaves the ice tray out to melt and overflow and join all the other liquids and sauces that dribble off the counter, rather than add some water or simply put it back in the freezer. Soon she's crunching on ice. She will later this day go to the McDonald's drive-thru to buy another large iced coffee, as a way of getting more ice. It's a daily ritual, and a huge expense on her small disability income. When I've asked her why she doesn't just make more ice in the ice cube trays, her answer has always been, "It takes too long."

Max leaves the room to go down to the cellar. I assume he's retreating for the day. But then he returns with forms I need to take to the bank. Steve has managed from California to guide Max through the process of printing them out and even filling out the needed information in ballpoint pen.

Margo asks to see the forms. But I know she'll see some word or phrase to send her off on a tirade. Then we'd be in the land of berserk, everyone screaming 'til we all go up in smoke.

Six years ago, my parents spent a long weekend talking with me and Steve about administering this "special needs" trust for the three. We were both ambivalent. "You realize we'll be doing this for the rest of our lives," Steve said. "We'll be buying their toilet paper forever." But the need was obvious and we finally agreed to take it on.

The main objective of the document was to protect the triplets' disability incomes, to protect them from homelessness, and to protect everyone from Margo. There was just enough money and property from all my father's working years to make it worth doing. But all Margo understands is that the trust gives us power over them. She doesn't grasp the necessity and purpose of this arrangement. Mum and Dad should have explained it to them. Maybe they did. I'm trying to do that now.

"Margo, you've got to trust us. I've explained why things have been arranged this way. I need Mum's copy of the trust to bring that to the bank. I believe you've taken it."

"You have your own copy."

"No. It didn't arrive before I left."

"I don't like what you're trying to do," she says, grinding away on her ice cubes.

"I told you exactly what we're trying to do," I say, snorting *Drosophila*. "No matter how carefully I spell it out, you fight us. No one is out to do you harm. No one wants to institutionalize you, as Marisol tells me you fear. We're acting to protect you three, according to Mum and Dad's wishes, written in this trust, back when they were in their right minds."

"Marisol doesn't understand this."

"Marisol does understand. Marisol takes her medication."

"You're not the executors. Ma is."

"Mummy is, Margo, but she does not want the duties and responsibilities that go with it." Why am I bothering to spell things out, if my words don't register? I persevere anyway. "She doesn't want to go to courthouses and file documents and get things notarized. She doesn't drive anymore. She doesn't even leave the house. I'm not sure she gets out of bed every day. She signed a form that gives Steve and me the right to do all this work. And we are willing to do it. But you must see how hard it is; we don't exactly live nearby. I'm still working and can't get here often. We need to go now."

Mum says, "Well, I just want to finish my coffee."

"Yes. Finish your coffee. I know you never miss your morning coffee."

I sit next to her on the couch, pitching north, waiting for Margo.

She finally emerges, firmly clutching the document between rigid covers. "Ma didn't drink coffee when she had cancer," she says. "She gave up coffee then."

"What?" says my mother. "I had cancer?"

"Yes, you did." Margo's words strain through her crunching.

"I did? Where?! You've gotta be kidding. You'd think I'd remember that."

"Yes, Mummy," I say. "It was a long time ago. You had breast cancer."

"And I forgot? I can't imagine." She sets her cup down on the coffee table, deeply concerned, and looks down at her chest, where she sustained a double radical mastectomy.

"I can't believe I'd forget something like that." Her tone is mournful. She turns silent and thoughtful, studying the flattened burgundy field of her chest, from left to right and back, then adds, almost childlike, "I keep wondering where they went."

"Yes," I say. "It was serious and you were very brave."

"Where did the other one go?"

"You had it twice. There were two mastectomies."

"My God, the things I'm forgetting."

"You came through it all very well. You couldn't have done better."

"I have always believed in the power of positive thinking. No matter what."

"I know, Mum. Down every dead-end road you've ever gone, you've encountered a sign that says 'Think Positive,' and you've come away with that. No complaint. No sorrow. No railing at Fate. And now you just live in the moment. Anyway, please drink your coffee so we can go."

"Margo, I need to see that trust. I need to see the date."

"I'm not letting this out of my hands."

"Why?"

"Ma told me not to."

"That is not your document."

"It's not yours either."

"Margo, you're not doing right by anything here. Legal or financial. There are bills not getting paid. The legal bills are not getting paid."

"That's because you're trying to say Ma is incompetent."

"Just paying the bill does not declare her incompetent." I don't want to be feeling my blood boil. I was hoping for a decent visit.

Margo is beyond her darkest years, I remind myself, recalling things she would not do now. She doesn't stalk priests anymore. There are no clergymen or veterinarians or politicians with restraining orders against her. No dead cats in her freezer. She hasn't accused any rapists lately and she has no lawsuits going that I know. She still calls the police every few days and sirens and cruisers and fire trucks come tearing up the road. And there are Max and Marisol too: three of them for Steve and me to oversee. Three is just too many. And Margo obstructs everything we try to do.

"Margo, I need to take that trust with me. Give it to me now."

"Well, I have to see those forms you have."

"No. You do not."

"Then I'm coming to the bank."

Well, this certainly is not going well!

Margo goes to stand at the door, clasping the trust firmly to her heart. She's not going to relinquish it and apparently she's going to stay in her pajamas. I wonder why I've taken on this aggravation. I remind myself that I do have a busy and demanding profession, and a developing social life, following a sorry divorce and the tragic death of my former husband. I don't need to be spending time on futile endeavors.

I swat fruit flies out of my blind spot.

Nothing more may be accomplished today than a visit to Mum. She appears to find my visits pleasant. And I feel I have my mother now, this moment. Beyond that, it's hard to know my meaning to her. And she's now retreating further into that mystery of her being, maybe purposefully escaping the experience of old age.

"You're eighty-eight years old, Mum," I say with awe and complicated affection.

"No, I'm not!" She accepts help getting her coat on. "Where did you say we're going?"

"Come on, Mum, it's a surprise."

"Look at this gray sky," she exclaims, coming through the door. "What is it they say? Heaven might wait . . . but not the tide or the snow? There's something I'm trying to say, but . . . well, Christ if I know."

Standing on the walkway, she looks around, as if revisiting an old, long-out-of-reach memory. This small yard once teemed with those magic Chinese lanterns, an orange miniature type of hibiscus Mum was able to grow even in our northern climate. Her extravagant trumpet vine spread out under the kitchen window, where I once washed dishes the livelong day. Those vines with their hummingbird retinue sustained me. Her morning glories were so splendid that my child-friend Ellie and I used to kiss their centers before they closed up for the day. Given how ghostly Mum looks now in the dim daylight, I'm certain she hasn't been outside for weeks. According to Margo, she refuses to go out.

"What a mess our yard is," Mum says, observing.

That's more than anyone else here does.

We help her step along, holding her elbows, avoiding the rough parts of the walkway. A V-line of Canada geese presses away overhead.

"Look at all our neighbors' yards," she goes on, "with their leaves all out in neat bags. It must be pickup day. What a mess we've got. One big wind is going to come along and blow all our leaves into their yards they're trying to keep so neat."

She and I laugh together over that.

A young couple with skipping children goes into the back door of Nickerson's old house. There's a whole new development where the Elo farm used to be. All our childhoods—including my father's—existed on that farm terrain. Those meadows and forests and streams still provide the settings of many of my dreams. Dad in his last days watched the territory of his nearly eighty-nine years through the bedroom window to see these rows of small square "boxes"—what I call McMuffies, more modest, aspiring versions of McMansions—materialize. Today's children scramble among the McTickyTack. I marvel at how each generation sweeps in and takes over the planet.

I settle Mum into the front seat of the car. She holds her pocketbook in her lap.

"Our yard looks like hell rose up and fell on it," she says, laughing again. "One good gust of wind and there they'll all be with our mess." Her laugh grows hearty. "Well, that's one way to get our work done."

I join my mother laughing, which she can still do. Margo, with one tight, serious face, gets into the backseat, clutching the trust. She has her tumbler full of ice and sounds like some Arctic animal gnawing its way through an ice floe.

She says again, "I need to see the form you're going to get Ma to sign."

I consider scrapping the mission. But I came all this way. So, hoping to head her off, I say, "You can see the form when we get inside the bank, but you must not snatch it. Please understand that Linda is going to take care of things."

"Just look at all their hard work," Mum keeps on, maybe recalling her and Dad's years of zealous yardwork. "I hope for their sake, the wind stays low. Then our leaves will stay under the trees they came from and we'll just have what we deserve."

"Or if the wind blows backward," I offer, "maybe it will put the leaves back on the trees."

Mum and I chortle. No laughter comes from the backseat.

"Where is it we're going?"

This is my dear little Mummy, who used to watch Arthur Godfrey, wearing his Hawaiian lei and playing his banjo weekday mornings during the 1950s, and who flopped down hard over her ironing board one day when her hopes were dashed just one time too many of becoming Queen for a Day. Winning allowed the "queen"—some housewife with too many children who was judged more oppressed than other housewives with too many children—to reign, just for that day, and receive a new washer or vacuum cleaner, presumed to be her heart's desire. Mum never won, though she was repeatedly nominated by her sisters and some neighborhood women.

The bank is a brick bastion, the most solid, well-constructed building in town. It stands in a row of leaning, waterlogged wooden storefronts of structures one or two stories high. It's surprising to step from the buckled sidewalk into an interior of firm plaster and polished wood. I ask for Linda, who appears promptly, a well-groomed, nondescript woman with short hair and glasses. Her office is enclosed by an L-shaped glass partition. Two chairs wait in front of her large, polished mahogany desk, and my mother and I are motioned to sit down. Someone brings another chair for Margo, the unexpected guest.

I confirm before I sit that Steve spoke to Linda yesterday from California and explained the situation. Mum nods happily, enjoying a social occasion. Margo sits, grim, under her tent of hair. "I need to see that form," she says as I start to give it to Linda.

"Yes. Take a look at it." I try to sound as if all is normal. I explain that this is the Trustee Certification form Mum has to sign with Linda as witness.

Margo grabs it. "What do I see?" she exclaims. "Look at that, you've got Daddy terminated from the trust."

"He's terminated because he's *dead*." I blow my cool. Linda visibly flinches and I recover my élan. "Margo, please give Linda the form now and let us talk."

I tell Linda that there are a couple of pieces of information that she can fill in by looking at the trust. That information has to go on the TC form. I ask Margo to please give Linda the trust so she can determine the date and put it on the form. "Mum can sign and we can all go home."

Margo tells Linda that she doesn't like what's going on here. She doesn't like what Steve and I are trying to do. And she won't let go of the trust.

Linda suddenly looks alarmed.

I assure Linda in my most calming voice, "We have some people here who are suspicious and shouldn't actually be here today. And some other family members who don't know why they're here." Mum nods and beams as if she's being introduced. "And in spite of these obstacles, which I think my brother told you about, I made the five-hour drive last night—not without traffic, of course—and we're trying to accomplish this very simple thing."

But Linda is looking under threat, and she wants out. "Family matters will have to be handled elsewhere," she says coldly, and I think she must have her finger ready to press the security button under her desk.

There's nothing to say. How did I forget the small-town mentality? We might as well be creeps off the street. "Never mind, we'll go." I take my mother's hand. "Let's go, Mummy. This isn't going to work." Mum sparkles and rises up as if she's been asked to dance. I move her as quickly as possible out the door. She comes smiling along, lit up like a happy little spinning top. Margo walks behind—hair in a blizzard, arms clutching the trust.

As we drive home in murderous silence, Mum says it looks like snow. "You can just feel the air turning to winter. Look at that man with his cane, going out to get his newspaper. Poor thing." Her face presses against the window as if she's leaning out to join him. "This is probably his only outing for the day. Winter is so hard on old people. At least it's not snowing yet. At least there isn't any wind."

Ahead, the steely old railroad tracks glint like frozen blades running into the bush.

"Soon winter will be down on us. Suffocate us all," Mum says, continuing her soliloquy. There's an absolutely pregnant stasis in the air.

Teeth on ice sounds calmly from the backseat. *Oh, how I don't want the weight of them*, I think. *Three of them! Three is just too many!*

"Margo." I can't help but let out my full fury. "I hope you know that you have no legal right to that document. Mum and Steve and I are the executors. I'd be within the family's legal rights to call the police right now to come and take that from you." I imagine her running with the trust up to her filthy apartment when we get home, and a police escort taking me up there after her, every step stirring dust bunnies up my nose.

"*I'm* going to call the police," she retorts.

Well, no, we're not going there. I remind myself that she calls the police as if they're her personal entourage.

I decide to be quiet. Talking only makes me madder. There is no way to remedy the roadblocks. She can't trust us and she can't help it. We drive past the clock tower, once reflected like a large, blank eye in the bloated elbow of the river, now a parking lot. It's almost noon, time for the bank to close. This is one of many New England towns dominated by a four-sided clock tower on top of a mill, even though time doesn't seem to register here until it's time to die—a silent presence until it gongs the hour.

"Just feel it all bearing down," my mother continues. "Any minute now the sky is just going to start. Old people have such a hard time in winter. It's a big deal even just to get the newspaper. You know it's coming when the air sits still like this, then the sky clamps down and lets loose and it's just flying those . . . what are those animals? The ones when it rains?"

Suddenly, Margo reaches forward from the backseat and places the trust in my mother's lap.

Great, I think. *Now that the mission is aborted.*

"One big white ghost surrounds you and you can't find the nose on your face. Poor old people. Winter's like that. It always comes."

"Margo. You know we all miss Daddy," I offer.

When we pull into the driveway, I pick up the trust, so my mother can get out. This provokes Margo to go shrieking mad in the backseat—a reaction that moves me to such rage that I turn and throw the trust at her. "Get out of my car," I command. "I can't stand the sight of you."

Suddenly, Mum starts shouting, as if we're children, "You kids, stop this fighting. Right this minute. I will not stand for this. I'm putting my foot down now."

I take off. I'm shaking. And on my drive back to the motel I'm so disoriented that I find myself halfway to Boston. As I turn the car around, I hear that forgotten tumbler of coffee and ice, overturned and rattling, oozing brown slush all over my backseat.

Good Day Darkness

Lemmy has stopped eating and drinking, the same way Qwerty did. He stayed under my bed for days. He'd come out doggedly and drink from a water bowl when I sat on the floor and called him. But that stopped. He was doing it for me. Then came his last day. I got him out from under the bed and cradled him in my arms all morning, until I went to see patients out in my office. I checked in with him every time I had a break.

When I returned late that evening, he lay cold on the floor. I thought he was dead, but as I leaned down to touch him, he suddenly reached up with his paw and touched my cheek. With that beautiful gesture, I took him into bed with me. He lay facing my left side as I lay on my back. About two in the morning I felt him press my shoulder once with each paw. Press. Press. And with that he died. I loved his last signal to me, last loving touch, firm good-bye, with conviction and wit—Lemmy was known for his wit—that conveyed such familiarity and some kind of knowing.

I've lost some deep loves. Pets are deep, easy loves.

Taking Power

I wish life allowed stopping points. Sometimes you simply can't go on.

"If we find life with a partner, that is frosting on the cake," I tell my patient who feels she has no life without a man. "But you are the cake."

It's hard to be without primary love, someone you know deeply who knows you and where you are most minutes of the day. Without that person, no one shares the details of living, thoughts about dinner, the need for coffee and toothpaste, the warm body to wrap around you at night. I try to accord myself with the Buddhist precept of letting go of what you cannot have, waking up to what you do have, not living in the state of something missing. I want to hold to Carlos Castaneda's principle of living a strong life. What would that look like? When the light turns that dismal mustard hue, I almost taste that indefinable dread. When did the light borne down through my beloved trees become oppressive?

There's the depression of not finding deep, lasting relationships—people to come through life with. The depression of finally finding yourself ordinary, when you had dreams beyond. Once I had a little recognition, publishing in small magazines, two stories numbering among the one hundred best in the annual Best American Short Stories collections. But I felt I lacked a subject and my peculiar condition finds so little to tell. I didn't publish enough to join the club. Now I just look most humbly for some path to wisdom.

This isolation is to some extent an affliction of place. A home office once seemed financially ideal and convenient. Just me. Just here. That old comfort. Now I find myself locked into something that has taken me fully out of the world. It feels as if I've been condemned to one of the unseen lives—under the trees, behind the hedge. The home office has proved hermetic. This is a university town, but for a single older woman, it's the suburbs. Could I ever move back to the city? I've thought I never would.

I seem to need to keep going back to the Ahlenberg family. Two needs: see how Mum is doing without Dad these nine months, and continue reconstituting an old, lost, cut-off self in the presence—or, I might say, in the shadow—of my mother. It doesn't matter that she's not all there. I need to sink to the bottom of a giant sob, need its deep brass pitch to release me after all these years into a life that merits gratitude. That's why I keep returning, and why I will continue to do so until my mother's gone.

Jason will be joining me this time. Susanna is working.

As usual, a message from Margo precedes my visit: "Hi Janis—Marisol's therapist told her that I must have a false memory disorder regarding the time she was carried off the ice by a child molester because she doesn't remember it and declares it never happened. If she could get to that memory of being raped in the woods that day when she was skating, she might not be having poor health and high blood-sugar levels, with her diabetes acting up. I don't think hypnosis is a good idea, but her therapist isn't helping her know what really happened."

I'm truly tired of this. Sorry for Margo. Tired. It's Mum I'm trying to return to.

The back porch is perfectly neat. This time, no bottles, no cans. No ashtrays or birds' nests full of butts. Max has not only stopped drinking, he's stopped smoking, too. He's made the porch positively pristine.

Max is a new person. He wears a black turtleneck and black corduroy pants—he looks good, except for his unsettling stare—and is heading off for a job interview.

"Hi Janis"—the voice of Marisol speaks out on my mother's speakerphone—"let me know what time we should get there? Call as soon as possible. Joshua has to eat by four."

I tell her to come tomorrow, not today.

My mother looks well. She smiles a lot, tells me I look good, and tells Jason how handsome he is. Then she repeats the whole round. Jason is sure she doesn't know who we are and she's faking it.

"You must be missing Dad," I say.

She answers, "Oh, yes."

Evening has fallen, and Max is back. He's been hired to do a website for a psychiatrist who specializes in schizophrenia. Interesting that the psychiatrist didn't ask about his mental health history. *Cool guy*, I think.

We take our places, all in a row, me and Jason next to Mum, stationed before the TV, which is on mute. Max switches over to the baseball game. The Red Sox are playing. I ask him to please keep the sound off so we can talk.

Usually no one asks much about mine and Jason's lives because they don't know what to imagine. But Margo does ask Jason how he likes living in New York City (he's been back there for three years now), how his audio-engineering career is going, and how Susanna is doing with her residency. Many people don't ask others about their lives. Margo has this sensitivity and personal interest, and I'm glad for her.

We make it an early evening and say good night. Jason and I go to our motel.

Today, Marisol and family arrive in the late afternoon with bags of food, including Oreos and Doritos, and there is pure, nonstop eating and shouting until they leave. Joshua screams and throws things. Marisol screams at Joshua, at Margo, and at Fred. Margo screams at Marisol. Mum sometimes tries to holler above all. The chorus gets interrupted when a canister of fish food, grabbed from the top of Max's fish tank, hurls through the air and just misses Mum.

I seize Joshua's arm hard as he aims his dish of macaroni. I take the dish away, give him an emphatic "No," and hold him firmly. I take him into the kitchen. When he quiets down, I give him the Koosh ball I've brought for this occasion. It's a brilliant toy, designed with love and humor and delight. It is the picture of friendliness. All children in my practice take to the Koosh. "This is the only thing to be thrown, Joshua." I speak in a loud enough voice to be heard over the disturbance, but I do not yell. "This is for you. It is to be thrown to another person who knows it is coming and has agreed to catch it and throw it back. Not *at* them, *to* them. The other person has to want to play. You have to ask them first."

He dissolves into tears.

"Will everyone be quiet and let this child regain himself?" I shout over the pandemonium. No one stops. Joshua proceeds to implode. He cannot be soothed. My nerves jangle for an hour after they leave. The fish in the tank slowly emerge from their caves. The cats peek out from behind doors. Additional debris lies everywhere.

I retrieve the spatula from the lampshade. Then Mum and Jason and I fall into conversation.

We talk about the '60s.

"The '60s was about upsetting power," says Jason.

Margo says that the '60s were not a good time for women. "Sex was bad for women," she says.

I hold my breath.

"They all felt under pressure to put out and it wasn't good for them. It was for the men, it wasn't for them."

I think this is a rational and thoughtful opinion—if she's not heading into delusion territory. Which she might not be. I say that young women today might not be under that same kind of pressure. Women may have become much more their own agents. But they seem to be mistaken in some of the choices they make. Some use their bodies now as weapons.

"Well," Margo says, "women today . . . relationships are very cold today. The whole mentality of these times is related to war." What lucid ideas from someone so outside of life herself, whose perceptions are often so skewed. These are some of her mellowed dimensions. We might actually be having a sane conversation. I want to love my sister. Sometimes I do.

Margo tells Mum we're not watching *The Godfather* tonight. Mum responds by shaking the pages out of the *TV Guide* she's searching: "Well, then"—she picks up one page—"tonight we're watching *The Good, the Bad and the Ugly*, and tomorrow we're watching *Hang 'Em High*."

"These Red Sox just hung 'em high!" Max calls out.

Max allowed Mum to surf the channels for a moment, but he has the baseball game back on now.

"Sorry, Max," I say. "You can join the conversation, if you want."

"Where is *The Godfather*?" Mum keeps asking.

"You've watched *The Godfather* every night this week and now you think everything you watch is *The Godfather*."

"What's wrong if I think that?"

Margo changes the subject. "The pediatricians are saying Joshua is retarded."

"Who can pluck him out of the air long enough?" I say.

"When Marisol takes him to the doctor," she continues, "he pushes the doctor away and says, 'No.' It's like he knows they aren't going to say good things. And Marisol is upset. The doctors know Joshua's natural mother is retarded. And they see how delayed his speech is. So they just take the easy way and say he's retarded too."

"You can't diagnose that child separate from his environment," I snap. "He barely has a chance of being human."

"Look, Marisol gets overwhelmed. She's got her hands full . . ." Margo, predictably, defends her twin. I back off. It's not worth voicing thoughts that won't do any good. I worked hard at one time to set Joshua up with expert diagnosticians and Marisol and Fred didn't follow through. It turned out that they would only go to professionals who are Christian. I gave up.

"You know, Mum," I say, "it is so profound that you just live purely in the moment now. Really, that is so deep. There is no past—because you don't remember—and no future."

"That's me," she says. "Love not and want not."

"But it's a wonderful thing to try to make your moments their best."

"Well, what else? The bridge has been crossed, the fork is long gone. The hill is over."

"Too bad Dad can't be here to enjoy these moments with you."

"Well, where is he?"

"We should all say a prayer for Dad," says Margo. She appears ready to lead us.

"We should all pray for Boston right now," says Max.

"Margo," I say, "each of us in our own way."

"What's wrong with saying a regular prayer?" she insists.

"Better safe than sorry," offers Mum.

"I believe Dad's in a good place," I say. "Whatever that might be. Something our tiny minds just can't imagine."

Again, I picture Dad in his last days, watching out his bedroom window as that noisy backhoe barged the dirt and made roadways on farmland that had remained unchanged in just about all of his eighty-nine years. Dad seemed perfectly accepting of the changes going on outside his window. He never complained. Goldfinches devoured the nyjer seed all day long from the Plexiglass feeder Max suction-cupped against that same window. There's an old swimming hole way back behind that old farm that had a whirlpool. Dad and his high school buddies used to run naked through the woods—young Olympian athletes—to dive from the high rocks into the pool. Dad loved a story he'd read in high school about a boy who fell into the maelstrom and emerged an old man. He never forgot the story, but—typically—didn't care to learn the name of the story or the author.

"Well, who'd have thought there'd be the day," I say, "when we'd all be sitting here without Dad?"

"I know," Margo agrees.

"Dad gone. David gone. Mum with Alzheimer's. You start to have a different view of who you are. Of what life is. Life is ultimately a tragedy!"

"Here's a tragedy. Boston's busted!"

Jason and I are laughing.

"Sorry, Max, another time for us and baseball," I say.

I share with everyone that I do constantly wonder how we're supposed to live with the losses in our lives. "We've lost two good men and, I do have to throw in, two good cats. We're without them. Without them," I repeat, to absorb the meaning.

Margo brings up that there were some confusing things about Dad. Ways he wasn't perfect. Then she retells the story none of us has ever believed or let her finish about a time he took Margo, Marisol, and a little neighborhood girl up to the lake house and that he went into his bedroom with the girl (who might have been ten) and closed the door.

This time, I venture, "Well, so what happened then?"

"Well, we phoned Ma."

"And what did Ma say?"

"She said, 'Open the door.'"

"So, what happened?"

"We pushed the door open."

"What happened then?"

"Nothing could happen then. The door was open."

"What does Marisol say about this?"

"Marisol says this never happened and she doesn't remember it."

"What are you talking about?" Mum pipes up. "I can't let you talk like this. You can't be saying what I think you are. He would never. Never. I know him, and he'd never in this world."

There's some back and forth between Margo and Mum, with Mum getting a bit riled.

Do I have to imagine this? Do I have to live with another uncertainty? I decide to change the subject. "Look, we all know what a sweet and loving man Dad always was. Let's leave it at that."

"Well something did happen," says Margo.

"What was that?"

"I lost my grasp of reality."

"I'd like to hear about that—when you lost reality."

Jason sits up straight to listen.

"Well! I'll tell you. There was a time when I wore a bicycle helmet. All the time. Everywhere. For years. I wore it because I thought someone was going to shoot me. I just walked around that way, with this bicycle helmet on my head. And no one ever asked me why I was wearing a bicycle helmet, even though they looked right at me. Even my therapist never asked. And it was winter. I didn't even own a bicycle. If they had asked me, I would have told them I was wearing it because people were going to shoot me. Then they would have said, 'What kind of family do you come from?'"

At this she laughs.

"How come you laugh at that?" I ask.

"Well, it's pretty funny."

"What part is funny?"

"That no one ever thought to ask me. Makes me wonder who the crazy ones are."

"I guess you have a point. Did you get back your grasp of reality?"

"I couldn't because I had that setback."

"Which one was that?"

"When I had my wisdom teeth out. My insides were sore when I came out of the anesthesia, and I knew right away what they did.

"What was that?"

"They took my eggs."

Like Marisol? Deprived of her eggs. I usually don't let her go on with this story either.

"So where are you with it all now?"

"I cope. I say to myself, 'I did everything I could to get justice.'"

She tried to sue that dentist. Probably no one would take on the case.

"So you don't let it bother you anymore?"

"For a long time, every once in a while, I'd notice some blond child—say in a shopping mall—and I'd wonder if it was conceived from my eggs. But that doesn't happen anymore."

"You don't let this upset you now."

"No. I figure these people aren't coming after me anymore. I think I'm safe."

Soon we all join Max, watching the ball game.

On my way to the bathroom, later, I find the cat's water bowl heaped with Joshua's macaroni. When I lift the lid of the toilet, there—floating—is the Koosh ball.

New Day

I see some gathering new light. I'm going to follow this beacon. I've decided to sell my house and move, before the ivy here claims everything, overgrows the house, and makes a topiary of me in my bed. After all, how many times am I going to sit in this patch of late afternoon, dazed by the same neurotic reflections on mistakes and wrong turns, trying to find the beginning, like following Ariadne's thread? When I can name the problem of myself, I'll have that much more to offer.

Otherwise, I walk around here talking to David as I did as a child to my make-believe playmates Ham and Hoatie, making mud pies in the back yard. "David, I miss you," I blurt out to his picture on the wall: young guy in 1971—looking like Bob Dylan—wearing his droopy sun hat, sitting on a doorstop in Les Beaux, southern France, playing with a cat. I'm not denying he's dead. But I wish he weren't.

"Everything felt like everything when I had you," I tell him. "Best days of both our lives. Divorce left a hole at my center. Then you died. First I was attached to you like a barnacle. Then came that point of independent resolve. Women aren't like I was anymore in western society. They have more choice and accomplishment—dare I say personhood—from birth. On the simplest level, I was always just trying to have my own identity and subjectivity, and that became the crisis of my middle age. Then we never got to talk about anything, never got to revisit . . . or repair . . ."

I need to find the meaningful life now—without you.

Water is pouring on my toes. I've been watering the plants. That's followed by a dish that drops and breaks and splatters applesauce on the floor and up my ankles. The blue teapot is over there with that missing chip in the broken lid. Lives are full of breakage. It wouldn't even help to stand still and not move.

The phone rings. I answer.

"Hello."

"Hi. It's me. I just left Reno. I spent last night in a motel looking out on high-desert plateau. Nevada is interesting. It has no corporate income tax. I don't know how they came to be so enlightened."

"Steve, do you think you might just want to know if maybe I'm having a heart attack, or fell in the shower and I'm lying here with a broken hip? Maybe in the middle of being kidnapped and murdered? Or just saying yes to a marriage proposal?"

"Let me finish. You've never seen friendly people like they have out here. You go into a bar and anyone will talk to you."

"I'm sure you must mean listen . . ."

"I'd live out here if it weren't for the sagebrush pollen. I've been here in the winter and you can see the haze hanging over the meadows. This is Donner expedition country and it was mining country back in the day. And I don't feel odd-man-out bearing a firearm here."

I keep the phone on speaker and open the mail. I've told him I don't like it when he calls and talks at me. I'm finding some really great new people, friends I hope to keep. I'll find more when I move to the city. Respectful, considerate people. I'm going to have mutual, reciprocal relationships.

"You know, you're supposed to ask how the other person is; if it's a good time to talk. You could ask how my weather is."

But not Steve, who goes on nonstop, making only himself exist by making the other person not exist. I finally tell him I have to go.

"Bye."

Night falls. Moon and stars rise. Without an object or a target, love must travel undefined out to infinity—and even if it dissipates, its particles must never diminish to nothing.

Sleep is blissfully comatose. The sun and birds staff my interior at dawn. World enters my soul first. Then I wake from the world within, from the inside out.

It's me alone—no longer two cats and me—sitting on the couch and reading the newspaper with morning coffee.

Margo's voice is carrying on: "... keep your nails clean ... moist ... drink plenty of water ... or ... they'll lose their feeling ... not a good thing to lose feeling."

"I'd like to lose feeling, Margo," I say to the air. "And ridges in the fingernails are probably just another cruelty of getting old."

As if on cue, the phone rings again.

"It's Me. I spent yesterday afternoon at Old Faithful."

"I thought you were the car repair, letting me know—"

"Listen to me. This place is wild. There are geysers going off everywhere. If I took a shot out here, you wouldn't even hear it."

My brother is clearly driving cross-country. I realize he must be heading to my mother's. Jason and I were about to visit her again.

"Why would you want to? Is that handgun to protect yourself? Are you taking it into your tent to protect yourself from bears?"

"No. Don't you know you can't bring a gun into a national park?" he scolds (the NRA taught him well, he's always claimed; the NRA was his more assertive father). "It's illegal. I just have it for target practice. I told you that already. I have to keep it in my trunk. Well, I gutta go. I've got dinner: Boston beans and hotdogs over the campfire."

He probably won't be sending a photo of this dinner. The last one, taken on the deck at the lake house—a boiled lobster sprawled across his plate next to a glass of white wine—looked like a 3-D predator charging toward me. The creature had a spatula inserted upright in one claw. Steve said it was waving a protest banner targeting some effort by Obama. He talked then about having rejoined a branch of the NRA, and having purchased this handgun in connection with them: "a group of very nice people." A group that included women and churchgoers. I forget the rest. I'm recalling his shooting career when it began at about age nine. Sometimes he'd bring home a dead squirrel.

More phone calls: "I came down to Twin Falls, Idaho, down from the Lewis and Clark Highway. This is where the Snake River Canyon is, where Evel Knievel tried to fly his motorcycle on rocket fuel. But I hate it here. Everything's paved over and it's hot as hell."

I call Jason. "I think Steve is headed to Grandma's. I don't think we want to be there."

"Oh. Are you kidding? I'm not going if he's there. You don't have to tell me."

Message left on my phone later: "It's me. I just had an experience I never imagined would have the effect on me it did. I went through the Rock & Roll Hall of Fame in Cleveland. I . . . I . . . just came unglued. You can probably hear it in my voice right now. I'm really just coming apart."

He is actually breaking up, crying.

"I mean . . . there were . . . John Lennon's . . . glasses.

He can barely get those words out.

"I gutta go."

I'm sad for my brother. He can't connect with his feelings, they just stab through. John Lennon's glasses won't hold him. I imagine the emptiness he must feel, and his fragility leaves me bereft. I'm sad for all of us—for all our foibles, including my own.

"David, if you could see Steve now. That cool guy who used to take you to dinner when you were out there, driving 100 miles an hour on Route One in his Lexus, which he still has. You'd always make use of some cognitive dissonance and say what a good driver he was—like a race-car driver—and what an amazing time you had."

My husband is not here to know the glorified and idealized status he has with me now. I flip one perfect single-egg, tomato, and Gruyere omelet. I've collapsed all the memories into that great vat of youth we shared together. I only have to do something about my state of mind. I can't live on an imaginary playmate: that once-tender scholar moved to love a hurt girl. I know too that it's my youth I'm missing.

"David, remember how we used to quote from *Call It Sleep*? How this young Jewish boy in Brooklyn hung a stocking at Christmas and 'mine fodder pud in a eggshells wid terlit paper,' whenever the thought struck." I feel myself swoon and crash backwards onto the couch into the sleep of glorious non-being.

Not So Sure About Thee

Steve has taken my mother to the lake house and given her his gun.

A phone call from Margo let me know.

Mum, who can barely be gotten out to her doctor appointments, is now vacationing with Steve, who has always lived alone except for that one short, failed attempt to live with Joanne. He's only taken care of himself.

It's hard to imagine being with either Steve or my mother in a small space. Mum is probably saying, "Oh, my, that lake is so beautiful. Look how beautiful that lake is." Then she'll say the same thing again.

Margo phones me, frantic.

"Ma just answered the phone and said she was all alone up there at the lake."

When Margo told her that Steve was there, Mum called out "Steve? Steve?" and searched the two bedrooms and called down to the laundry. Steve was not there.

"Then Ma said, 'Is someone going to come up here to get me before winter?'"

This concerns me too, so I call him on his cell phone.

"Steve, what are you doing with Mummy up there? Are you leaving her alone?"

"She doesn't need someone glued to her."

"Well, that's a question."

"I've been out doing target practice. Gun rulings are so stringent in some states. How am I supposed to know them all?"

"I thought the NRA..." (And what about crossing state lines?)

"These progressive states are so dimwitted. I wanted to go to a California shooting range last year and target-shoot with my handgun. First I had to take a gun safety course and pass an exam for my California Firearms Safety Certificate. Then I had to pass a handgun safety exam. Then, on your first visit, you have to be accompanied by someone who knows you personally and can attest that you're not a nut." (That would have been Joanne?) "Then the kind of firearm you can use is limited. No automatics, for example, or other 'politically incorrect' weapons like an AR-15 or an AK-47. And of course the rest of the population will label you as a right-wing fanatic. Here, it's 'Come on down and shoot.' All you need is a driver's license and you can rent any firearm in their arsenal, or bring your own. This includes fully automatic military machine guns you can rent for $150 an hour, and no concern about the nut factor. I'm going tomorrow. I hope I don't hurt myself."

Hopes he doesn't hurt himself! He says these things.

"What about Mum?"

"The other night I put my gun in Ma's hands and had her point it and then I took her photograph."

"That's bizarre."

"I emailed it to Margo. I'll send it to you. Of course, Margo called me right away and said"—he imitates an upset, fluttering female voice—"'What... what... what if she pulled the trigger?' And I said, 'Do you think I'd give Ma a loaded gun? I mean, come on.'"

"This is disturbing, Steve."

"She was so cute. She kept saying, 'I've never held a gun before.' I've got a lot of nice photographs of Ma holding the gun."

"Did you have her point it at you?"

"I'll send you the picture."

All this time I thought that Steve and I had a bond of some sanity in a sea of cuckoos. Now every time we talk he goes on about guns and shooting. The number of sane people in my family keeps dwindling. When do I discover that I'm nuts too? I've read that many therapists are unhappy. I wouldn't characterize myself as unhappy. Melancholy, though. I love melancholy. You can thrive on it like a mushroom on a disintegrating log, bedded on silken pine needles under black, feathered hemlocks dappled with sun.

I met John Keats in such a clearing in a forest when I was sixteen. His poem "When I Have Fears" had me in its grip for one whole phase of my life. I dwelt on that deepest predicament of wanting to make time stop, and how it did in Keats's "Ode on a Grecian Urn." How horrible to know you are young and are going to die soon. But not without a basic strain of melancholy happiness. There is a you to die.

My basic temperament is happy and warm. I don't fail to count my good fortune now and then. It's a fact that I feel less unreal than I once did. The loss of David remains unbearable, and though I feel swallowed by sadness—I do keep finding I'm still here.

The Ahlenbergs are taking me out of my own life too much. Now I'm worrying about Steve. Too often he refers to suicides by gun. I'm recalling a phone message last fall, when he told me he was ready to "shoot myself" after enduring a visit from Marisol and Joshua at the lake, during which Marisol kept losing everything she touched. Would he hurt my mother? Shoot himself? Get my mother to shoot him? That would be one mean, poetic ending.

He's telling stories again about that interesting old Melvin in his neighborhood who so smartly "put a bullet through his head." He had something of a friendship with this man. He's said more than once now that he likes Melvin's handling of his own fatal diagnosis.

"I gotta tell you," he says again, "I admire the guy. That's exactly what I'd do. Put my gun to good use. Get it over with. Why go through the hell of an illness?"

"You leave out the people who care about you—that they'd be devastated," I say.

I know Steve heard that.

But throughout my father's deterioration and demise, my brother still said things like, "You know, I can't respect Dad for letting himself just go like this. I wish I could put my gun next to his bed. I'd never go through what he's going through. I couldn't bear the indignity."

At this I said, "There's a rational, mature, and responsible way to end your own life, involving the people who care about you and having their love and support. There's a right way to do these things. You don't have to be some reckless lone wolf."

I send Steve an email: "I'm worried about you. Should I be? I think Dad's death hit you hard. Will you let me be your friend?"

I follow up with a phone call next day.

"How are you?" I say to start.

"I'm sick. I have vomiting and diarrhea and I can't get out of bed."

"Can you talk?"

"No. That's the point."

"Maybe we'll talk tomorrow?"

He emails the following day. "There's no danger. Not to worry. We can talk Sunday."

At eleven o'clock Sunday morning, I pick up the ringing phone and Steve launches into a high rant: "I'm done with this place. It's a permanent mess. I pulled a pony tail of blond hair out of the bathroom sink. How do people who rent this place for $1,800 a week put up with plugged bathroom drains? Max comes up and just sits in front of the TV while rain pours in through the open sliding door, leaves dirty dishes all over the place. They all do that. Joshua's fingerprints cover every window in the living room. The kitchen floor tiles have sat in puddles of orange juice and gravy and they're starting to buckle. The plumbing is fucked up. The basement toilet I put in overflows, the faucets don't run. All the water goes the wrong way. You can't sit on the toilet in the bathroom off the kitchen if it's raining without the skylight dripping on your head. I've tried caulking all around it. Now I have to wait 'til it rains to see if it's worked and I just want to get outta here..."

"Where's Mummy?"

When he's back in California, Steve sends me a long email expressing regrets about what happened the night before Dad's memorial service—but placing most of the blame on me and Jason. I write back:

> Steve: I appreciate your handling of the estate and the financial advice you've given me over these last years. But I'm worried about your stability right now and for the safety of yourself and maybe those around you. I'd like to find ourselves on a better note. I don't want us to have any more trouble together.

He replies:

> You are giving me mixed messages. Why would you want any contact with someone who threatens you so much you won't even come to your own mother's house when he's there?

I respond:

> Because I don't want to lose you. And there will be more family gatherings. Because we are locked in

this family situation as executors and overseers. And because I don't ever want to have things become scary and threatening again.

No reply.
Am I trying to turn a chair into a bird? Trying and trying. The chair remains a chair.

Love Is Not Enough

What will happen to the inhabitants of my mother's domain? I repeatedly question how much it is possible to care without destroying myself. If we had all died in our forties, as life spans were in centuries past, there would not have been time to destroy love. Though we might all have gone out with question marks over our heads (probably still will). A jumble of visits has shown me that just as you can't ask for love, you might not be able to refuse it. Steve and I will forever have watch over the three. We're trapped. What love is that? Not the lustrous love of poetry and song. It's snot-nosed and begrudging; it has guilt and disappointment, and a weary hopelessness. But it's a persistent love. As real as any other.

Here in my hometown again, on a love excursion, one fine day in September. Max and Mum and I go to Gloucester, a place we know well. Max has another job interview, having completed the website for the psychiatrist. He spells out his negotiating points while driving. He makes sense and appears confident, even outgoing, and I grab on to this carrot of hope.

While he's interviewing, I take my mother to lunch.

Her spoon hovers over her bowl of white clam chowder on the red-and-white-checkered oilcloth. "You say I'm sitting in Gloucester," she says.

A fleet of fishing boats loom skyward outside the window. She's riveted on those boats on the water, is forgetting to eat her chowder. "I have every reason to have dozens of memories here."

"Yes?"

"I don't have any."

I take her hand.

Today I take Margo to Wingaersheik Beach, also in Gloucester, a bay inlet with ancient rock domes the size of single-story buildings that kids climb. My child-footprints are all over those worn rocks. I brought David here. I wanted him to know this place.

I watch Margo wade into the water, a tall, lumpen (due to her medication), but not ungraceful woman who looks much younger than she is. The vision of her against the sea and sky puts a chokehold on my heart. Who's going to care about the Ahlenberg triplets?

I take her for fried clams, a rare treat. She talks about a high school classmate she ran into in town. "When we were in high school and Marisol had her operation"—the surgery Marisol had at age thirteen to construct the uterus she lacked, she means—"this girl started calling her an 'it.'"

"How did she know about the operation?"

"Everyone knew."

"Who told them?"

"Anyways, I have no use for this girl. She's the one who just stood there while Charlie Pafnauer raped me—"

"Margo, I don't want to hear about this."

"You never do. You've never been able to give me—"

"I give you my company and sometimes fried clams. That's it."

I return to my own home. Then Steve comes back East and stays at Eden for a night before heading to the lake house. He and

Margo fight until Margo has a near-psychotic break. She calls me on the phone and I manage to pull her out of it. Because I can do that, it has probably become my role.

I'm angry with Steve for his cruelty. I try to make him understand her fragility.

Two days later, I'm on Steve's side. Margo decides she's discovered a $10,000 "error" in my mother's checking account and so Steve must be embezzling. A couple months ago, Steve invested $10,000 of my mother's money. He notified all of us at the time and has already managed to make a good return on it.

"He's entrusted to do this, Margo. You are not supposed to be snooping in the family bank account and jumping to your paranoid conclusions."

But nothing can stop Margo.

She drags my mother to the bank and walks in there yelling and alarming everyone that there's a state of emergency, that Steve Ahlenberg has embezzled $10,000 from my mother's account. My mother follows, grabbing on to people, asking "Who are you? Where am I? What am I doing here?"

When the people at the bank reach Steve by phone, they let him know they're about to put a restraining order on Margo. She will not be allowed in the bank anymore or the police will be called. They stopped just short of reporting her for "elder abuse."

Margo insists that she was right and that she has her lawyers.

"Steve doesn't need Mum's money, Margo. Do you understand that Steve is a wealthy man?"

This means nothing to her. However, she does finally quiet down, at which point she starts phoning me with cute kitten stories. I cut her off and tell her that after all the trouble she's caused, I don't know when I'll want to talk to her again.

You will always be dragged to the lowest common denominator.

Two days later, I receive a holy card in the mail—the Virgin Mary holding baby Jesus—that says, "Sorry I made so much trouble. But Steve and Max should have explained it to me."

"Don't you read your emails?" I say when I call her. "Steve explained it all." But here we drop it. For her, it's out in the ether.

This scenario will be repeated many times to come. Steve and I will become more firmly bonded as a result of this never-ending travesty.

Do I really want this job of love—love extorted, love as responsibility? Necessity? I think there is such a thing as plain, corny love. It's the "you'll-miss-them-when-they're-gone" kind. Love us all because we die.

But I've known what must be meant by true love. Given who I was, how I was endowed, and where I was in time and place, survival was going to depend on the man I married. Not that I knew that consciously. But that love held joy and happiness, the kind that deepens. Love as survival. Then we make each other live.

It's sad that my folks were incapable of grasping complexity. The snobbery they saw in me was about my being alone and trying to invent myself. Or maybe that idea about my going above them gave them their ticket to let go of me in pursuit of their dream house on the lake. They could have offered more encouragement of my aspirations, if not financial help. But they saw me as simply gone to the realm of the urban and educated, and deemed me all taken care of and okay, and outside of them; they chose the not-knowing kind of ignorance.

Is ignorance a kind of innocence? The profound cruelty of ignorance may not be intended. But does it make any difference? The ignorant get off scot-free—because they didn't know better, as my mother used to say of Mimay. Forgive limitation? You have no choice. Feel the disappointment? No choice.

I wish I'd found a way to cut through a lot of smoke. I don't know how much I touched my parents on my return. Was that my motive? We could have talked about all the years they dealt with three young adults with mental illness. Have I been as compassionate and honest as I might—and increasingly do—hope I was? Toward all of us?

Don't You Turn Your Back On . . .

My mother died of pancreatic cancer on December 28, 2012. Mummy is dead.

She'd not been feeling well. Margo and Marisol had her screamed to the hospital in an ambulance with flashing lights, themselves aboard. Their usual hospital disruption followed. While Mum lay contented with a therapy dog who joined her in her hospital bed, my sisters tried to commandeer the place, force their medical opinions, fire the people in charge, and camp out at Mum's bedside. The hospital threatened restraining orders. But then came the diagnosis and Mum was returned home to die in her own bed.

Steve flew back to Eden to sleep in the little room from the time Mummy returned from the hospital until she died. Then he stayed some three weeks more. The police, the social worker—everyone concerned—refused to deal with Margo and Marisol. They suggested Steve get a restraining order against Margo. But he said no. He started coming across as a reasonable, self-controlled person—no pressured speech. And he became quite effective there.

When I learned of my mother's illness, I set out with a hastily packed bag to the train, but on the way developed crushing chest pain. Soon I was sitting in an emergency room in agony so great that I cried and nearly passed out.

Over two days, every possible test was done. Nothing was found. Just as suddenly, the pain lifted. They said, "This is a strong heart." The diagnosis was panic attack. Panic pain can be that severe. Jason called as I was ready to set out again; he wanted to come with me. He drove us in his car for a two-day stay.

Meantime, Steve had taken a stand on dirty dishes everywhere. Any dirty dishes not put in the dishwasher by day's end would be placed out in the trash barrels in the garage. He kept one set for himself. When all the dishes in the cabinets were gone, Margo and Max simply went out to the trash for a spoon or a bowl. Nobody said anything. What's needed there is a case manager, or a house parent.

I found Mum in bed and not with it at all. No recognition of anything or anyone. She had bouts of struggling discomfort, clutching at her blankets, then periods of sleep. I felt that strain of melting tenderness and empathy it seems one can only feel for their own mother facing her departure from the universe. Again, it's that sublime, tender feeling—as with Dad—I liken to feelings toward a newborn. Is there a complementary innocence to being born in dying?

I also felt the full weight and tragedy of death, the greed of Time, our mysterious journey. Maybe I was in communion with Mum's soul more than with her person, gone to dementia. Where my mother was within herself will remain a question consistent with her full mystery, but I have always been deeply touched by Mummy.

In one move, while restless, she threw off her blanket. She was naked. She'd refused a nightgown. I gasped when I saw her chest. Her breasts had been "radically" removed (radical mastectomies) so long ago. They didn't replace the nipples then. Her once-buxom chest was not just flat; it actually looked almost concave. I reeled with the tragedy of what she must have gone through, at that time when I was no longer part of anything here and only vaguely aware of what was happening.

Mummy, you too were abandoned in childhood. That hard life made you hard. I feel you deeply, for qualities that are so uniquely you, I couldn't put a name to them. But you lived so that love could never touch you. As if that touch would kill. I can love you now. I always did. Spent most of my life rebelling against it.

This time is not that time. Our life is always new. Until it's gone.

Steve and Jason and I sat at Mum's bedside that evening. Just us three. Jason and I were digesting our surprise at Steve's clean manner, the fact that his voice stayed at a normal pitch. He brought up politics only once, and when Jason firmly stated that he didn't want to go there, Steve respected his wishes.

At some point Steve talked about our mother's fiery temper and about the time she threw the catsup bottle through the door and it smashed against the wall in this room, causing the stain that I named Dribble Man. So he remembers that too.

Mum didn't respond to my talking, so I began singing "I'll Be Home for Christmas," which I always thought of as "their" song, picturing Dad in his sailor uniform, trying to come home. I sang in the falsetto voice I've cultivated, as a giant frog sits in the middle of my throat these days. I sing around it. But it's a good voice and I can carry a tune. Next I sang "I'll Be Seeing You," imitating Rosemary Clooney, and Mum sighed and seemed to swoon into a soothed comfort.

Steve did go on about the family's best era up on the lake. I react less each time he talks about that glorious past. "You weren't there" seems to be the refrain, referring to my absence. "You didn't know the Coleman stove, the lantern we had. Those were amazing days, the family's best times. Aunt Sunday and Uncle Pye there making pizza together. The neighbors, their kids. Everyone grew up together. We'd hear the loons all night. Those are the times I miss."

I won't let go of my brother. Can my attachment be explained just by the fact that I was there in the backseat that day at the hospital, waiting while silent snow pawed the windshield and breath of anticipation steamed the windows? Then Mum brought that bundle through the blizzard, and I saw his little tongue's first taste of the world in snowflakes. I was transfixed by awe of the newborn, a child loyalty to first things, a faith in beginnings. I'll accept, but I won't let go. Love can be that primitive.

At some point over the two days, I heard Steve telling Jason how lucky the family was to have had health insurance just after the triplets were born and my father had his accident. He said that my father's bosses visited every Friday afternoon. Could this be true? Where was I? Well, out working, of course, then at the Pizza House with all my high school classmates—the popular and the marginal, all in one place on Friday night, the only hangout there was.

If JW and Viki did indeed walk in past that whole mountain range of dishes and diapers waiting for me, and if there was health insurance, and Mum had me believe that there wasn't—convinced me we were poor when we were not—how do I parse that? Maybe we were only poor for a while and she forgot to tell me when it was over.

Mum deserves my rancor, I have to admit. And given that I only want to love Mum, the hurt of it will simply hurt. But I can hold my love and hate for Mum in the same heart. It's her whole person I embrace. But did she lie to me? This new question assaults me. The riddle of it all will have to remain a riddle. There will be no certainty.

Mummy's memorial is beautiful. Large photos of her reel across the wall above the altar of my sisters' modern Christian church: my mother from youth—the skinny, knock-kneed child—through middle and old age, all the way through to her last months, with her halo of glowing hair.

Margo gives a thoughtful, graceful speech recognizing all who helped my mother through her last years. She thanks everyone, including me and Steve and Jason and Susanna. She looks beautiful and her manner is elegant. Max doesn't speak, of course. I speak as well, then Marisol rants about God and the Bible for half an hour. Jason pays a musical tribute to his grandmother: a Dave Brubeck piano piece he once played for her long ago. Steve has asked to go last.

Steve tells the audience that one of his most meaningful times with my mother was when the family all sang Christmas carols in the car returning from Aunt Sunday's home at Christmas. I think he's talking about him and the triplets in the backseat, not the many Christmases he and I spent in the backseat, coming home from Aunt Sunday's, before that. It seems they all stopped singing when my mother began singing "Silent Night," because she sang it so beautifully.

Suddenly, out over the whole congregation, a woman's voice is singing "Silent Night." The attendees are stunned. It's Mummy's voice. The pictures continue. She sits on the deck, framed by the lake. Then there she is, pointing a pistol. The audience laughs. They don't understand it's a real gun. At the end of her song, Mum says, "Good-bye, everyone. I loved you all very much."

Mum you have left us. This time forever and for good. You did it by degrees. You grew old, and you lost yourself gradually along the way. You lost memories. You lost contact. But you hid your absence well, as you always did.

Mummy, I miss you. I have always missed you.

My mind still rides past those Mummy places, the places where she lived as a girl. Sometimes a giraffe or a happy monkey or a stealthy, feathered warrior wanders through. And Mum and I are in song. I can still rerun those times when my spirit soared. In her way, my mother touched me—just never for too long.

Steve recently asked me, "Do you think Ma loved us? Any of us? Including Dad?"

Shall we again consider what love is?

I love "Mummy" with my first broken heart. And I have her patchy love of me to love. Mum will always have the face of my longing.

Book of Love

The Rhode Island triplets will turn fifty-seven soon. The estate's financial affairs are mine and Steve's last, probably never-ending, chapter. But this naturally devolves into responsibility for all their well-being. Margo and Max live together on Eden Avenue in a state of hostile dependency. Max was awarded the first floor, deemed earned by all those years patiently waiting in the coal bin. Margo has her apartment upstairs but uses the first floor as if it were her own, believing it should be. The place deteriorates more. The front steps are crumbling and a tree grows out of the middle of the second step. The row of hemlocks in back has grown in to cover the entire backyard and tower over the two-story house.

I suggested they start pruning them from below.

"Oh, no. That would cost too much," said Margo.

"I was thinking that you could do a little every day yourselves, as I did in my own yard. Get rid of the lowest branches and you can at least have use of the yard."

I wonder if this is how they feel about the housework: it would just cost too much to hire someone, so it isn't done. They don't wash dishes. They reuse the dirty ones. Max claims Margo's messes in his space are hopeless, so there's no use in his maintaining order. My childhood home rots beneath this rubble.

Then, for a while, we couldn't make contact. Margo had taken it upon herself to change the home phone number. She said this was necessary because Max's debtors were calling all day long. But she ignored the major inconvenience to Steve and me.

Her studies have added up to a degree and she finally has a job, teaching special-needs children in a preschool nursery. She spends five-hour days there, invests her own money in goods and supplies, and engages deeply with the children. She's lovely with them; she treats them like the little people they are. Margo at her best has my respect. She can only be paid for three of her five hours a day, in order not to lose her benefits. Either way, we're talking about less than $1,000 a month she has to live on. She'd like to get off the dole, but it's scary. She has to trust her ability to survive—and that ability remains in question.

Disability benefits are always under fire and more and more people are taking advantage of the system. Where should the taxpayers' money go? Some would think a school, a road, or a hospital rather than my sister. At times I think the same.

"You cannot reveal my mental illness," she explained to the Social Security field-office. She'd gone there in person. "I work with children." She volunteered to make copies of her paychecks and bring them personally. Her request was not honored. Social Security sent a letter to the school, requesting income information. The director expressed surprise. (I can't imagine the school hasn't done background checks, but I don't say this.)

We determine she should say her temporary disability was serious depression. But the experience causes her to unravel. She has the Parkinsonism caused by tardive dyskinesia that manifests in the form of trembling. Frequently, her chin quivers. She's in tears, telling me. I'm near tears hearing about it. Her doctor tries to keep her on the lowest dose of Stelazine possible, along with benzotropine to control these side effects.

"Sometimes the kids point and laugh at me," she says in a despairing tone.

"Just distract them," I say. "Point to something across the room or out the window. Remember how beautiful you are."

She tells me that a little boy of four said, "You're a crazy lady!"

"Four-year-olds don't know what they're talking about."

"He had to get that from an adult."

"Many adults don't know what they're talking about either." I tell her to drop it. "Don't give it another thought. You'll get paranoid and then you'll be in a terrible place. Don't do that to yourself."

This advice seems to work.

She calls again later. "I'm just going to tell them I'm a rape survivor."

"No, Margo. Don't do that. That's not the way to go."

The estate is complicated. Two properties are to be sold, and a large share of the proceeds is to go into a family trust. This trust will own Eden Avenue as Section 8 housing, as already arranged by my parents with HUD, and allow Margo and Max to remain living there. Their benefits will be protected. The condominium should be sold right away.

Max says he cannot live with Margo, who is impossibly bossy. But to remain living there is the only viable financial deal for both of them. They have very little to live on forevermore. Finding and holding jobs is something each of them does only sporadically.

Steve will buy the lake house immediately, pay the family trust, and invest some of the money to start it growing. Even with all the aggravations to come, I'm cautiously optimistic. This new stage of the family responsibility is bringing out the best of my brother. Will he be changed by the loss of my parents? Will I know a better person?

But nothing is easy. Margo and Marisol have refused to sign the release form allowing Steve to buy the cottage. We are all legally required to sign this form because Steve is both our sibling and an executor of the estate.

They hire a Christian lawyer, who has to be paid with limited estate money, and though he has explained the situation correctly to them, they don't understand and they don't relent. The release form refers—*pro forma*—to "any progeny" the purchaser of the property might have. They take this to mean Steve has children; they review all his past girlfriends, expect these children to turn up, and it's not clear what will happen if they do. They seem not to care that they're depriving themselves and poor Max of some immediate financial support. So they prevent this property sale.

This irrationality and suspicion will prevail throughout the whole estate process.

After I tell Margo I'm so angry that I don't want to talk to her or Marisol again, she calls the next day in the late afternoon. I'm in New York, walking up Columbus Avenue by my treasured Museum of Natural History.

"It's an emergency!" she cries when I answer. "Marisol has had a 51-A filed against her." She goes on and on and I can't understand what she's telling me.

"What's a 51-A?" I'm impatient; I shouldn't have answered the call. "Ten words or less, please." I'm walking to my new office. I'll soon be living here permanently. And I probably don't want to know anything about this.

"Marisol's been accused of neglect." Then something about sexual abuse.

"By whom? I can't hear another word about sexual abuse."

The rest of the story is worthy of an out-of-body experience on my part. In a capsule: Marisol has made a public issue of the fact that Joshua has a habit of inserting his fingers into his rectum. "Margo, please. Enough." She goes on, telling me that this clearly indicates he's been the victim of sexual abuse.

Marisol spoke to the people who run the school he attends, and apparently accused them of this sexual abuse. And, as a perfect non sequitur, told them that this is the same thing that official from the senator's office, whom she dated in her twenties, did: he sodomized her.

"Margo, I'm hanging up. Marisol has obviously said really dumb things and got herself in a stupid predicament."

"She's your sister."

"My misfortune!" I just can't do the subject of Marisol and her child. I don't want the hopeless number-three burden of Marisol. And here I am, yelling, as I have all their lives, "I can't do three of you. Three is just too many."

She screams louder. I end the call. People on the sidewalk are staring.

Months drag on. I hear nothing more about the 51-A. They finally sign the releases.

I have another meeting on the Cape, and I invite Margo to drive up. She is thoroughly lucid. She knows she interrupts Max's privacy. But she can't stop herself from half-living in his quarters on the first floor. She finds the upstairs rooms, which my grandparents once called home, cramped and uncomfortable (I do see her point). But she can't recognize how she intrudes, bosses him mercilessly, and makes appalling messes in his living space. She knows she faces a life of poverty; already she is sometimes forced to eat in soup kitchens. She wants to remain in the family home, but she wants the downstairs, and she wants Max to leave because he's smoking again.

"You can't afford the house alone," I tell her.

She knows, but says she'll find roommates.

"No one can live with you, Margo," I say. "You order people around, don't honor boundaries. You'd be thinking your roommates were stealing from you, poisoning your cat, or violating you in some way. You lose jobs for these reasons." (She's lost her teaching job and is now doing some babysitting for a small income.)

She wants to find a way. I'm distraught with compassion and helplessness. She only wants to have a life. That's Margo.

Margo tells me next that Max sits outside on the ground after dark with his back pressed to the side of the house, staring longingly at the house next door, because that (single) woman who lives there now has smiled at him and said hello. I spend one sleepless night worrying about this. It is in keeping with Max's personality. But nothing in my talk with him the next day corroborates this. He tells me not to worry—that he's not pining for anyone, and he continues to get freelance work.

The irony of it all is dismaying. The M&Ms's central place in the family from birth gave my sisters—not Max—the truly misleading sense of entitlement that now pans out at the other end as nothing. A dupe. An empty promise. They're emerging from crippling mental illness and endeavoring to find life in their late fifties. It's a far reach to have hope. I will soon have to admit I can't do more than very little good here.

"Love not, want not," my mother often said.

Steve at the lake has his hunting down to one red squirrel. He got rid of the four others. He's in a wrangle with this defiant one—a deadlock. The last-standing creature seems to have his respect and admiration. Life often supplies brilliant metaphors.

I left the family at eighteen, but I never left my brother. I wrote him during my freshman year of college. He wrote to me. I plotted to get him out of our little backwater. I thought to educate him from afar. I told him about the Fine Arts Museum in Boston—my first experience of a museum. Some of my part-time jobs were in offices; there, I photocopied the Constitution, the Declaration of Independence, and the Gettysburg Address, and sent them with a note that he should read and memorize them. It was the key to his future. But he told me later that what saved his life was when I sent him The Beatles's *Rubber Soul* album. "That's when I knew I wouldn't be spending my life pumping gas," he said. "That's what I got from you."

    Steve told me a sweet story about Max. Max took a job as janitor in a big-box store. He arrives at five thirty in the morning to mop the floors and clean the toilets. One morning, when all the staff had just come in, a sparrow swooped in and flew around in seeming panic. Confusion reigned. Everyone dropped everything, but no one knew what to do. Then Max just reached a hand in the air and caught the bird in flight. All were stunned as they watched Max gently release the bird out the door. Now they call him "the bird whisperer."

Flowers In the Teapot

There's a new baby. Jason and Susanna are married, and they've just had a baby boy.

His name is Derek. He was born on January 1, 2015, and he is the sublime zenith in the long chain of babies that has filled the stages of my life.

I consider all that these different babies have meant to me. Steve was my wish for a sibling come true. My love of my first little brother remains. I feel he began with me. The triplets—tiny perfections dropped from heaven—sadly, became too much (and not only for me). New little Derek is a planned and wanted baby. My own baby's baby. He glows with unencumbered light. This is the sweetest love yet.

My son was my most extraordinary first. The high point of my young-adult years. He, too, was planned and wanted. I set out to be the best mother. But was I as easily smooth-running with him as I am with my grandson? All those bumpy-road times when a new mother doesn't know what to do. Then too soon it's over. Grandmother doesn't have those challenges. And everything is different when you reach the age of "wisdom," thriving on a hard-earned serenity. Babies who are your own progeny seem to be an automatic, inescapable, lasting love.

Derek is just walking. He claps and smiles and squeals with pleasure as he moves along. Jason and Susanna and I sit on the floor, sharing his delight that this body he inhabits does new things every day. We vocalize with him the sounds he makes. There aren't words yet to his wonder. When he helps himself to an apple, he holds it out in front of himself, seemingly for balance but also to treasure it. He walks forward with his prize and finally bites into it with his four budding teeth. Jason says, "What a nice apple you've got there. Look at that fine, wonderful apple you found."

Derek is not yet about self-satisfaction or self-consciousness. He's about the apple. Everything has this thrill—a set of measuring spoons, a Tupperware container, a potholder. He courses around the room heralding the shoehorn in his grip as if it's the Holy Grail. The focus is not on his getting the prize, it's on the prize itself. The apple is the joy of everything.

The wonder of life increases. Babies make for life renewal. Derek draws me more purely than ever into the mystery of being. He didn't exist. Now he does. Now I see the shoehorn as I haven't before.

"The lady is by herself," says the maître d' as he seats me at the table and instructs the waiter to bring my champagne. Lobster Thermidor follows. Peach Melba for dessert. I live in a box in the sky. I sold my house. And now that I'm here in New York City, I don't know where else I could be. This world has no husband, no mother, no father. The home I sold, the last ten years, my treasured gardens, that stage of my blood and mood, is all washed over the temporal waterfall. Books and possessions were given away so I could shrink into a smaller, more essential space—the size to contain not more than the present moment. I keep the music. My beloved musicians will all be gone one day, but the music will go on. My city living room with one south-facing wall of glass looks out on sky and tall buildings, admits luxurious light in on new houseplants. Mum's cobalt teapot, absent the lid, sits on the coffee table holding a mixed bouquet. Flowers in the teapot. I have new friends here and still have the friends I finally found out in divorce-land—a long, rich story I've not taken the room here to tell.

I walk home from dinner out with myself singing "I'll Be Seeing You." Billie Holiday is in my head this time. Feelings—like the tide—pull between the pain and the joy of life. David and I lived here for more than twenty, mostly happy years. This is our "old country," our "old hunting ground." That basic layer of the love of us, that smile and laugh of us, lives on in me. I alone inhabit our old familiar places—and I'll always be seeing you. But a new layer sprouts beyond all that, just because of each new day. A beyond-you, David, gains increasing existence, the simple result of time.

I don't know yet that Jason and Susanna will have a baby girl and I'll be doubly enchanted. I'll remain loyal to the triplets, whose sweetness and gratitude will win my generosity and affection, though now from a distance. Steve will stop speaking to me over a petty exchange and following the jolt of receiving such primitive treatment, I'll just finally, at last—as I never thought I would—let go.

Key in the lock. Door swings open. Bach's "Concerto for Harpsichord in F minor" is playing. It's lighted and welcoming here, where I keep my sorrow of the survivor.

It's only me who comes home, but—when I go—I leave the lights on when I go.

www.ingramcontent.com/pod-product-compliance
Lightning Source LLC
Chambersburg PA
CBHW020351080526
44584CB00014B/981